MICROCOMPUTER APPLICATIONS
THIRD EDITION

WordPerfect 4.2/5.0/5.1, Lotus 2.2/VP Planner Plus, and dBASE III Plus Edition

ROBERT T. GRAUER
University of Miami
Coral Gables, Florida

PAUL K. SUGRUE
University of Miami
Coral Gables, Florida

Mitchell McGRAW-HILL
New York St. Louis San Francisco Auckland Bogotá
Caracas Lisbon London Madrid Mexico Milan
Montreal New Delhi Paris San Juan Singapore
Sydney Tokyo Toronto

Mitchell McGraw-Hill
55 Penny Lane
Watsonville, CA 95076

Laboratory Manual to accompany
Microcomputer Applications, Third Edition

Copyright © 1991, 1989, 1987 by McGraw-Hill, Inc. All rights reserved. Printed in
the United States of America. Except as permitted under the United States Copyright Act of 1976,
no part of this publication may be reproduced or distributed in any form or by any means,
or stored in a database or retrieval system, without the prior written permission of the publisher.

4 5 6 7 8 9 0 MAL MAL 9 0 9 8 7 6 5 4 3 2

ISBN 0-07-024151-1

Library of Congress Catalog Card Number 90-83372

 This book is printed on recycled paper containing a minimum of 50% total recycled fiber with
10% postconsumer de-inked fiber.

Table of Contents

To The Student

PC/MS DOS
Introduction 3
Exercise 1: Turning on the Computer 3
Exercise 2: Formatting a Disk 7
Exercise 3: Practicing DOS Commands 9
Exercise 4: Subdirectories 12
Exercise 5: Advanced DOS Commands 16
Exercise 6: The DOS Shell 21
Exercise 7: The File System 26
DOS Reference 29
PC/MS DOS Self-Evaluation 39
Answers to PC/MS DOS Self-Evaluation 42

WordPerfect 4.2
Introduction 44
Exercise 1: Creating a Document 44
Exercise 2: Retrieving a Document 50
Exercise 3: Reformatting a Document 53
The WordPerfect Template 58
Exercise 4: Using a Dictionary and Thesaurus 59
Exercise 5: Block Commands and Other Operations 62
Exercise 6: Sending Form Letters 65
WordPerfect 4.2 Reference 68
WordPerfect 4.2 Self-Evaluation 70
Answers to WordPerfect 4.2 Self-Evaluation 71

WordPerfect 5.0/5.1
Introduction 72
Requirements 72
Exercise 1: Creating a Document 73
Exercise 2: Retrieving a Document 77
Exercise 3: Reformatting a Document 81
Understanding WordPerfect 87
    The WordPerfect Template 87
    The Help Facility 88

   Hidden Codes 88
   Pull-Down Menus 90
 Exercise 4: Using a Dictionary and Thesaurus 91
 Exercise 5: Block Commands and Other Operations 94
 Exercise 6: Sending Form Letters 97
 Exercise 7: Combining Text and Graphics 101
 Exercise 8: Introduction to Desktop Publishing 106
 WordPerfect 5.0/5.1 Reference 111
 WordPerfect 5.0/5.1 Self-Evaluation 117
 Answers to WordPerfect 5.0/5.1 Self-Evaluation 118

Lotus 2.2/VP Planner Plus

Introduction 119
Exercise 1: Installation and Loading 119
Exercise 2: Creating a Simple Spreadsheet 124
Exercise 3: Basic Spreadsheet Commands 126
Exercise 4: Variable Rate Mortgages 132
Exercise 5: A Financial Forecast 136
Exercise 6: Extended Grade Book 141
Exercise 7: Combining Spreadsheets 146
Macros 150
Exercise 8: Macros 152
Exercise 9: Business Graphics 158
Lotus/VP Planner Plus Reference 168
Lotus/VP Planner Plus Self-Evaluation 172
Answers to Lotus/VP Planner Plus Self-Evaluation 174

dBASE III Plus

Introduction 176
Installation 176
Exercise 1: Loading dBASE 177
A First Look at dBASE 181
Exercise 2: File Maintenance 182
The Basics of dBASE 188
 The Record Pointer 189
 The dBASE Notation 189
 The dBASE Help Facility 192
 The dBASE Assistant 194
Exercise 3: Data Analysis 195
Exercise 4: Menu-Driven Programs 198
dBASE Reference 204
dBASE Self-Evaluation 214
Answers to dBASE Self-Evaluation 217

To the Student

Microcomputer Applications is a generic text, with no reference whatsoever to specific software. You will soon discover however, that there comes a point when you want (indeed must) learn the commands of particular application programs in order to apply the concepts learned in class. Indeed the truly "fun" part of the course occurs in the PC laboratory, when you sit down at the computer and make it perform for you.

The Laboratory Manual is divided into four sections: **PC/MS DOS**, **WordPerfect** (Versions 4.2, 5.0, and 5.1), **Lotus 1-2-3** (Version 2.2/VP Planner Plus, and **dBASE III Plus**). Each section contains program specific hands-on exercises corresponding to the generic versions in the text. As you do the exercises you will become proficient in the individual applications, and in so doing learn to make the computer a useful tool in your business career.

In addition to the hands-on exercises, each section ends with a convenient reference listing the most commonly used commands of each program. There is also a self-evaluation test (with answers) at the end of each section to help you measure your progress.

We suggest you begin with the first three exercises on DOS (which are reproduced from Chapters 1 and 2 in the text for your convenience), then proceed to the application areas as directed by your instructor. All of the exercises are written for both a PC with two floppy drives as well as a system with a hard disk. Hence if you have access to the latter configuration, you may find it useful to do the additional DOS exercise on subdirectories (reproduced from Chapter 14) before proceeding to the application areas.

Good luck and enjoy,

Robert T. Grauer
Paul Sugrue

IBM Program License Agreement

BEFORE OPENING THIS PACKAGE, YOU SHOULD CAREFULLY READ THE FOLLOWING TERMS AND CONDITIONS. OPENING THIS PACKAGE INDICATES YOUR ACCEPTANCE OF THESE TERMS AND CONDITIONS. IF YOU DO NOT AGREE WITH THEM, YOU SHOULD PROMPTLY RETURN THE PACKAGE UNOPENED AND YOUR MONEY WILL BE REFUNDED.

This is a license agreement and not an agreement for sale. IBM owns, or has licensed from the owner, copyrights in the Program. You obtain no rights other than the license granted you by this Agreement. Title to the enclosed copy of the Program, and any copy made from it is retained by IBM. . .The Section in the enclosed documentation entitled "License Information" contains additional information concerning the Program and any related Program Services.

LICENSE INFORMATION

You may:

1) Use the Program on only one machine at any one time, unless permission to use it on more than one machine at any one time is granted in the License Information.

2) Make a copy of the Program for backup or modification purposes only in support of your Authorized Use. However, Programs marked "Copy Protected" limit copying.

3) Modify the Program and/or merge it into another program only in support of your Authorized Use, and

4) Transfer possession of copies of the Program to another party by transferring this copy of the IBM Program License Agreement, the License Information, and all other documentation along with at least once complete, unaltered copy of the Program. You must, at the same time, either transfer to such other party or destroy all your other copies of the Program, including modified copies or portions of the Program merged into other programs.

You shall not:

1) Use, copy, modify, merge, or transfer copies of the Program except as provided in this Agreement

2) Sublicense, rent, lease, or assign the Program or any copy thereof.

*This excerpt from the IBM License Agreement for DOS is typical of the agreements on all software. Note well that while you are permitted to make backup copies of the software in support of your authorized use, it is clearly **illegal** to make copies for any other purpose.*

PC/MS - DOS

Introduction

This section contains the hands-on exercises which appear in Chapters 1, 2, 14, and 15. The exercises are reproduced for your convenience so that you do not have to bring the text itself into the PC lab. Remember, too, that there are minor variations in all of the exercises, depending on whether or not you are using a hard disk. Accordingly pay close attention to the parenthetical remarks and use the commands appropriate for your system.

      Proficiency in DOS comes with time; i.e. the more you work on the computer the better you become. Do not try to master all the material in this section yet. Instead do only Exercise 1 (turning on the computer) and Exercise 2 (formatting a disk) for now. Glance at exercise 3 (practicing DOS commands) and refer to it continually as you go through the later chapters on word processing, spreadsheets, and data management. Save the remaining exercises (tree structures, advanced commands, and DOS 4.00) until you are more comfortable with the computer.

Hands-On Exercise 1: Turning on the Computer

Objective: Turn on the computer, load a DOS system disk, and answer the date and time prompts. Use the PrtSc key to obtain a printed record of your session at the computer. (Corresponds to Hands-On Exercise 1 in Chapter 1.)

Step 1: Locate a DOS System Disk (with two floppy drives)
Skip this step if your system has a hard disk. Otherwise, you will need a floppy disk containing the operating system, which is called a DOS disk. Place the DOS disk, with the label side up and the label toward you in drive A, the drive on your left as you face the computer. (Some systems will have the drives one on top of another, in which case drive A is usually the drive on top.) Close the door on the disk drive.

Step 2: Turn on the Computer
The number and location of the on/off switches depends on the nature and manufacturer of the devices connected to the computer. (The easiest possible setup is when all components of the system are plugged into a

surge protector, in which case only a single switch has to be turned on.) In any event you must:

1. Turn on the printer.
2. Turn on the monitor.
3. Turn on the system unit

Step 3: **Wait**

Each time the power is turned on, the computer conducts a series of self-checking diagnostics (see insert). *Be patient.* Soon you will hear the sound of the disk drive followed by a beep; then you will see a red blinking light on the door of the disk drive. This means that the computer is reading (writing) information from the disk. Do not open the drive door when the red "in use" light is on.

Step 4: **Answer the Date and Time Prompts**

Your system may or may not request the date and time, depending on whether it has an internal battery operated clock. You can proceed to step 5 if you do not see the request; otherwise comply with the instructions provided. The request for a date will appear as follows:

```
Current date is Tue 1-01-1980
Enter new date:
```

Supply the date, *if asked*, using either hyphens or slashes to separate the month, day, and year. 3-16-1990 and 3/16/90 are both valid entries for March 16, 1990 (year may be entered as either a two- or a four-digit number). The system will then return a message of the form:

```
Current time is: 0:00:20.00
Enter new time:
```

Time is expressed in hours:minutes:seconds.hundredths (on a twenty-four-hour military clock). To enter the time, colons are required between hours, minutes, and seconds, and a period between seconds and hundredths of a second. Any value which is omitted is assumed to be zero. 11:30 am. may be entered as 11:30 or 11:30:00 (hundredths are generally omitted). In similar fashion, 11:30 p.m. would be entered as 23:30 or 23:30:00.

Should you enter the date or time incorrectly, you will see the message:

```
Invalid date
Enter new date:
```

or Invalid time.
Enter new time:

It won't take long for you to realize that it is possible to bypass the date and time requests by pressing the enter key twice in a row. We recommend very strongly, however, that you take the trouble to enter the date and time properly so that the operating system will automatically stamp the date and time on every file (for example, a spreadsheet or word processing document) you create.

Step 5: **Recognize the DOS Prompt**
The system should now be up and running, the proof of which is the appearance of the DOS prompt on the monitor. The DOS prompt indicates the default drive and further that the operating system is ready to receive commands. Accordingly, you should see either **A>** or **C>**, depending on whether you are using two floppy drives or a hard drive. (The concept of a DOS prompt and default drive is fully explained in Chapter Two.)

Step 6: **Correct Problems**
You can skip this step provided you ended with the DOS prompt in step 5. Otherwise, you need to address any one of a number of potential problems, the most common of which is using the wrong disk in drive A or using the right disk but forgetting to close the door of the disk drive. Should you make a mistake, you are apt to see the messages:

```
Invalid COMMAND.COM in drive A
```

or `Non system disk or disk error`

or ```
The IBM Personal Computer Basic
Version C1.00
Copyright IBM Corp
61404 Bytes free
```

The procedure to correct these problems depends on whether or not you have a hard drive. Accordingly:

*On systems with two floppy drives:* Check that there is a DOS disk in drive A, with the label side up and toward you. Now close the door of drive A and press the **Ctrl**, **Alt**, and **Del** keys simultaneously.
```

On systems with a hard disk: Leave the door of drive A open, then press the **Ctrl**, **Alt**, and **Del** keys simultaneously.

Either way, the screen should clear and the process begin anew.

Step 7: **Reboot the System**

There may be times when the system locks and the cursor refuses to move. Although this condition does not occur often, and certainly should not be the case now, we will practice the procedure for a warm start.

Use your left hand to hold down the **Ctrl** and **Alt** keys, and while keeping these keys depressed, use your right hand to press the **Del** key. Almost immediately, you will hear the sound of the disk drive, see the red light come on, and view the date (and time) prompts on the monitor.

This process (a warm boot) restarts the computer, causing it to lose everything previously in RAM. The process is faster than a cold start (when the machine is initially turned on), as the machine bypasses the self-checking procedure of step 3. As you might have guessed, the placement of the Ctrl, Alt, and Del keys is deliberately awkward to avoid an accidental rebooting of the system, with its associated memory loss.

Step 8: **Print the Screen**

Be sure the printer is turned on. Most printers have two indicator lights, one to show the power is on, and one to show it is "on-line" to the computer. Check that both of these are on.

The contents of the screen may be sent to the printer at any time. Press the **Shift** key, and while holding it down, press the **PrtSc** key as well, and the contents of the screen will be reproduced on the printer. Obtaining hard copy in this fashion is a useful practice to record a command, and can help in solving any problems you may have. *It is impossible for an instructor to answer questions unless he or she has an exact copy of what happened, as provided by the PrtSc key.* You can also use this technique to create your own reference manual.

Step 9: **Shut the System Down**

You have now completed the first Hands-On Exercise and are ready to begin using the computer effectively. You have turned on the machine and its peripheral devices, loaded a disk, initialized the date and time, and obtained printed copy of your session at the computer.

Turn the power off to shut down the system. (The disk in drive A may be removed from the drive either before or after the power is turned off.)

Hands-On Exercise 2:
Formatting a Disk

Objective: Format a disk and use the DIR and COPY commands. Remember also that the messages returned by the FORMAT command, regarding the number of bytes used and the available space, will differ depending on the size and capacity of the disk, as well as the version of DOS you are using. (Corresponds to Hands-On Exercise 1 in Chapter 2.)

Step 1: **Boot the System**
Boot the system following the procedure used in the first Hands-On Exercise.

Step 2a: **Format a Disk (with two floppy drives)**
Place a DOS disk in drive A and the disk to be formatted in drive B. Enter the command **FORMAT B:/S** to format the disk with the system files to which the system will respond:

```
Insert new diskette for drive B:
Strike ENTER key when ready
```

Be sure that the disk to be formatted is in the proper drive, that is, in drive B. Strike the enter key (earlier versions of DOS allowed you to press any key), then relax for about one minute. The system will respond:

```
Formatting . . .
Format complete
System transferred

   362496   bytes total disk space
    60416   bytes used by system
   302080   bytes available on disk

Format another (Y/N)?
```

Respond **N**, for no, and the formatting operation is complete.

Step 2b: **Format a Disk (with a hard drive)**
Place the disk to be formatted in drive A, then change to the subdirectory on the hard drive containing the DOS utility programs. (Subdirectories are explained fully in Chapter 14.) Enter the command **CD\DOS** (where

DOS is the name of *our* subdirectory), then enter the command **FORMAT A:/S** to format the disk in drive A. The remaining messages parallel those in step 2a.

Step 3: **View the Directory (DIR Command)**
Type **DIR B:** or **DIR A:** (depending on which drive contains the formatted disk.) You should see a directory resembling the following, although the size of COMMAND.COM will depend on the version of DOS you are using:

```
Volume in drive B has no label
Directory of B:\

COMMAND   COM   22042   8/14/84   8:00a
  1 File(s)  302080 bytes free
```

At first this directory may appear slightly puzzling in that the formatting messages in step 2 indicate that 60,416 bytes were used by the system (the exact amount will depend on the version of DOS that you are using), yet COMMAND.COM takes only 22,042. What happened to the remaining 38,374? The answer is that the portion of the operating system which was transferred to the formatted disk consisted of three files, not one. Only COMMAND.COM is visible, but there are also two hidden files which aren't listed in the directory.

Step 4a: **Copy a File (with two floppy drives)**
Enter the command **COPY A:FORMAT.COM B:** to copy the file FORMAT.COM from the disk in drive A to the disk in drive B. (Your DOS release may contain the file FORMAT.*EXE* rather than FORMAT.*COM*.)

Step 4b: **Copy a File (with a hard disk)**
The only difference between this command and the one in step 4a is the specification of the source and destination drives. Accordingly, enter the command **COPY C:FORMAT.COM A:** to copy the file from the hard disk in drive C to the floppy disk in drive A.

Step 5: **Change the Default Drive**
Enter **A:** or **B:** to change the default drive, depending on which drive contains the newly formatted disk. Now enter the **DIR** command to obtain the directory of the new default drive, and observe the following:

```
Volume in drive B has no label
Directory of B:\

COMMAND     COM     22042     8/14/84     8:00a
FORMAT      COM      9015     8/14/84     8:00a
    2 File(s)   292864 bytes free
```

The disk in drive B contains the FORMAT.COM file in addition to COMMAND.COM, reflecting the results of the COPY operation.

Hands-On Exercise 3: Practicing DOS Commands

Objective: Illustrates various DOS commands and how to write-protect a disk. *Remember, as with the previous exercises, there are differences in the commands depending on whether or not you are using a hard disk.* (Corresponds to Hands-On Exercise 2 in Chapter 2.)

Step 1: **Starting Out**

Continue where you left off in the previous exercise. *On a two-drive floppy system* place a DOS disk in drive A and a formatted disk in drive B. *On systems with a hard disk*, change to the DOS subdirectory with the command CD\DOS, then place a formatted disk in drive A.

Step 2: **The CHKDSK Command**

Type the command **CHKDSK B:** or **CHKDSK A:** depending on which drive contains the formatted disk. You should see a message similar to the following appear on the monitor (with the size of the various files dependent on the version of DOS you are using):

```
362496  bytes total disk space
 37888  bytes in 2 hidden files
 22528  bytes in 1 user file
302080  bytes available on disk

655360  bytes total memory
618336  bytes free
```

Now you see the approximately 38,000 bytes in the hidden files which were "missing" from the directory in the first Hands-On Exercise. Note, also, that the sum of 37,888 and 22,528 is 60,416, which matches the number of bytes used by the system, as indicated by the FORMAT command in step 2 of the previous exercise.

The indication of 655,360 bytes is the total amount of RAM in the system of which 618,336 are still available. Note, too, that although 640Kb (655,360/1024) is a common configuration, your system may register a different amount, depending on the amount memory in your system.

Step 3: **The COPY Command with Wild Card**
We will use the wild card designation in conjunction with the COPY command to copy all files whose file name begins with the letter D. (There will be at least two such files, DISKCOPY.COM and DISKCOMP.COM, and possibly others, depending on your version of DOS.) Note too, that the precise format of the COPY command depends on whether or not you have a hard disk, that is whether you are copying from drive C or drive A. Thus:

With two floppy drives, enter the command **COPY A:D*.* B:** because you are copying from drive A to drive B.

With a hard drive, enter the command **COPY C:D*.* A:** because you are copying from drive C to drive A.

Step 4: **The RENAME Command**
The name of an existing file can be changed through the RENAME command, but again the precise command will depend on your system. Accordingly:

With two floppy drives, enter the command **RENAME B:D*.*   X*.*** because you are renaming the files on drive B.

With a hard drive, enter the command **RENAME A:D*.*   X*.*** because you are renaming the files on drive A.

Either way you are changing the names of all files beginning with the letter D to begin instead with the letter X. You can verify the results of the RENAME command by taking a directory of drive A or B, before and after issuing the RENAME command.

Step 5: **The ERASE Command**
This time we will erase the files copied in step 3 and renamed in step 4. Again the precise command depends on the drive containing your files. Thus:

With two floppy drives, enter the command ERASE B:*.* to erase all files on drive B

With a hard drive, enter the command ERASE A:*.* to erase all files on drive A

Step 6a: DISKCOPY (with two floppy drives)
Place a DOS disk in drive A and a blank disk in drive B (or leave the current disk in). Type the command **DISKCOPY A: B:**. The system will tell you to place the source disk in drive A and the target disk in drive B, and to strike any key when ready. When the copy operation is finished, it will ask you whether you wish to copy another. Respond N for no. The disk in drive B now contains a duplicate copy of the original DOS disk.

Step 6b: DISKCOPY (with a hard drive)
Place the source disk (the disk you want copied) in drive A, then issue the command **DISKCOPY A: A:**. The system will tell you to place the source disk in drive A at which point it will read as much data from the disk as possible into memory. It will then instruct you to remove the source disk and replace it with the target disk at which point it will copy the data in RAM to the target disk. It will continue prompting you to switch the source and target disks until the source disk has been copied.

Step 7: The DISKCOMP Command
The DISKCOMP command checks whether two disks are identical to one another. Type the command DISKCOMP A: B: or DISKCOMP A: A: depending on whether you have two floppy drives or a single floppy drive (in which case the system will tell you to switch disks as necessary).

Step 8: Write-Protecting a Disk
Step 5 illustrated the ERASE command and showed how files can be deleted provided the disk was not write protected. To illustrate the concept of write protection follow the appropriate procedure depending on the size of your floppy disk. Thus:

With 5 1/4 inch floppies: Cover the write-protect notch of the disk with a piece of **opaque** tape

With 3 1/2 inch floppies: Move the built in-cover on the disk so that the write-protect notch is open.

Return the floppy disk to drive A, close the door, and issue the command **ERASE A:*.*** The system asks if you are sure (type **Y**), and then prints the message:

```
Write protect error writing drive A
Abort, Retry, Ignore?
```

In effect, DOS is telling you that you are trying to erase data from a disk which has been write protected. Answer **A** to abort the command.

Step 9: Removing the Write Protection
This time we write-enable a disk by reversing the procedure of step 8:

With 5 1/4 inch floppies: Uncover the write-protect notch of the disk by removing the piece of opaque tape

With 3 1/2 inch floppies: Move the built-in cover on the disk so that the write-protect notch is closed.

Return the floppy disk to drive A, close the door, and issue the command **ERASE A:*.*** The system asks if you are sure (type **Y**), then erases all of the files on drive A.

Hands-On Exercise 4: Subdirectories

Objective: Use DOS commands associated with subdirectories, namely, MD, CD, RD, TREE, PATH, and PROMPT. The exercise will create the tree structure of Figure 1. (Corresponds to Hands-On Exercise 1 in Chapter 14.)

Step 1a: Starting Out (with a hard disk)
Boot the system, then place a newly formatted disk in drive A. Enter the command **A:** to make drive A the default drive.

Step 1b: Starting Out (with two floppy drives)
Boot the system (with a DOS system disk in drive A), then place a newly formatted disk in drive B. Enter the command **B:** to make drive B the default drive.

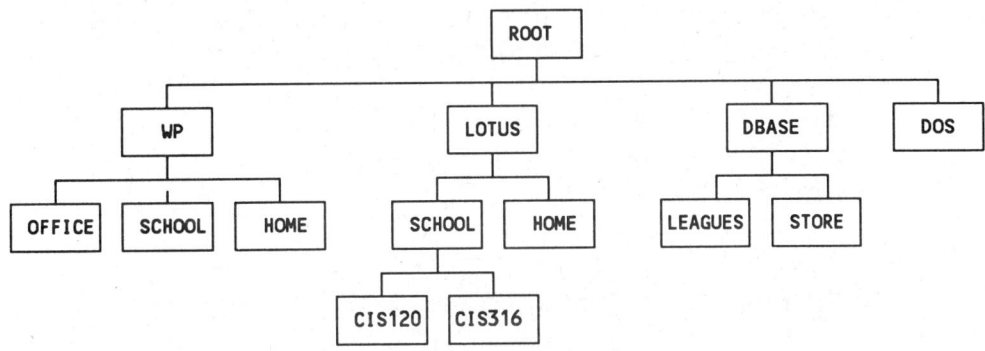

Figure 1 - Tree Structure

Step 2: **The PROMPT Command**

Enter the command **PROMPT pg** to change the prompt to include the currently logged directory whereupon the next prompt should be A:\> or B:\> depending on whether you followed step 1a or 1b (for systems with and without a hard disk, respectively). In either case the backslash indicates you are currently in the root directory of the default drive.

Step 3: **The MD Command**

Create the four subdirectories under the root directory by entering the following commands in succession:

    MD WP
    MD LOTUS
    MD DBASE
    MD DOS

Note too, that since each of the subdirectories belongs directly to the root, a backslash could have been included in each MD command, for example, MD \WP. Execute the **DIR** command after you have created the subdirectories. Your directory will resemble the listing below (COMMAND.COM may or may not appear depending on how the floppy disk was formatted.)

```
Directory of  A:\

COMMAND    COM        37637  06-17-88   12:00p
WP                   <DIR>          05-11-90   11:00a
LOTUS                <DIR>          05-11-90   11:00a
DBASE                <DIR>          05-11-90   11:00a
DOS                  <DIR>          05-11-90   11:00a
        5 File(s)      1348096 bytes free
```

Step 4: **Create Additional Subdirectories**
Create the three subdirectories in the WP directory with the commands:

    MD \WP\OFFICE
    MD \WP\SCHOOL
    MD \WP\HOME

The backslashes show the path to the subdirectories; for example, OFFICE belongs to WP, which in turn belongs to the root directory. Now enter the additional commands necessary to create the remaining subdirectories in Figure 1.

Step 5: **The CD Command**
Type the command **CD \WP** (or equivalently, CD WP without the backslash, since you are still in the root directory) to enter the WP subdirectory. Now issue a **DIR** command to obtain the directory listing below:

```
Directory of  A:\WP

.              <DIR>      05-11-90    11:00a
..             <DIR>      05-11-90    11:00a
OFFICE         <DIR>      05-11-90    11:01a
SCHOOL         <DIR>      05-11-90    11:01a
HOME           <DIR>      05-11-90    11:01a
        5 File(s)     1343488 bytes free
```

Now enter the command **CD \WP\OFFICE** (or simply CD OFFICE since you are in the WP directory) then enter a final **DIR** command to obtain the directory below.

```
Directory of  A:\WP\OFFICE

.              <DIR>      05-11-90    11:01a
..             <DIR>      05-11-90    11:01a
        2 File(s)     1343488 bytes free
```

Step 6: **Copying Files**
This step copies the TREE.COM program file (associated with the external TREE command) to the newly created DOS subdirectory. The commands differ however, depending on whether you are copying the file from a hard disk or from the DOS system disk. Enter the appropriate command for your system:

With a hard disk: **CD A:\DOS** and **COPY C:\DOS\TREE.COM   A:**
With two floppy disks: **CD B:\DOS** and **COPY A:TREE.COM B:**

Step 7:   **The PATH Command**
Change to the root directory with the command **CD ** then issue the **TREE** command. The system will not, however, display the tree structure, but instead will return an error message of the form, "Bad command or file name". You did not make an error; the system is simply saying it can't find the program TREE.COM program in the current (root) directory.

Enter the appropriate PATH command to allow DOS to search additional directories for the TREE.COM program (which you copied in the previous step). Thus:

With a hard disk: **PATH A:\DOS**
With two floppy disks: **PATH B:\DOS**

Repeat the **TREE** command and this time you will get the desired output.

Step 8:   **The RD Command**
Enter the command **RD DBASE** to remove the DBASE subdirectory, to which the system responds, "Invalid path, not a directory, or directory not empty". DOS is preventing you from removing the DBASE directory because it (DBASE) contains additional subdirectories. Accordingly you need to enter the following:

CD \DBASE
RD LEAGUES
RD STORE
**CD **
RD DBASE

You can confirm the success of these commands by issuing another **DIR** command from the root directory.

Hands-On Exercise 5:
Advanced DOS Commands

Objective: Demonstrate the FIND, SORT, and MORE filters; use the ANSI.SYS and VDISK.SYS device drivers; use CHKDSK to locate lost files on disk; implement an AUTOEXEC.BAT file. The exercise requires the creation and/or modification of the AUTOEXEC.BAT and/or CONFIG.SYS files. We suggest therefore that you do the exercise from drive A so as not to disturb these files if they already exist which in turn requires preparation of a bootable floppy disk from which to work. **The exercise requires DOS 3.00 or higher.** (Corresponds to Hands-On Exercise 1 in Chapter 15.)

Step 1: Formatting

Boot the system. Place the disk to be formatted in drive A or drive B depending on whether you are working with a hard disk or two floppies, then issue the following commands:

With a hard disk: **CD C:\DOS** followed by **FORMAT A:/S**
With two floppy drives: Place a DOS disk in drive A, then enter the command **FORMAT B:/S**

The floppy disk in drive A (or drive B depending on your configuration) should now be bootable.

Step 2: Create the DOS Subdirectory

You need to create a DOS subdirectory on the newly formatted disk. Accordingly:

With a hard disk: **MD A:\DOS**
With two floppy drives: **MD B:\DOS**

The floppy disk in drive A (or drive B) now contains a DOS subdirectory.

Step 3: Copying Files

This step copies the external program files you will use in subsequent steps to the DOS subdirectory you just created. (Note that the program files are specified with a wild card extension, as different versions of DOS use different extensions, COM or EXE for these files. The asterisk accommodates any version.) Enter the indicated commands.

DOS Hands-On Exercises 17

With a hard disk: (These commands change the default to drive C, copy files to the disk in drive A, and finally make drive A the default.)

C:
CD C:\DOS
COPY SORT.* A:\DOS
COPY MORE.* A:\DOS
COPY FIND.* A:\DOS
COPY TREE.* A:\DOS
COPY CHKDSK.* A:\DOS
COPY VDISK.SYS A:\DOS
COPY ANSI.SYS A:\DOS
A:

With two floppy drives: (These commands change the default to drive A, then copy files to the disk in drive B.)

A:
COPY SORT.* B:\DOS
COPY MORE.* B:\DOS
COPY FIND.* B:\DOS
COPY TREE.* B:\DOS
COPY CHKDSK.* B:\DOS
COPY VDISK.SYS B:\DOS
COPY ANSI.SYS B:\DOS

Step 4: **Check Your Progress**

From this point on, all subsequent instructions are identical regardless of your hardware configuration. Accordingly, place the newly created floppy disk in drive A and enter the command **PATH A:\DOS** followed by **TREE/F**. Your results should parallel those in Figure 2a, reflecting that you have created a bootable disk with a DOS subdirectory, and further that all external files necessary for this exercise are in that subdirectory. If this is not the case, repeat steps 1, 2, or 3 as necessary.

Step 5: **Redirecting Output**

Enter the command **TREE/F>LPT1** whereupon the output of the TREE command will be directed to the printer. You can redirect output of the DIR command as well, with the command **DIR>LPT1**.

Step 6: **The SORT Filter**

Enter the command **CD\DOS** to change to the DOS subdirectory. Enter a DIR command to list the directory as it was created, then enter the command **DIR ¦ SORT** to list the files in alphabetical order, and finally

```
Directory PATH listing
Volume Serial Number is 2613-12FD
A:\
├── COMMAND.COM
│
└──DOS
      SORT.EXE
      MORE.COM
      FIND.EXE
      TREE.COM
      CHKDSK.COM
      VDISK.SYS
      ANSI.SYS
```

(a) Tree Structure

```
 Volume in drive A has no label
 Volume Serial Number is 2613-12FD
 Directory of  A:\

COMMAND   COM      37637 06-17-88   12:00p
DOS            <DIR>       01-07-90   11:56a
        2 File(s)       563200 bytes free
```

(b) Root Directory at Beginning of Step 4

```
 Volume in drive A has no label
 Volume Serial Number is 2613-12FD
 Directory of  A:\

COMMAND   COM      37637 06-17-88   12:00p
DOS            <DIR>       01-07-90   11:56a
CONFIG    SYS         46 01-07-90   12:02p
AUTOEXEC  BAT         38 01-07-90   12:07a
        4 File(s)       561152 bytes free
```

(c) Root Directory at End of Step 9

Figure 2 - Directory for Exercise 5

enter the command **DIR ¦ SORT/+14** to obtain the files in ascending order of file size. You can also list the files in descending order by including the /R parameter at the end of the command; i.e., **DIR ¦ SORT/R/+14**.

Step 7: **Create a CONFIG.SYS File**
Change to the root directory with the command **CD **, then create the CONFIG.SYS file shown below. The configuration file establishes a virtual disk of 100KB, loads the ANSI.SYS device driver, and changes the DOS defaults for files and buffers. The easiest way to create the CONFIG.SYS file is with the COPY CON command as shown:

    COPY CON: CONFIG.SYS
    DEVICE=\\DOS\\VDISK.SYS   100
    DEVICE=\\DOS\\ANSI.SYS
    FILES=20
    BUFFERS=15
    Press the **F6** key then the **enter** key

The COPY CON command is in fact an ordinary COPY command where the source file is the CONsole (keyboard) and the destination file is CONFIG.SYS. Pressing the F6 key signifies the end of the source file (that is, no more commands will be entered from the console).
    Enter a DIR command to be sure that newly created CONFIG.SYS file appears on the root directory.

Step 8: **Create an AUTOEXEC.BAT File**
This step creates a simple AUTOEXEC.BAT file to accept the date and time, establish a path to the DOS subdirectory, and change the prompt to include the current subdirectory. You can use COPY CON to create the AUTOEXEC.BAT file (or alternatively you can create it with any word processor provided you create it as an *ASCII* file). Enter the commands:

    COPY CON: AUTOEXEC.BAT
    DATE
    TIME
    PATH A:\\DOS
    PROMPT PG
    Press the **F6** key then the **enter** key

The COPY CON command copies commands from the CONsole (keyboard) to the file specified; in this case, AUTOEXEC.BAT which consists of four DOS commands: DATE, TIME, PATH, and PROMPT, as indicated. When the last command (PROMPT) has been entered, press the F6 key (to indicate the end of the file to be copied) followed by the enter key, as indicated. Enter a DIR command to be sure that newly created AUTOEXEC.BAT file appears on the root directory.

Step 9: **The Virtual Disk**
Press **Ctrl, Alt, and Del** to reboot the system, whereupon the newly created CONFIG.SYS and AUTOEXEC.BAT files will take effect. The availability of a virtual disk will be confirmed by the messages:

```
VDISK Version 1.0 virtual disk D:
   Sector size adjusted
   Directory entries adjusted
   Buffer size: 100 KB
   Sector size: 128
   Directory entries: 64
```

You can also enter the command **DIR D:** to view the contents of the RAM drive (which is empty at this time).

Step 10: **The Cluster Concept**
Figure 2b shows the root directory at the start of step 4, and 2c shows it after step 9 has been completed. Observe the root directory contains only three files (COMMAND.COM, CONFIG.SYS, and AUTOEXEC.BAT), in addition to the DOS subdirectory, and we urge you to set up your hard drive in a similar, uncluttered fashion.

Note, too, the difference in available disk space between the two figures (563,200 bytes in Figure 2b versus 561,152 bytes in Figure 2c). The latter figure contained two additional files (CONFIG.SYS and AUTOEXEC.BAT), which collectively are 84 bytes in length; yet they decreased the available disk space by 2048 bytes (563,200 - 561,152). The discrepancy is due to the fact that every file is assigned a minimum of one cluster (equal to two sectors or 1,024 bytes) regardless of its size.

Step 11: **Finding Lost Files**
Enter the command **CHKDSK/V** whereupon every file on the disk (in both the root and DOS subdirectory) will be listed. Now enter the command **CHKDSK/V¦FIND ".SYS"** and only those files with an extension of SYS will be found. Three such files will be displayed (CONFIG.SYS on the root directory, and ANSI.SYS and VDISK.SYS in the DOS directory); i.e. the system has located the latter files in the DOS directory even though you are currently in the root directory.

Step 12: Experiment with ANSI.SYS
You can change the colors displayed on your monitor as described in the box on ANSI.SYS in Chapter 15 of the text. For example, to change the display of your monitor to white letters on a blue background, enter the commands:

PROMPT PG$E[44;37m   (the m **must** be in lower case)
CLS

The colors will *not* change until after you enter the CLS command. Note too the CONFIG.SYS file must contain the ANSI.SYS driver (as was done in step 7) after which the system has to be rebooted. Different color combinations are possible; e.g., the command PROMPT PG$E[41;33m gives yellow letters on a red background.

Step 13: The MORE Filter
The utility of the MORE filter comes into play only if a file contains more lines than can be displayed on the monitor at one time. Although this is not the case with the floppy disk in drive A, the MORE filter is one of DOS' most useful features, so keep it in mind when you return to your other disks.

Hands-On Exercise 6:
The DOS Shell

Objective: Illustrate the DOS shell and various options within the Start Programs menu. Add, change, and delete a program and/or a group to the opening menu. **This exercise requires DOS 4.00 and a hard disk.** (Corresponds to Hands-On Exercise 2 in Chapter 15.)

Step 1: Load the DOS Shell
Change to the DOS subdirectory or include this directory in the active path. Type **DOSSHELL** to enter the shell, whereupon the Start Programs screen of Figure 3a will come into view. Your screen, however, will contain only the first four options (as we have modified our menu), and further the display on your monitor may be different from ours. (The shell can be displayed in either text or graphics mode; our illustrations are in the graphics mode.)

22 DOS Hands-On Exercises

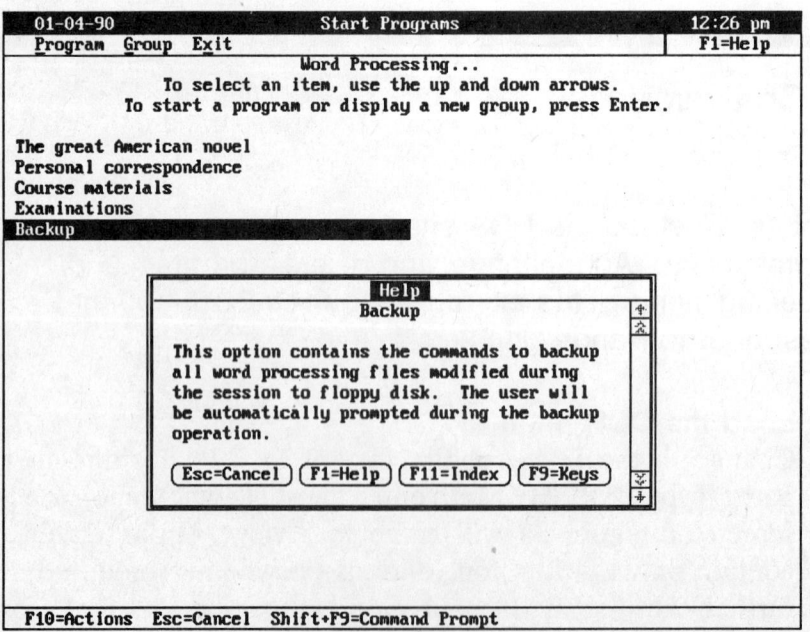

(a) Start Files (With Choices Added)

(b) Secondary Menu

Figure 3 - The DOS Shell

Step 2: Explore the Main Group
The procedure to start (execute) a program depends on whether you are using the keyboard or a mouse. Thus:

To start programs with a mouse: Move the mouse pointer over the program, then **double click** (press the selector button twice) to start the program.

To start programs from the keyboard: Move the cursor with the up and down arrow keys to highlight the desired option, then press the **enter** key.

Step 3: Change Colors
This option is useful only on systems with a color monitor. Start this program (click twice or highlight and press return), then follow the on-screen instructions to select the color combination you like best. You can also press the **F1** function key at any time to enter the online help facility, then press **Esc** to return to the previous screen.

Step 4: The Command Prompt
Select **Command Prompt** to temporarily leave the DOS Shell and return to the normal DOS prompt from where you can execute any desired DOS command(s). Type **Exit** at the DOS prompt and you will be returned to the DOS shell. (Note well, however, that this procedure is different from permanently exiting the shell by selecting Exit from the action bar. The latter action requires the DOSSHELL command to restart the shell.)

Step 5: DOS Utilities
The three dots indicate that DOS utilities is a group rather than a program, which in turn produces a secondary menu. Select one or more choices from the DOS utilities menu, e.g., DISKCOPY or FORMAT, (the choices are disappointing) then press **Esc** to return to the opening screen of the shell.

Step 6: Add a Program
The major advantage of the shell is the ability to add additional programs (e.g., Lotus) and/or groups (Word Processing...) to the opening menu. Double click on **Program** at the top of the screen (if you have a mouse), or press the F10 and enter keys (on systems without a mouse) to select Program. You will see the pull down menu of Figure 4a. Select Add and Figure 4b appears.

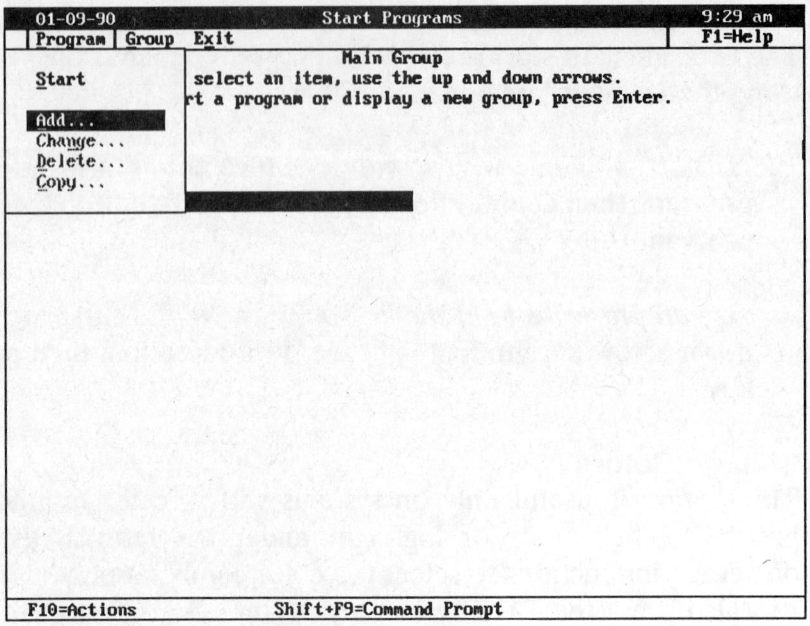

(a) Pull Down Menu

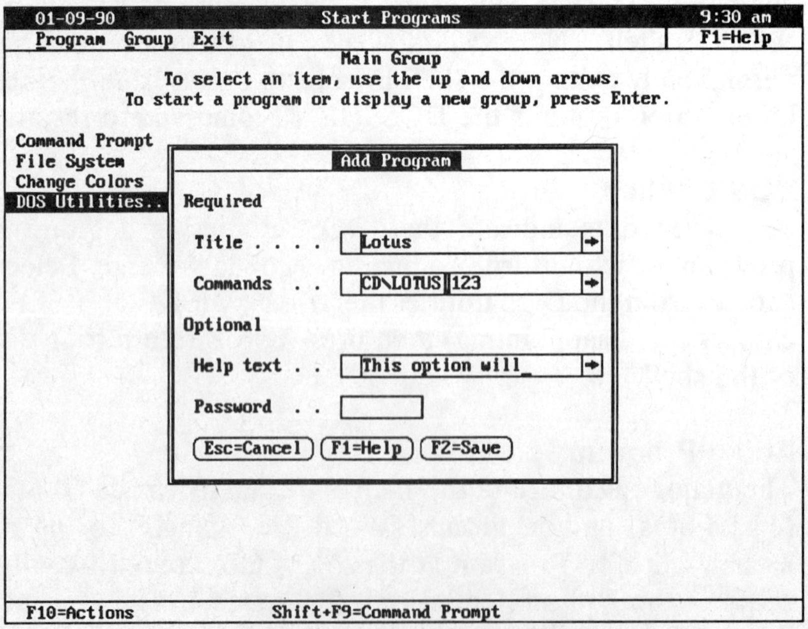

(b) Entering the Commands

Figure 4 - Adding a Program

For the title, enter the descriptive information as it is to appear in the Main Group; e.g., Lotus. Press the enter key. Next enter the individual DOS commands you would normally use to run Lotus; namely CD \LOTUS to change to the LOTUS subdirectory, and 123 to execute the program. *You must press the F4 function key to separate the commands from each other.* Press the enter key after entering the second command (123). The Help Text and Password entries are optional as indicated. Help text contains the screen (or screens) that will appear in conjunction with the F1 function key whereas password restricts access to this program to individuals knowing the password you establish.

Press the **F2** function key to save your work and return to the opening menu.

Step 7: **Add a Group**

A group (e.g., Word Processing...) is added in much the same way as an individual program (e.g., Lotus) except that the **Group** option (rather than Program) is selected from the action bar. (Recall that a group is distinguished from a program by the three dots and implies the existence of a second menu.)

Select the Group option and add the group name Word Processing. You will see a screen similar to Figure 4 except that it calls for a filename rather than individual DOS commands. Choose any valid name, then press **F2** to save the group and return to the opening screen. Select the newly entered Word Processing group, then add individual programs within this group according to the procedure described in the step 6. The individual programs can load different word processors, or they can load the same word processor but log into different subdirectories for the different documents.

Step 8: **Changes and Deletions**

You can change and/or delete any group or program you have created by selecting the appropriate command from the action bar. (You cannot however change or delete the four original options in Start Programs.)

Step 9: **Exit the DOS Shell**

Double click over **Exit** (or press the F10 key to return to the action bar and select Exit) to leave the DOS shell and return to the DOS prompt. Unlike the temporary exit from step 4, however, you must now type DOSSHELL should you wish to reenter the shell.

26 DOS Hands-On Exercises

Hands-On Exercise 7
The File System

Objective: Illustrate the File System within the DOS shell and the use of pull down menus to copy, delete, and rename files from multiple directories. Explore how subdirectories can be created and renamed, and how their associated files are displayed. **The exercise requires DOS 4.00 and a hard drive; a mouse is recommended.** (Corresponds to Hands-On Exercise 3 in Chapter 15.)

Step 1: Enter the File System

Change to the DOS subdirectory and type **DOSSHELL** to enter the shell as in the previous exercise. Select File System from the main group whereupon the system will pause briefly with the message, "Reading Disk Information," then display the contents of the root directory.

On systems without a mouse, press the Tab key repeatedly to move the cursor to the various elements on the screen: the action bar listing the available commands (File, Options, Arrange, and Exit), the drive identifier indicating the selected drive, the directory tree (graphic description of the disk), and the file list for the currently selected subdirectory. Once the cursor is at the appropriate portion of the screen use the arrow keys to highlight the desired option then press the return key to select that option.

It is much easier on systems with a mouse as all you do is move the pointer over the option, then click once to select that option.

Step 2: Single File List (Figure 5a)

Select different directories from the tree structure, observing that as each new directory is highlighted its corresponding file list appears in the right side of the screen.

Step 3: Sort a Directory

Highlight the DOS (or any other) subdirectory, then move to the action bar and select the **Options menu**. Choose **Display Options** and select one of the listed options (Name, Extension, Date, Size, or Disk Order) to list the files according to the option chosen.

Step 4: Multiple File List (Figure 5b)

Return to the action bar and select the **Arrange menu.** Choose **Multiple file list** to display two directories with their associated files.

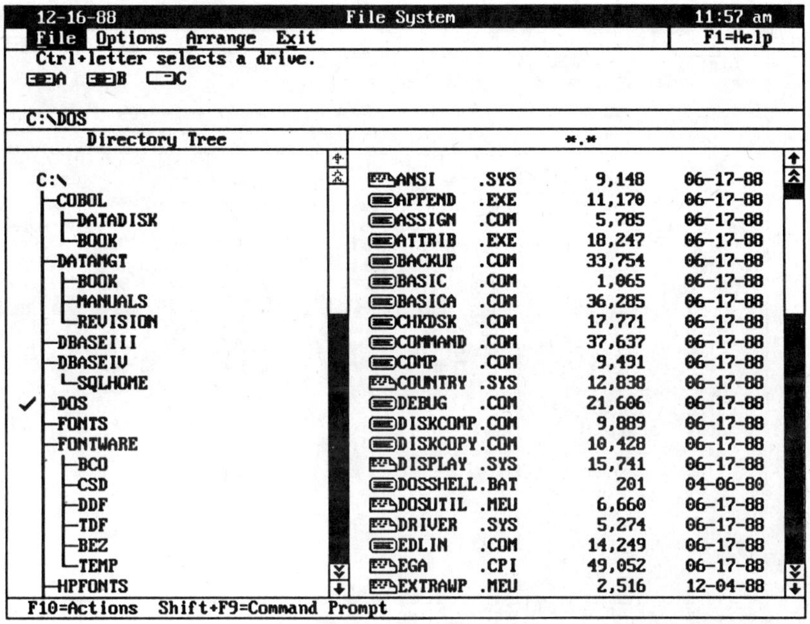

DOS Hands-On Exercises 27

(a) Single File List

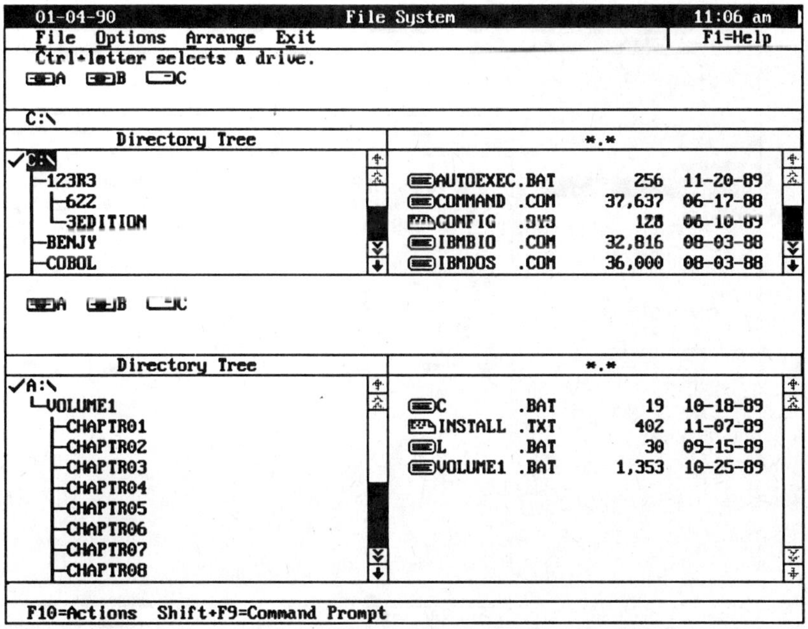

(b) Multiple File List

Figure 5 - DOS File System

28 DOS Hands-On Exercises

```
 01-04-90                File System              12:41 pm
 File  Options  Arrange  Exit                     F1=Help
 Ctrl+letter selects a drive.
 [==]A  [==]B  [=]C

 C:\JESSICA
                                         *.BK!
 File
   Name  : PLANTS.BK!      CHAPTR04.BK!   84,709   01-03-90   2:46pm
   Attr  : ...a            CHRISTIN.BK!    6,406   01-02-90  12:20pm
 Selected          C       FIG1TO5 .BK!   86,404   12-18-89   8:23pm
   Number:         1       FINDIT  .BK!      256   02-01-89   3:39pm
   Size  :    18,411       HANDSON .BK!    3,734   01-03-90   2:13pm
 Directory                 INVITE  .BK!    7,824   01-01-90  12:10pm
   Name  : JESSICA         PLANTS  .BK!   18,411   01-01-90   7:48pm
   Size  :    99,277       TEMP    .BK!    2,587   12-31-89   8:54am
   Files :        13       TEMP    .BK!    7,343   12-31-89  11:59am
 Disk                      TEMP    .BK!   72,136   01-02-90   1:59pm
   Name  :
   Size  : 120,315,904
   Avail :  57,221,120
   Files :       2,687
   Dirs  :         145

 F10=Actions   Shift+F9=Command Prompt
```

(c) System File List

```
 01-04-90                File System              12:42 pm
 File | Options  Arrange  Exit                    F1=Help
               drive.
 Open (start)...
 Print...
 Associate...
                                         *.BK!
 Move...
 Copy...                   CHAPTR04.BK!   84,709   01-03-90   2:46pm
 Delete...                 CHRISTIN.BK!    6,406   01-02-90  12:20pm
 Rename...                 FIG1TO5 .BK!   86,404   12-18-89   8:23pm
 Change attribute...       FINDIT  .BK!      256   02-01-89   3:39pm
 View                      HANDSON .BK!    3,734   01-03-90   2:13pm
                           INVITE  .BK!    7,824   01-01-90  12:10pm
 Create directory...       PLANTS  .BK!   18,411   01-01-90   7:48pm
 Select all                TEMP    .BK!    2,587   12-31-89   8:54am
 Deselect all              TEMP    .BK!    7,343   12-31-89  11:59am
                           TEMP    .BK!   72,136   01-02-90   1:59pm
   Name  :
   Size  : 120,315,904
   Avail :  57,221,120
   Files :       2,687
   Dirs  :         145

 F10=Actions   Shift+F9=Command Prompt
```

(d) Pull Down Menus

Figure 5 - DOS File System (Continued)

Step 5: **System File List (Figure 5c)**
Select the **Arrange** menu once more, but this time choose **System file list**. The system will pause briefly, then display *every* file on the selected disk (but of course, you won't see them all at the same time).

Now choose the **Options menu** and select **Display options** from this menu. The cursor is positioned in the file name area which currently reads *.*, meaning that all files are displayed. Change the display to read *.BK! (since only the BK! files are desired), press return, and only the BK! will be listed.

Step 6: **Deleting Selected Files (Figure 5d)**
Select the **File** menu once more and choose the **Select all** option from this menu. All files on the right hand side of the screen should now have their respective file markers highlighted. *Verify that only the BK! files are shown.* Select the **Delete** command from the File menu and all of the BK! files on your entire disk will be deleted.

In similar fashion you can the use other commands from the File menu (e.g., Copy, Rename, Change attribute, and so on) to work with other groups of selected files.

Step 7: **Creating Subdirectories**
Subdirectories can be easily created, deleted, or even renamed without a thought for the backslash. Choose the **Arrange menu** once again, and choose the **Single file list**. To create a new subdirectory, simply highlight the existing subdirectory under which the new directory is to go. Return to the File menu, choose **Create directory**, and enter the new directory name.

Step 8: **Exit the File System**
Select the **Exit menu**, choose **Exit file system** and you will be returned to the Start Programs screen of the DOS shell.

DOS Reference

You will find it extremely useful to have essential DOS information in a single place. Accordingly we present a reference section with specific illustrations of some of the more commonly used commands, with the commands listed in *alphabetical order*.

Realize, however, that this manual is not intended to be a substitute for the IBM DOS Reference manual; hence we do not list some of the more esoteric options of various commands nor do we list all of the DOS commands. You are referred to the IBM DOS manual for complete information.

ATTRIB Command

Purpose: Changes or displays the read-only and archive bits of a file; identifies all occurrences of a particular file anywhere on disk

Type: External (Requires DOS 3.00 or higher)

Format: ATTRIB [+/-R][+/-A][d:][path] filename[.ext][/S]

Examples:

ATTRIB +A XYZ	Sets the archive bit to one for file XYZ
ATTRIB +A C:*.* /S	Sets the archive bit to one for all files on drive C (/S parameter is for DOS 4.00 only)
ATTRIB -R *.*	Turns off read-only bit for files in directory
ATTRIB +A +R *.*	Turns on both the archive and read-only bits for all files in this directory
ATTRIB \BENJY/S	Finds all occurrences of the file BENJY on the default disk
ATTRIB FILE.ONE	Displays the attributes of FILE.ONE (which must be in the current directory)

BACKUP Command

Purpose: Copies (backs up) files from one disk to another, typically from a hard disk to a series of floppy disks. The command accommodates large files unable to fit on a single floppy by prompting for additional disks. Used in conjunction with the RESTORE command.

Type: External

Format: BACKUP [d:][path][filename[.ext]][d:][/S][/M][/L]

Examples:

BACKUP C:\WP\BOOK A:	Backs up the file BOOK from the directory WP to the floppy disk(s) in drive A.
BACKUP C:*.* A:/S	Backs up all files on drive C to drive A, prompting for additional disks as necessary.
BACKUP C:*.* A:/S/M	Backups every file that was modified or created since the last BACKUP operation

CD (Change Directory) Command

Purpose: Changes the current directory and/or displays the current directory path

Type: Internal

Format: CD [d:] path

Examples:

CD \LOTUS	Changes to the Lotus subdirectory which branches off the *root* directory

	CD LOTUS	Changes to the Lotus subdirectory which branches off the *current* directory
	CD \LOTUS\HOME	Changes to HOME which branches off LOTUS which branches off the root
	CD \	Changes to the root directory
	CD ..	Changes to the parent of the current directory

CHKDSK (Check Disk) Command

Purpose: Analyzes files and/or directories on the default or designated drive; produces a disk and memory status report; can be used with FIND filter to locate files on disk.

Type: External

Format: CHKDSK [d:][/F]

Examples:
CHKDSK	Checks the disk on default drive
CHKDSK A:/F	Checks disk on drive A; the F (fix) parameter causes DOS to correct any problems it discovers
CHKDSK LARGE.FIL	Indicates whether or not the file is in contiguous sectors

CLS (Clear Screen) Command

Purpose: Clears the display screen (monitor)

Type: Internal

Format: CLS

Examples: CLS — Clears the screen

COMP (Compare Files) Command

Purpose: Compares the contents of the first file to the second file; may be run after a copy operation to guarantee that the two files are identical.

Type: External

Format: COMP [d:][path]filename[.ext] [d:][path]filename[.ext]

Examples:
COMP A:TAX B:TAX	Compares the file TAX on drive A to file TAX on drive B
COMP A:*.* B:	Compares all files on drive A to files with the identical file specifications on drive B

COPY Command

Purpose: Copies individual files; requires that destination disk be formatted; will not erase any pre-existing files on the destination disk

Type: Internal

Format: COPY [d:][path] filename[.ext] [d:][path] filename[.ext]

Examples:

COPY A:HW.WK1 B:HW.WK1	Copies file HW.WK1 from drive A to drive B, naming the copied file HW.WK1
COPY A:HW.WK1 B:	Copies file HW.WK1 from drive A to drive B, naming the copied file HW.WK1 (the existing file name is the default name for the copied file)
COPY HW.WK1 B:	Copies file HW.WK1 from the default drive to drive B, naming the copied file HW.WK1

DIR (Directory) Command

Purpose: Lists all files and/or subdirectories in the current directory

Type: Internal

Format: DIR [d:][path][filename[.ext]][/P][/W]

Examples:

DIR	Lists all entries in the default directory
DIR>LPT1	Directs output of the DIR command to the printer
DIR/W	Lists directory entries in column format without date and time
DIR/P	Lists directory entries once screen at a time

DISKCOMP (Disk Compare) Command

Purpose: Compares the contents of two floppy disks; normally run after a DISKCOPY operation

Type: External

Format: DISKCOMP [d:][d:]

Examples:

DISKCOMP A: B:	Compares the contents of the disk in drive A to the disk in drive B
DISKCOMP A: A:	A single drive operation; the command will prompt the user to continually switch the source and destination disks in drive A

DISKCOPY Command

Purpose:	Copies the contents of the source disk to the target disk; formats the target disk and erases any files which were there previously
Type:	External
Format:	DISKCOPY [d:][d:]
Examples:	DISKCOPY A: B: — Makes a duplicate copy of the disk in drive A on the disk in drive B
	DISKCOPY B: A: — The *opposite* of the first command as it copies the disk in drive B to the disk in drive A. You should write-protect the source disk prior to using the command so as not to copy the wrong disk
	DISKCOPY A: A: — A single drive disk copy operation (used to duplicate a floppy disk when only one drive is available).

DOSSHELL Command (DOS 4.00 Only)

Purpose:	Enters the DOS Shell (See hands-on exercises 6 and 7)
Type:	External
Format:	DOSSHELL
Examples:	DOSSHELL — Assumes DOSSHELL program is in current directory or in a directory in the current path

ECHO Command

Purpose:	Enables (prevents) the display of DOS commands executed from a batch file
Type:	Internal
Format:	ECHO text [ON][OFF]
Examples:	ECHO OFF — Suppresses DOS commands
	ECHO Help me — "Help me" echoed to the montior
	@ECHO OFF — @ sign suppresses the ECHO OFF command itself (DOS 3.00 or higher)

ERASE (DEL) Command

Purpose: Erases (deletes) designated files from the current directory

Type: Internal

Format: ERASE [d:][path] filename[.ext]
DEL [d:][path] filename[.ext]

Examples:

ERASE A:MYFILE	Erases MYFILE from the disk in drive A
ERASE MYFILE	Erases MYFILE from the default drive
ERASE *.BK!	Erases every file with the extension BK! from the default drive
ERASE *.*	Erases all files from the default drive

FIND Filter

Purpose: Identifies all lines from the designated file(s) containing the specified character string; can also be used with CHKDSK and piping to find the location of any file(s) on the disk

Type: External

Format: FIND [/V] string [d:][path][filename[.ext]]

Examples:

FIND "111" FILE1	Displays all lines in FILE1 containing 111
FIND /V "111" FILE1	Displays lines in FILE1 not containing 111
FIND "222" FILE1,FILE2	Finds all occurrences of 222 in FILE1 and FILE2
CHKDSK/V ¦ FIND "ABC"	Finds all occurrences of file ABC
CHKDSK/V ¦ FIND ".BK!"	Finds all files with the extension BK! (Be careful; CHKDSK ¦ FIND "*.BK!" won't work)

FORMAT Command

Purpose: Initializes (and simultaneously erases) the disk in the designated drive.

Type: External

Format: FORMAT [d:][/S][/F:size]

Examples:

FORMAT A:	Formats the disk in drive A
FORMAT B:/S	Formats disk in drive B as bootable disk (with COMMAND.COM and two hidden files)
FORMAT A:/F:720	Formats the disk in drive A as a 720Kb disk (even if the drive is 1.44M); this parameter is available only in DOS 4.00

MD (Make Directory) Command

Purpose: Creates a new directory (subdirectory)

Type: Internal

Format: MD [d:][path]

Examples:

MD \LOTUS	Creates a Lotus subdirectory under the *root* directory
MD LOTUS	Creates a Lotus subdirectory under the *current* directory
MD \LOTUS\HOME	Creates a HOME subdirectory under the existing LOTUS subdirectory which in turn is under the root directory

MORE Filter

Purpose: Displays once screen at a time, pausing with the message --More-- at the end of each screen (pressing any character causes another screen to be displayed)

Type: External

Format: MORE

Examples:

TYPE MY.FILE ¦ MORE	Displays MY.FILE one screen at a time
DIR ¦ MORE	Displays the directory, pausing at the end of each screen of data
DIR ¦ SORT ¦ MORE	List directory in alphabetical order, one screen at a time

PATH Command

Purpose: Causes designated directories to be searched for commands not found in the current directory.

Type: Internal

Format: PATH [d:][path][;[d:][path]...]

Examples:

PATH \DOS	Sets a path to the DOS directory of the current drive
PATH C:\DOS	Sets a path to the DOS directory on drive C
PATH C:\DOS;C:\NORTON	Sets a path to the DOS and NORTON directories on drive C
PATH	Displays the current path
PATH;	Cancels the current path

PROMPT Command

Purpose: Sets a new system prompt

Type: Internal

Format: PROMPT [prompt-text]

Examples:

PROMPT pg	Includes the currently logged directory, for example, C:\WP\HOME>
PROMPT $	Eliminates the prompt character entirely (something you wouldn't do ordinarily)
PROMPT tg	Displays the time, for example, 9:44:00:00> (The seconds and hundredths of a second appear as well and are distracting.)
PROMPT ng	Restores the prompt to its default value, for example, C >

RD (Remove Directory) Command

Purpose: Removes a directory; the directory to be removed must be empty

Type: Internal

Format: RD [d:][path]

Examples:

RD \SCHOOL	Removes the SCHOOL directory from the root directory (SCHOOL must be empty)
RD SCHOOL	Removes the SCHOOL directory from the current directory

RENAME Command

Purpose: Changes (renames) an existing file

Type: Internal

Format: RENAME [d:][path] filename[.ext] filename[.ext]

Examples:

RENAME A:HW.1 HW.ONE	Changes the name of file HW.1 on drive A to HW.ONE; the drive designation is specified only for the oldname
RENAME OLD NEW	Changes the name of file OLD to NEW on the default drive
RENAME *.2 *.TWO	Changes the extension of all files with extension 2 to TWO (the file names are retained)

RESTORE Command

Purpose: Restores (to a hard disk) one or more files previously created in a BACKUP operation; you *must* use the same DOS release for both BACKUP and RESTORE

Type: External

Format: RESTORE d: [d:][path] filename[.ext]

Examples:
RESTORE A: C:\WP\BOOK	Restores the BOOK file from the backup disk to its original subdirectory on drive C
RESTORE A: C:*.*/S	Restores all files on the backup disk to their original subdirectories on drive C

SORT Filter

Purpose: Reads data, sorts it, then writes the result to the standard output device

Type: External

Format: SORT [/R][/+n]

Examples:
SORT < TEST.DAT	Sorts the file TEST.DAT, displaying results on the monitor
SORT < IN > OUT	Sorts the file IN storing results in file OUT
DIR ¦ SORT	Produces an alphabetical directory
DIR ¦ SORT/R/+14	Sorts the directory beginning in column 14 (file size), listing files from largest to smallest

TREE Command

Purpose: Displays all directory paths in the specified drive; optionally lists all files in each directory. DOS 4.00 lists the structure from the current directory down, whereas earlier versions list the structure of the entire disk, regardless of current directory.

Type: External

Format: TREE [d:][/F]

Examples:
TREE	Lists all subdirectories from the current directory down (in DOS 4.00).
TREE C:\	Lists all subdirectories for drive C regardless of the current directory
TREE A:\ /F	Lists all subdirectories and associated files for the disk in drive A
TREE > LPT1	Directs output to the printer.

TYPE Command

Purpose: Displays the contents of an ASCII file on the output device; will not however work with other types of files.

Type: Internal

Format: TYPE [d:][path] filename[.ext]

Examples:

TYPE AUTOEXEC.BAT	Displays the contents of AUTOEXEC.BAT from the current directory
TYPE BIG.FILE ¦ MORE	Displays the contents of BIG.FILE one screen at a time
TYPE C:\SUB1\FILE1>LPT1	Displays the output of FILE1 in the directory SUB1 on the printer

XCOPY Command

Purpose: Copies individual files; requires that destination disk be formatted; will not erase any pre-existing files on the destination disk

Type: External

Format: XCOPY [d:][path] filename[.ext] [d:][path] filename[.ext]

Examples:

XCOPY C:*.* A:	Copies every file from the current directory to drive A. (Omitting the path defaults to the current directory.)
XCOPY C:\LET*.* A:/S/P	Copies every file in the LET directory as well as all its subdirectories, prompting (with Y/N?) before each file is copied.
XCOPY C:\LET*.* A:/S/E	Copies every file in LET and all its subdirectories to drive A, creating empty directories on drive A should they exist on drive C.
XCOPY C:*.* A:/S/D:1-21-90	Copies all files in all subdirectories on drive C, which have been modified or created on or after 1/21/90.
XCOPY C:*.DBF A:/S/M	Copies all DBF files on drive C (including subdirectories), which have been created or modified since the last XCOPY operation.

PC/MS DOS Self-Evaluation

1. Indicate the DOS command which (in the absence of subdirectories) will:
   (a) Copy the contents of an entire disk onto another while also formatting the destination disk.
   (b) Copy every file from drive A to a formatted disk in drive B without erasing what was previously on the disk in drive B.
   (c) Erase the screen.
   (d) Display the name of every file on the disk in drive B.
   (e) Indicate the amount RAM.
   (f) Erase every file on the disk in drive A.
   (g) Copy the file MY.BK on drive B to drive A, naming the copied version YOUR.BK.
   (h) Format a blank disk in drive B, placing the system files on the formatted disk.
   (i) Display all files on drive B which have the extension COM.
   (j) Compare the contents of two disks to see whether they are identical.

2. Indicate what each of the following commands will accomplish. (Some of the commands, however, are deliberately invalid and will produce error messages; identify these as invalid.)
   (a) DIR
   (b) DIR C:
   (c) DIR *.INT
   (d) DISKCOMP A: B:
   (e) FORMAT B:
   (f) FORMAT
   (g) DISKCOPY B: A:
   (h) CHECKDSK C:
   (i) COPY A:FILE.ONE B:
   (j) COPY B:FILE.ONE A:FILE.TWO
   (k) COPY *.* B:
   (l) DIR ?.*

3. State the difference between the following:
   (a) The single command DIR B: versus two commands, B: followed by DIR
   (b) COPY A:*.* B: and DISKCOPY A: B:
   (c) DIR and DIR/W
   (d) DIR FW.* and DIR *.FW
   (e) DIR F?.WK1 and DIR F*.WK1
   (f) The source and target disk
   (g) FORMAT and FORMAT B:
   (h) FORMAT B: and FORMAT B:/S
   (i) Covering versus uncovering the write-protect notch
   (j) COPY A:F1 B: and COPY A:F1 B
   (k) COPY A:F1 B: and COPY B:F1 A:
   (l) DISKCOPY A: B: and DISKCOPY A:

4. (a) What are the commands to format a disk with, and without, the system files? What is the advantage of each?
   (b) What is the difference between formatting a disk with the system files, versus formatting without the system, and then copying COMMAND.COM onto the formatted disk?

5. Assume the following files are on a disk in the drive A, and that a blank formatted disk in drive B. *Assume drive A is the default drive in all instances.*

   TEST1F89.120   TEST1S91.316
   TEST1S90.120   ASSGNWP.120
   TEST1F90.120   ASSGNSS.120
   TEST1S91.120   ASSGNDOS.120
   TEST1F89.316   ASSGNWP.316
   TEST1S90.316   ASSGNSS.316
   TEST1F90.316   ASSGNDOS.316

   (a) Enter a command to copy all files with an extension 120 from drive A to the disk in drive B.
   (b) Which files will be copied to the disk in drive B, given that the command COPY TEST*.120 B: is entered from the A>?
   (c) Which files will be copied to the disk in drive B, given that the command COPY TEST?F89.120 B: is entered at the A>?
   (d) Enter a command to copy all of the assignment files for both courses to the disk in drive B

(e) Enter a command to erase all files with the extension 316 from the disk in drive A
(f) Which files will be erased from the disk in drive A by the command, ERASE 120*.*, given that the command is entered at the A>?

6. Explain what each of the following commands will do. (Some of the commands, however, are deliberately invalid and will produce error messages; identify these as invalid.)
   (a) A> COPY MYFILE B:
   (b) A> COPY MYFILE B
   (c) A> COPY MYFILE
   (d) A> COPY B:MYFILE
   (e) B> COPY MYFILE A:
   (f) B> COPY A:MYFILE
   (g) A> COPY A:MYFILE B:MYFILE

7. Show the tree structure that would be created by issuing the following commands in succession:

    CD \
    MD SUB1
    MD SUB2
    MD SUB3
    CD SUB1
    MD SUB4
    MD SUB5
    MD SUB6
    CD SUB6
    MD SUB7
    MD SUB8

    Assume now that *you are in the SUB1 directory* and that the following commands are issued from this directory. Indicate whether there is a problem, and if so, state the nature of the problem. Answer with respect to the tree structure just created.
    (a) CD SUB2
    (b) RD SUB6
    (c) MD SUB5
    (d) MD SUB9\SUB10
    (e) PATH C:\SUB1
    (f) PATH C:\SUB1;C:\SUB2
    (g) CD ..

8. Describe the precise effect of each command, assuming that *each command is issued from the root directory of drive C*. Note, however, that some commands will not execute in which case you should indicate the nature of the error.
   (a) COPY A:*.* C:
   (b) COPY A:*.*
   (c) COPY C:*.*
   (d) XCOPY A:*.* C:
   (e) XCOPY A:*.* C:/S
   (f) XCOPY A:*.* C:/S/M
   (g) COPY A:\WP\FILE.1 C:

9. Indicate the commands needed in the AUTOEXEC.BAT file to accomplish the following:
   (a) Change the prompt to show the current directory and the default drive.
   (b) Change the colors displayed on the monitor to show yellow letters on a blue background.
   (c) Enable programs contained in the WP50, LOTUS, and DOS directories to be run from anywhere on the disk.
   (e) Load the RAM resident program SideKick (located in the SIDEKICK directory with the command SK).

10. The command CHKDSK/V ¦ FIND ".BAK" will locate all BAK files, regardless of where they are located on the disk.
    (a) What is the function of the piping symbol?
    (b) Explain why the command will not work if ".bak" or "*.BAK" is substituted for the ".BAK" entry.
    (c) How would you generalize the command to find any file, not just a file with a BAK extension?
    (d) Assume that you do in fact create the necessary batch file called LOCATE.BAT, and further that you place the batch file in a UTILITY subdirectory. What PATH command has to be in effect for the command, LOCATE MYFILE, to search the disk for a file called, MYFILE?

11. Supply the XCOPY command to do the following:
    (a) Copy all of the files in the currently logged directory of drive C to the currently logged directory in drive A
    (b) Copy only the WK1 files in the currently logged directory to the disk in drive A
    (c) Copy all of the WK1 files on drive C to the disk in drive A
    (d) Copy all of the WK1 files on drive C that were modified or created since the last XCOPY command was issued
    (e) Copy all of the WK1 files on drive C that have been modified or created since July 4, 1990

12. Both of the commands will below will copy all of the WK1 files from drive C, to the disk in drive A.

    Command 1:
    XCOPY C:*.WK1 A:/S

    Command 2:
    BACKUP C:*.WK1 A:/S

    (a) What advantage does command 1 offer over command 2? does command 2 have over command 1?
    (b) Assume the WK1 files are in four subdirectories (C:\LOTUS\SUB1, C:\LOTUS\SUB2, C:\LOTUS\SUB3, and C:\LOTUS\SUB4.) Indicate the individual COPY commands which collectively would be the same as command 1.

13. Given the tree structure below enter commands to do the following:
    (a) Show the directory you are in (without changing the current prompt):
    (b) Change from the GRADE subdirectory to the MISC subdirectory.
    (c) Create a new CIS120 subdirectory under the SCHOOL subdirectory
    (d) Create a new subdirectory, OFFICE, under the existing LOTUS subdirectory. Assume you are already in the LOTUS subdirectory.
    (e) Could you also create an OFFICE subdirectory under SCHOOL? If so, what command would you use?
    (f) Show the command to copy all of the files from the DOS subdirectory to the disk in drive A.
    (g) Copy all of the files with a 120 extension from the GRADE subdirectory to the disk in drive A.
    (h) Remove the EASTERN subdirectory (several commands will be necessary)
    (i) Enable the execution of external DOS commands without having to log in to the DOS subdirectory
    (j) Display the current path setting
    (k) Cancel the current path setting
    (l) Change the prompt to show the currently logged subdirectory
    (m) Display the tree structure of the disk, showing all files in each subdirectory.
    (n) How could you restore the last command issued to the command buffer?

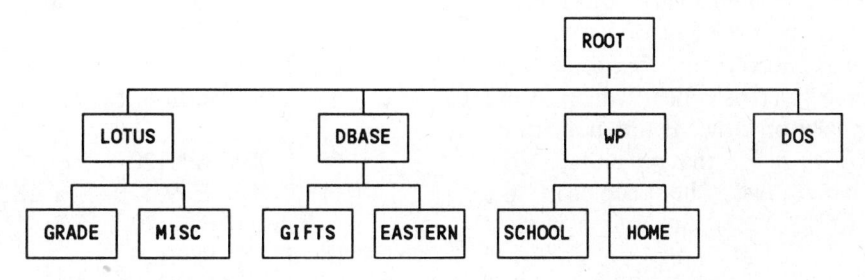

Figure 2 - Tree Structure for Problem 13

Answers to PC/MS DOS Self-Evaluation

1. (a) DISKCOPY A: B:
   (b) COPY A:*.* B:
   (c) CLS
   (d) DIR B:
   (e) CHKDSK
   (f) ERASE A:*.*
   (g) COPY B:MY.BK A:YOUR.BK
   (h) FORMAT B:/S
   (i) DIR B:*.COM
   (j) DISKCOMP A: B:

2. (a) Directory of the current drive
   (b) Directory of drive C
   (c) Lists all files with extension INT in the current directory
   (d) Compares the disks in drives A and B
   (e) Formats the disk in drive B
   (f) Formats the disk in the default drive
   (g) Duplicates the contents of the disk in drive B to drive A (formatting drive A in the process)
   (h) Error - CHKDSK (misspelled)
   (i) Copies FILE.ONE from drive A to drive B
   (j) Copies FILE.ONE from drive B to drive A, naming it FILE.TWO
   (k) Copies all files from the default drive to the disk in drive B
   (l) Lists the names of all files with a one character name and any extension

3. (a) The single command list the contents of drive B; the two commands change the default drive to B, then lists its contents.
   (b) The COPY command copies all files in the current directory on drive A to drive B and requires that drive B be formatted (the files which were originally on drive B are not erased and it is possible that not all files from drive A will be copied); the DISKCOPY command makes an exact copy of the disk in drive A
   (c) DIR lists the file size together with date and time of creation; DIR/W command lists files in columns and omits this information.
   (d) The first command lists all files with filename FW regardless of extension; the second lists all files with the extension FW
   (e) DIR F? lists all two character file names (beginning with F); DIR F* lists all filenames (regardless of length) beginning with F
   (f) The source disk is the disk you are copying from; the target (destination) disk is the one you are writing to
   (g) The first command formats the default drive; the second formats drive B
   (h) The /S options makes the formatted disk bootable
   (i) Write enabling or write protecting the disk (with the procedure dependent on whether 5 1/4 or 3 1/2 disks are used)
   (j) The first command copies the file F1 to the disk in drive B, naming the copied file F1; the second command copies F1 to the disk in drive A naming the copied file B
   (k) The first command copies from drive A to drive B; the second command copies from drive B to drive A
   (l) The first command is a two drive operation; the second command will prompt the user to switch source and destination disks in drive A.

4. (a) FORMAT A: and FORMAT A:/S
   The system (/S) option makes the disk bootable but requires additional space for COMMAND.COM and the two hidden files; formatting without the system allows more room for data.
   (b) The /S options includes the hidden files in addition to COMMAND.COM.

5. (a) COPY A:*.120 B:
   (b) TEST1F89.120, TEST1S90.120, TEST1F90.120, TEST1S91.120
   (c) TEST1F89.120
   (d) COPY ASSGN*.* B:
   (e) ERASE A:*.316
   (b) No files will be erased

Answers to PC/MS DOS Self-Evaluation 43

6. (a) Copies MYFILE from drive A to drive B, naming copied file MYFILE
   (b) Duplicates MYFILE on drive A, naming the second file B
   (c) Error (no destination file)
   (d) Copies MYFILE from drive B to drive A, naming the copied file MYFILE
   (e) Same as part (d)
   (f) Same as part (a)
   (g) Same as parts (a) and (f)

7. The easiest way to check your answers is to do the exercise on a formatted floppy disk; hence the resultant tree structure (as printed by the TREE command is:

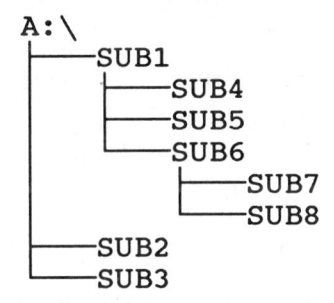

   ```
   A:\
   ├───SUB1
   │   ├───SUB4
   │   ├───SUB5
   │   └───SUB6
   │       ├───SUB7
   │       └───SUB8
   ├───SUB2
   └───SUB3
   ```

   In similar fashion the error messages produced in executing the remaining commands are shown:
   (a) Invalid directory
   (b) Invalid path, not directory, or directory not empty
   (c) Directory already exists
   (d) Unable to create directory
   (e) OK
   (f) OK
   (g) OK

8. (a) Copies all files from current directory in drive A to the root directory
   (b) Same as part (a)
   (c) Error (no destination file)
   (d) Same as part (a)
   (e) Copies all files (including subdirectories) from drive A to drive C, placing copied files in subdirectories
   (f) Copies all files modified or created since the last XCOPY operation
   (g) Copies one file (FILE.1) from the WP subdirectory on drive A to drive C

9. (a) PROMPT PG
   (b) PROMPT PG$E[44;33m
       CLS
   (c) PATH C:\WP50;C:\LOTUS;C:\DOS
   (d) CD \SIDEKICK
       SK

10. (a) Chains output of CHKDSK command to the FIND filter
    (b) The CHKDSK command displays filenames in uppercase
    (c) Place it in a batch file with a replaceable parameter as follows: CHKDSK/V ¦ FIND "%1"
    (d) PATH C:\DOS;C:\UTILITY

11. (a) XCOPY C:*.* A:
    (b) XCOPY C:*.WK1 A:
    (c) XCOPY C:*.WK1 A:/S
    (d) XCOPY C:*.WK1 A:/S/M
    (e) XCOPY C:*.WK1 A:/S/D:7-4-90

12. (a) XCOPY copies files in a form that can be read without having to restore the files as required by the BACKUP command. BACKUP, on the other hand, can accommodate files which are too large to fit on a single disk.
    (b) COPY C:\LOTUS\SUB1*.WK1 A:
        COPY C:\LOTUS\SUB2*.WK1 A:
        COPY C:\LOTUS\SUB3*.WK1 A:
        COPY C:\LOTUS\SUB4*.WK1 A:

13. (a) CD
    (b) CD ..\MISC or CD \LOTUS\MISC
    (c) MD \WP\SCHOOL\CIS120
    (d) MD OFFICE
    (e) Yes; MD \WP\SCHOOL\OFFICE
    (f) COPY \DOS*.* A:
    (g) COPY \LOTUS\GRADE*.120 A:
    (h) CD\DBASE\EASTERN
        ERASE *.*
        CD ..
        RD EASTERN
    (i) PATH C:\DOS
    (j) PATH
    (k) PATH;
    (l) PATH PG
    (m) TREE/F
    (n) Press the F3 key

WordPerfect 4.2

Introduction

WordPerfect has become the acknowledged leader among full featured word processing programs, with annual sales for the privately held company approaching $300 million (see Corporate Profile in Chapter 4). The success of WordPerfect is all the more remarkable in that the company was late in entering an already crowded market, with WordStar the then undisputed champion, and MultiMate, Volkswriter, IBM's DisplayWrite and Microsoft Word as formidable competition. Who would have thought that an obscure company based in Utah, with only two employees and no venture capital, could possibly succeed, let alone unseat the entrenched leaders of word processing? Yet it happened, and WordPerfect today is the standard against which other word processors are judged, with an estimated 60 percent share of the market.

WordPerfect is truly an incredible program and includes virtually every feature you could want in a word processor. At the same time the program is remarkably simple to use, and you can learn the basics in a session or two. Our objective is not to teach you all of WordPerfect (we couldn't possibly), but only a subset of commands needed to do the hands-on exercises contained in the text. The exercises do, however, contain sufficient material to enable you to use WordPerfect productively for your work in your other courses.

This section describes WordPerfect 4.2 and is intended for use with the Educational version of this release. (The software is packaged with this manual.)

Hands-On Exercise 1:
Creating a Document

Objective: Load WordPerfect; create, save, and print a simple document. (Corresponds to Hands-on Exercise 1 in Chapter 3).

Step 1: Installation (Hard Disk Only)

You will find it convenient to copy the WordPerfect program files from the floppy disk to an appropriate directory on your hard drive. In addition you should create a separate directory to hold the documents you will create. Boot the system and end at the C prompt. Type the command

MD C:\WP42 to create a directory for the WordPerfect program files. Type **MD C:\WP42\PRACTICE** to create a second directory for the WordPerfect documents. (The latter directory will be referenced in step 2a when we describe how to load WordPerfect.)

Now place the WordPerfect program disk in drive A and enter the following commands. Type **CD C:\WP42** (to change to the WordPerfect directory), then **COPY A:WP*.*** followed by **COPY A:*.WP** (to copy the WordPerfect program files from the disk in drive A to the disk in drive C.)

Step 2a: Load WordPerfect (Hard Drive)

As indicated, the installation procedure in step 1 uses one directory for the WordPerfect program files, and a different directory for the WordPerfect documents you create. Thus the command sequence to load WordPerfect first logs into the document directory (C:\WP42\PRACTICE), then sets a path to the WordPerfect program directory. Type the following commands as indicated:

CD C:\WP42\PRACTICE	Makes C:\WP42\PRACTICE the default directory (to hold documents created by WordPerfect)
PATH C:\WP42	Indicates to DOS where to find the WordPerfect program
WP	Loads WordPerfect

The opening message of Figure EWP.1 should briefly appear on the monitor, followed by the text in Figure EWP.2. (See step 3 if the latter figure does not appear.)

Step 2b: Load WordPerfect (Two Floppy Drives)

Locate the WordPerfect program disk and place it in Drive A. Take a formatted disk and place it in Drive B. Type the following commands to load WordPerfect:

B:	Makes drive B the default directory (to hold documents created by WordPerfect)
PATH A:	Indicates to DOS where to find the WordPerfect program
WP	Loads WordPerfect

The opening message of Figure EWP.1 should briefly appear on the monitor, followed by the text in Figure EWP.2. (See step 3 if the latter figure does not appear.)

```
                    ┌─────────────────┐
                    │   WordPerfect   │
                    ├─────────────────┤
                    │   Version 4.2   │
                    └─────────────────┘

              (C)Copyright 1982,1983,1984,1985,1986
                       All Rights Reserved
                     WordPerfect Corporation
                        Orem, Utah  USA




         * Please Wait *
```

Figure EWP.1 - WordPerfect's Opening Message #1

```
                  WordPerfect 4.2 -- Training Version
                  Copyright 1986 WordPerfect Corporation


     This special training version is    The training version of
     provided to help you get to know    WordPerfect has been limited in
     WordPerfect.  It is protected by    the following ways:
     Federal Copyright Law and
     international trade agreements.     * Saved documents are limited in
                                           size to about 50,000
     You are allowed to copy and use       characters;
     this software for demonstration
     and training purposes.  You are    * Printed output occasionally
     not allowed to use copies of the     contains "*WPC";
     software, in whole or in part,
     for any other purpose.             * Advanced printing features are
                                          not allowed;
     WordPerfect Corporation retains
     title to the software.             * LPT1 (PRN) is the only port
                                          that can be used for printing.


                         Press any key to continue
```

Figure EWP.2 - WordPerfect's Opening Message #2

Step 3:   Correcting Problems

One common occurrence, especially with beginners, is that Figure EWP.2 does not appear immediately, and that you are instead confronted with the message:

```
     Are other copies of WordPerfect currently running (Y/N)
```

If this message appears it means that you (or whomever used the WordPerfect disk last), did not exit properly. Simply type **N** (to indicate that no other copies are running), press the return key, and continue with the exercise.

You should now be presented with a "clean screen" (i.e. a blank screen except for the status line at the lower right of the monitor) for creating and editing documents as shown in Figure EWP.3. The clear, uncluttered screen is a trademark of WordPerfect.

                                                    Doc 1 Pg 1 Ln 1   Pos 10

Figure EWP.3 - WordPerfect's Clear Screen and Status Line

The status line indicates the document number (two separate documents may be created and/or edited at the same time), and the page, line, and cursor position for the current document.

Step 4:   Create the Document

You are now in a position to enter your document. Type as you would on a regular typewriter, but do not press the return (enter) key until you come to the end of a paragraph, as WordPerfect goes automatically from one line to the next (word wrap) as the document is entered. If you make a mistake, use the backspace key to erase the last letter(s) that were typed. Figure EWP.4 shows the screen after we have entered a short one paragraph document.

```
       You should not attempt to develop a long document until you
   are confident of your ability to save and retrieve the documents
   you create.  Nothing is more frustrating than to spend an
   extended time entering text only to learn that you are unable to
   save or retrieve it._
```

                                                    Doc 1 Pg 1 Ln 5   Pos 29

Figure EWP.4 - Creating a Document

Step 5: Correct the Document (Insertion versus Replacement)
Check your document to see that it is correct. Remember that WordPerfect, like all word processors, is always in one of two modes, insertion or replacement (typeover). In the insertion mode, new text is added to the document (to the left of the cursor), with existing text pushed to the right. The typeover mode, on the other hand, causes new text to replace existing text on a character by character basis.

The **Ins** key functions as a toggle switch which alternates between the two modes; i.e., pressing the Ins key switches from one mode to the other. Try it. Press the Ins key a few times, observing that the left side of the status line will contain the word *Typeover* whenever you are in the replacement mode. Practice entering text in each of these modes.

Step 6: Save the Document
Press the **F10** function key to save the document (and continue editing); the following message will appear in place of the status line at the bottom of the screen:

```
Document to be saved:
```

Type **FIRST** (as the name of the document) and press the return key. (The document will be saved on the default drive established in your loading procedure; i.e. in the directory C:\WP42\PRACTICE if you followed step 2a and on drive B if you followed step 2b.)

Step 7: Print the Document
Be sure that the printer is turned on and is on-line. (This can be verified by checking the indicator light(s) on the top or front of the printer.)

To initiate the printing process, press the **Shift** key, and while holding the shift key down, press the **F7** function key. We use the notation **Shift+F7** to indicate that the keys are pressed at the same time. You should now be in the print menu shown below:

```
1 Full Text; 2 Page; 3 Options; 4 Printer Control; 5 Type-thru; 6 Preview: 0
```

Type **1** to print the document.

Step 8: Exit WordPerfect
Press the **F7** key whereupon you will be presented with a series of messages to: 1) save the current document and exit WordPerfect, or 2) save the current document, clear the screen, and begin work on a different document. Either way you will see the prompt:

```
Save Document? (Y/N) Y                        (Text was not modified)
```

Type **N** (since the document has not been modified since the previous save operation (in Step 6). Next you will see:

```
Exit WP? (Y/N) N                              (Cancel to return to document)
```

Type **Y** to exit WordPerfect and return to DOS. (Note, however, that were you to respond No to this prompt, *you would remain in WordPerfect with a clear screen* and hence could begin work on another document. The command sequence to clear a screen, and thus go from one document to another, is one of the most important, and most misunderstood, in all of WordPerfect.)

New Commands - Exercise 1	
To load WordPerfect (with a hard drive)	CD\WP42\PRACTICE PATH C:\WP42 WP
To load WordPerfect (with two floppy drives)	B: PATH A: WP
To erase a letter	Backspace
Toggle between insertion and replacement (typeover)	Ins
To save and resume editing	F10
To exit WordPerfect	F7 Y/N to save current document Y to exit WordPerfect
To clear the screen	F7 Y/N to save current document N to remain in WordPerfect
To print a document	Shift+F7 1 (Full text)

50   WordPerfect 4.2 Hands-On Exercises

Hands-On Exercise 2: Retrieving a Document

Objective: Retrieve an existing document; revise it and save the revision; print the revision (Corresponds to Hands-on Exercise 2 in Chapter 3).

Step 1:   Load WordPerfect
Load WordPerfect as described in step 2 in the previous exercise, following the instructions for your particular configuration. This is the process you will follow in the rest of the manual.

Step 2:   Retrieving a Document
Press the **F5** (list files) function key whereupon WordPerfect will display the default directory (B: or C:\WP42\PRACTICE) where the documents are stored. Press the return key to see a listing of the files on the default directory (e.g. drive B if you are using two floppy drives) as shown in Figure EWP.5.

```
11/01/90  10:14               Directory B:\*.*
Document Size:       0                            Free Disk Space:   361472

.  <CURRENT>  <DIR>            |  ..  <PARENT>   <DIR>
FIRST    .         276  11/01/90 10:14




1 Retrieve; 2 Delete; 3 Rename; 4 Print; 5 Text In;
6 Look; 7 Change Directory; 8 Copy; 9 Word Search; 0 Exit: 6
```

Figure EWP.5 - The List Files Command

Use the arrow keys to highlight the file named FIRST, but do *not* press the return key. Instead you must type **1** (retrieve) as indicated in the menu at the bottom of the screen. The FIRST file from exercise 1 should now appear on your monitor.

An alternate means of retrieving a file is to press the Shift key with your right hand, and while holding the Shift key down press the F10 function key with your left. We use the notation **Shift+F10** to show that these keys are pressed at the same time. WordPerfect will prompt with the message:

```
Document to be Retrieved:
```

Type **FIRST** as the name of the document to be retrieved.

Step 3: **Editing (revising) a Document**
The original document from Figure EWP.4 should be displayed on the monitor. You will now edit this document to include an additional sentence at the end.

Use the arrow keys to move the cursor to the end of the document. [Alternatively you can press **Home, Home,** and the down arrow (↓) keys to move to the end of the document.] Now press the return key to end this paragraph and enter the following sentence in the next paragraph.

```
Success - I can save and retrieve documents with my word processor!
```

When WordPerfect is in the insert (versus typeover) mode, any text which is entered is inserted at the cursor position, with the existing text pushed to the right of that line. To type over an existing character (i.e., to switch to the typeover mode) press the Ins key. The word Typeover should appear on the status line to indicate that WordPerfect has switched from the insertion to the typeover mode. Press the **Ins** key a few more times, observing that the word *Typeover* flashes on and off the status line, to indicate switching (toggling) between modes.

Step 4: **Deletions and the Undelete Command**
You can delete text within a document; for example, a letter, a word, or an entire line. To delete a letter, position the cursor under the letter and press the **Del** key. In similar fashion, a word is deleted by placing the cursor anywhere in the word, and pressing the **Ctrl** key and the **Backspace** key (**Ctrl+Backspace**). An entire line may be deleted by placing the cursor at the beginning of the line and pressing the **Ctrl** key and the **End** key (**Ctrl+End**).

WordPerfect also has an *undelete* (cancel) function which can restore your last three deletions, regardless of whether the deletion consists of a character, word, line, or a block. To illustrate this very useful capability, we will ask you to delete a line, then restore it. Accordingly move to the beginning of the document [you can press the **Home, Home,** and up arrow (↑) keys] and press **Ctrl+End** to delete the line. Now press the **F1** (cancel) key and the deleted text reappears in reverse video with the following prompt at the bottom of the screen:

```
Undelete  1 Restore; 2 Show Previous Deletion: 0
```

Type **1** to restore the deleted text.

Step 5: Save the Document

Press the **F10** function key as in the first exercise. This time, however, WordPerfect will not ask for the name of the document, but instead will prompt you with the following message:

Document to be Saved: B:\FIRST   **or**   C:\WP42\PRACTICE\FIRST

WordPerfect already knows the file name because you retrieved it earlier in step 2. Note too, that the file name is preceded by the drive on which it is stored (e.g., B: if you are using two floppy drives) Press the enter key to save the edited version as the document FIRST. WordPerfect will then prompt with a second message:

Replace B:\FIRST? (Y/N) N

In other words WordPerfect wants to be certain that you intend for the edited version (i.e., the document currently in memory) to overwrite the original file. Type **Y**, and WordPerfect will replace the file that was created in the first hands-on exercise with the edited version.

Step 6: Print the Document

Press **Shift+F7** as in the previous exercise to initiate the printing process. Type **1** to print the full document.

Step 7: Exit WordPerfect

Press the **F7** function key, answer **N** indicating that you do not wish to save the document (as it was previously saved in step 4), then answer **Y** to exit WordPerfect and return to DOS.

New Commands - Exercise 2	
To retrieve a document from a directory listing	F5 (List Files) 1 (Retrieve)
To retrieve a document when the file name is known	Shift+F10
To delete a word	Ctrl+Backspace
To delete to end of line	Ctrl+End
To restore previous deletion	F1 1 (Restore)

Hands-On Exercise 3: Reformatting a Document

Objective: Create a new document, then change its margins and line spacing; introduce underlining and boldface (Corresponds to Hands-on exercise 3 in Chapter 3).

Step 1: **Enter the Preamble to the Constitution**
Load WordPerfect as in the previous exercises, then enter the Preamble to the Constitution as shown in Figure EWP.6. Remember not to press the return key until you come to the end of the paragraph.

```
We, the people of the United States, in order to form a more
perfect Union, establish justice, insure domestic tranquility,
provide for the common defense, promote the general welfare, and
secure the blessings of liberty to ourselves and our posterity, do
ordain and establish this Constitution for the United States of
America._
```

                                                    Doc 1 Pg 1 Ln 6   Pos 18

Figure EWP.6 - The Preamble

Step 2: **Cursor Movement**
Check carefully that the preamble has been entered correctly. In so doing you may want to take advantage of WordPerfect's ability to move more rapidly than one character at a time, as shown in the table below.

Cursor Movement	
Left one word	**Ctrl+left arrow**
Right one word	**Ctrl+right arrow**
Beginning of document	**Home, Home, Up arrow**
End of document	**Home, Home, Down arrow**
To next page (large document)	**PgDn**
To previous page	**PgUp**
To page number nn	**Ctrl+Home** **nn** (desired page number)

Note too, that there is one curious feature about cursor movement of which you should be aware, namely that the cursor may not be moved past the end of a document. In other words, when the cursor is positioned at the end of the preamble, the right and/or down arrow keys have no effect.

Step 4: **Change Margins**
Press the **Home, Home,** and **up arrow** keys to move to the beginning of the preamble. Check the status line at the bottom of the screen and observe that the left margin of the document is in position 10 (WordPerfect's default margin). Press **Shift+F8**. The following options will appear at the bottom of the screen:

```
1 2 Tabs; 3 Margins; 4 Spacing; 5 Hyphenation; 6 Align Char:  0
```

To change the margins, select option **3**. The status line shows the current margin settings, and a prompt to enter a new left margin:

```
[Margin Set] 10 74 to Left =
```

Type **20** and press the return key. WordPerfect will next prompt for the new right margin:

```
Right =
```

Type **70** and press return, and the document will realign itself according to the new margins.

Step 5: **Reveal Hidden Codes**
WordPerfect embeds special formatting codes (which are normally hidden from view) into a document to instruct the printer as to how text is to appear in finished form. Position the cursor at the beginning of the preamble, then press **Alt+F3** to reveal the hidden codes and produce the display of Figure EWP.7.

WordPerfect uses a split screen format when codes are revealed, with the text of the document on the upper half of the screen, and the text with the embedded codes displayed on the lower. Separating the two is a ruler line; the triangles represent tab settings, and the brackets { } indicate the left and right margins. Press **Alt+F3** a second time to exit the hidden codes mode and return to your document.

Anything contained in square brackets is a WordPerfect hidden code. The first such hidden code indicates Margin Settings of 20 and 70 (left and right, respectively). Recall too that WordPerfect automatically wraps words from one line to the next when the right margin is encountered; this is called a soft return, and is shown as [SRt] when codes are revealed.

```
                    We, the people of the United States, in order to
                    form a more perfect Union, establish justice,
                    insure domestic tranquility, provide for the common
                    defense, promote the general welfare, and secure
                    the blessings of liberty to ourselves and our
                    posterity, do ordain and establish this
                    Constitution for the United States of America.
A:\PREAMBLE                                    Doc 1 Pg 1 Ln 1    Pos 20
▲▲▲▲(▲▲▲▲▲▲▲)▲▲
[Margin Set:20,70]We, the people of the United States, in order to[SRt]
form a more perfect Union, establish justice,[SRt]
insure domestic tranquility, provide for the common[SRt]
defense, promote the general welfare, and secure[SRt]
the blessings of liberty to ourselves and our[SRt]
posterity, do ordain and establish this[SRt]
Constitution for the United States of America[HRt].
```

Figure EWP.7 - WordPerfect's Hidden Codes

The Reveal Codes command is useful because it shows the formatting commands in effect. You can use the arrow keys to move within the document, and further you can delete any hidden code (and remove its effect) with the **Del** or **Backspace** key. (The Del key deletes the hidden code to the right, while the Backspace key deletes the code to the left). Table WP.1 lists some of the more common codes.

Symbol	Meaning
[B][b]	Bold (begin and end)
[HPg]	Hard Page
[HRt]	Hard Return
[Margin Set]	Left and right margins
[Rt Just Off]	Right Justification Off
[Rt Just On]	Right Justification On
[Spacing Set]	Line spacing
[SRt]	Soft Return
[U][u]	Underlining (begin and end)

Table WP.1 - WordPerfect Hidden Codes

Step 6:   Double Space the Preamble
Press **Shift+F8** (be sure that the cursor is at the beginning of the document). Once again WordPerfect will display the options that appeared when the margins were changed:

    1 2 Tabs; 3 Margins; 4 Spacing; 5 Hyphenation; 6 Align Char: 0

Choose **4** (spacing), then type **2** and press the **F7** (exit key) to return to your document; the paragraph will be double spaced automatically.

Step 7: Underlining and Boldface

Any portion of a document may be underlined, but the procedure varies depending on whether a document is being created for the first time, or whether text in an existing document is to be underlined. To underline text as the document is being created, press the **F8** key and continue typing, and underlining takes place. (Note however that on a color monitor the "underlined" text will appear in a different color, e.g., green.) Press the **F8** key a second time to end the underlining.

You need to follow a slightly different procedure to underline text that has been previously created. Move the cursor to the beginning of the intended underlining; for example, the *U* in *U*nited States in the first line of the preamble. Press **Alt+F4** to begin marking the text to be underlined, and the words "Block On" will flash on at the bottom left of the screen. Use the right arrow key to move the cursor to the end of the block (i.e. after the lowercase *s* in State*s*); as you do so each character in the block will be highlighted in reverse video. Finally press the **F8** key and the block of text, i.e. the words "United States", no longer appear in reverse video, but is underlined instead.

Boldface functions in similar fashion as underlining except with a different function key, F6 rather than F8. Thus you press the **F6** function key before and after the text to be emphasized when entering a document for the first time, or by blocking existing text and then pressing F6, as just described. (On color monitors, boldfaced text may appear in a different color, e.g., orange). On a monochrome monitor, however boldfaced text should be brighter, and if this is not the case, i.e. you can't discern a difference between bold and regular text, you need to adjust the contrast control on your monitor.

Step 8: Obtain a Clear Screen

The process of obtaining a clear screen; i.e. saving the current document and remaining in WordPerfect, is critical and easily misunderstood. Press the **F7** (exit) key as in previous exercises which produces the prompt:

```
Save Document? (Y/N) Y                    (Text was not modified)
```

Type **Y** to save the document, enter **PREAMBLE** as the document name, and press return. Next you will see the prompt:

```
Exit WP? (Y/N) N                          (Cancel to return to document)
```

Type **N** to remain in WordPerfect, but with a clear screen and ready to begin a new document, with the cursor positioned at line 1 column 1 of an empty document.

Step 9: Practice
Figure EWP.8 contains the text of a second document. Enter the document as indicated, executing the appropriate formatting commands as implied by the document itself. Press **Alt+F3** at the end of the document to reveal the hidden codes in effect.

```
This document will help you review what you have learned, but
remember you must have obtained a clear screen in order to begin.
The exercise includes underlining and boldface, and shows how
different margins can be in effect for different parts of a
document.  From now on we will use double spacing and a left
margin of 20.

        This text appears in boldface

        This text is underlined

We now return to the regular left margin of 10 and single
spacing.  Press Alt+F3 to reveal hidden codes._


C:\WP42\PRACTICE                         Doc 1  Pg 1  Ln 13   Pos 56
```

Figure EWP.8 - Additional Practice

Step 10: Exit WordPerfect
Press **F7** to save the document and exit WordPerfect. Save the document as **PRACTICE** then type **Y** to exit WordPerfect and return to DOS.

New Commands - Exercise 3	
To highlight a block	**Alt+F4**
Reveal codes	**Alt+F3**
Underlining (new text)	**F8** (before and after)
Underline (existing text)	Highlight block (**Alt+F4**) **F8**
Boldface (new text)	**F6** (before and after)
Boldface (existing text)	Highlight block (**Alt+F4**) **F6**
To change margins	**Shift+F8, 3** (Margins)
To change spacing	**Shift+F8, 4** (Spacing)

The WordPerfect Template

The exercises just completed illustrate the basics of WordPerfect and some of its many formatting capabilities. To the inexperienced beginner however, many of the commands, e.g. Shift+F10, Alt+F3, etc., may appear haphazard and/or difficult to remember. Fortunately however, there is a way around this problem in the form of the WordPerfect template, which comes with the Educational Version. As you will soon discover, the template is indispensable.

The WordPerfect template is designed to rest on your keyboard and serve as a convenient reference. WordPerfect makes two distinct templates, depending on whether your function keys are grouped together on the left side or whether they are located in the top row.

Next to each function key is a color-coded description of what the key does, with black denoting the key by itself, and red, green, and blue meaning the key in conjunction with the Ctrl, Shift, and Alt keys, respectively. Figure EWP.9 depicts the WordPerfect template with different type styles used in lieu of the different colors.

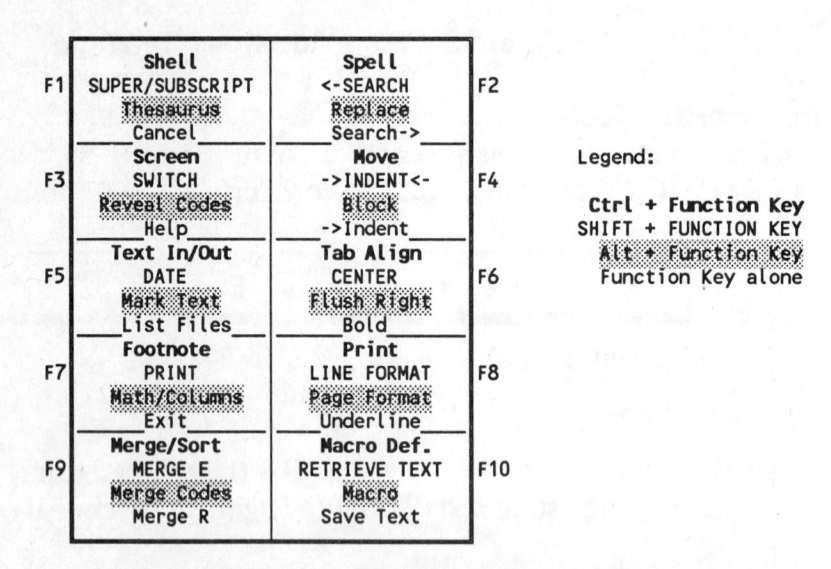

```
         Shell            Spell
F1  SUPER/SUBSCRIPT     <-SEARCH        F2
        Thesaurus        Replace
         Cancel          Search->
         Screen            Move                 Legend:
F3       SWITCH         ->INDENT<-       F4
      Reveal Codes        Block              Ctrl + Function Key
          Help           ->Indent          SHIFT + FUNCTION KEY
       Text In/Out      Tab Align           Alt + Function Key
F5        DATE            CENTER        F6    Function Key alone
        Mark Text       Flush Right
        List Files        Bold
        Footnote           Print
F7        PRINT         LINE FORMAT      F8
       Math/Columns     Page Format
          Exit           Underline
       Merge/Sort       Macro Def.
F9       MERGE E        RETRIEVE TEXT   F10
       Merge Codes        Macro
         Merge R         Save Text
```

Figure EWP.9 - Function Key Template (Version 4.2)

You can see how the template helps in finding keystrokes to perform the various functions in WordPerfect. Verify, for example, that the F6 and F8 function keys in isolation provide boldface and underlining respectively, that Alt+F3 reveals hidden codes, Shift+F10 retrieves a file, and so on.

You can also press the **F3** (help) key by itself to produce an online version of the template. The F3 key produces expanded help screens in the commercial version of WordPerfect but is limited in the Educational version.

Hands-On Exercise 4:
Using a Dictionary and Thesaurus

Objective: Use the WordPerfect Dictionary and Thesaurus.

Step 1: **Load WordPerfect**
Load WordPerfect as in the previous exercises, once again following the instructions for your particular configuration. Alternatively, if you are already in WordPerfect, follow the procedure to obtain a clear screen so that you can begin working on a new document.

Step 2: **Retrieve an Existing Document**
The commercial version of WordPerfect includes an extensive dictionary and thesaurus. Understandably however, these functions are limited in the Educational Version, and contain only enough entries to demonstrate their use; i.e. the dictionary and thesaurus can be used only in conjunction with an existing document provided by WordPerfect.

Press **Shift+F10** to retrieve an existing document at which point WordPerfect prompts you for the name of that document; your response depends on your configuration:

With a hard disk: **C:\WP42\README.WP**
With two floppy drives: **A:README.WP**

Figure EWP.10 displays the beginning of the README.WP document which will be retrieved on either system.

```
This "readme" file is designed to show you how the WordPerfect
thesaurus and speller operate.  Because of space restrictions,
the thesaurus and speller on this disk are quite limited.
However, the words needed to correct the famous aphorism on this
page are loaded into the partial thesaurus, and the words needed
to spell check the familiar paragraph on page two are loaded into
the speller.

Instructions: Put the cursor on a word in the following
famous aphorism, and while holding down the Alt key, push F1.
(*Words in the thesaurus that are preceded by dots are
"headwords"--push their corresponding letter for further
selection, or follow the options on the status line in the bottom
left-hand corner of the screen.)

            Fools rush in where angels fear to tread.

A:\README.WP                              Doc 1 Pg 1 Ln 1 Pos 10
```

Figure EWP.10 - Partial text of README.WP

Step 3: The Thesaurus

As indicated, the thesaurus is limited in the Educational Version but nevertheless sufficient to demonstrate the feature. (The thesaurus is implemented for the words in boldface in Figure EWP.10 - fools, rush, angels, fear, and tread.)

Use the arrow keys to highlight the word *fools* in Figure EWP.10 then press the **Alt+F1** key to activate the thesaurus. You will see the screen of Figure EWP.11 on your monitor.

```
┌fool-(n)────────────────────────────────────┐
│ 1 A  blockhead           cheat             │
│   B  dolt                defraud           │
│   C  dunce                                 │
│   D ·idiot          5    jest              │
│   E  oaf                 joke              │
│                                            │
│ 2 F  buffoon        6    feign             │
│   G  clown               pretend           │
│   H  harlequin                             │
│   I  jester        fool-(ant)──────────    │
│                     7   ·genius            │
│ fool-(v)────────────    ·sage              │
│ 3 J  deceive                               │
│   K  dupe                                  │
│   L  mislead                               │
│   M  trick                                 │
│                                            │
│ 4 N  bilk                                  │
└────────────────────────────────────────────┘
```
1 Replace Word; 2 View Doc; 3 Look Up Word; 4 Clear Column: 0

Figure EWP.11 - Thesaurus Entries in WordPerfect

To replace the word *fools* with *idiot*, type the number **1**. WordPerfect will prompt you to enter the letter of the word; type the letter **D**. Note, however, that *idiot* is not inserted in its plural form and thus the document must be edited accordingly.

Observe also how the thesaurus contains antonyms as well as synonyms which can be inserted automatically as well. It's also possible to look up synonyms of synonyms (although this capability is again limited in the Educational version.) Highlight any of the other boldfaced words in Figure EWP.10 and experiment as you see fit. It's easy and it's fun.

Step 4: The Dictionary

Press the **PgDn** key to move to page two in the README.WP document which in turn produces Figure EWP.12. The dictionary is also limited in its implementation in the educational version, but nevertheless functions sufficiently so that you can appreciate its power and potential. Follow the instructions in the README.WP document as they are described on the next page.

Instructions: While holding down the Ctrl key, push F2. Next, push 2 to check a page, and then follow the prompts and status line as you like.

```
We hold theese truths to be self-evedent, that all men are
are created equal, that they are endoud by their Creator
with certain unalienable Rights, that among these are Life,
Liberty and the prusuit of Happiness.  That to secure these
rights, Goverments are instituted among Men, deriving their
just powers from the consent of the governed.


A:\README.WP                              Doc 2  Pg 1  Ln 1  Pos 10
```

Figure EWP.12 - Additional text in README.WP

To initiate the dictionary, press **Ctrl+F2** then type **2** to check the entire page. WordPerfect scans the page, stopping at, and highlighting, each word it doesn't recognize. It's a little tricky, because the dictionary stops first at *F2*, which appears in the document, but which is not a recognized word in the dictionary. Type **2** to skip this word and continue.

Figure EWP.13 shows the screen at the next misspelling. The misspelled word *theese* is highlighted, with the various user responses displayed at the bottom of the screen. Type **A** and the substitution, *these* for *theese* in the example, is made automatically. Alternatively, you can select one of the prompts at the bottom of the screen; 1 or 2 to skip the correction, 3 to add a word, and so on. Press the F1 key at any time to cancel the spelling checker and return to the document.

```
We hold theese truths to be self-evedent, that all men are
are created equal, that they are endoud by their Creator
with certain unalienable Rights, that among these are Life,
Liberty and the prusuit of Happiness.  That to secure these
rights, Goverments are instituted among Men, deriving their
just powers from the consent of the governed.
================================================================

  A. these              B. this              C. those

Not Found!  Select Word or Menu Option (0=Continue): 0
1 Skip once; 2 Skip; 3 Add word 4 Edit; 5 Look Up; 6 Phonetic
```

Figure EWP.13 - Correcting spelling errors

New Commands - Exercise 4	
To use the thesaurus	Alt+F1
To initiate the dictionary	Ctrl+F2

Hands-On Exercise 5:
Block Commands and Other Operations

Objective: Move and copy text within a document; introduce the search and replace command (Corresponds to Hands-on exercise 1 in Chapter 4).

Step 1: **Create the Document**
Enter the document in Figure EWP.14. The creation of this document is straight forward, and should not pose a problem. We do, however, ask you to try the following as you enter the text:

a) Center the title by pressing **Shift+F6** before typing the text to be centered (Microprocessors), and then pressing the return key.
b) Press the **Tab** key to indent each paragraph.
c) Save the document at the end of each paragraph by pressing the **F10** function key. Saving a document repeatedly is a good habit to get into, due to the possibility of power fluctuations or other problems, to minimize the amount of work that would be lost.
d) Press the return key at the end of the second paragraph.

```
                          Microprocessors

     Microprocessors are often misleadingly described with a
single parameter, such as 8-bit, 16-bit or 32-bit.  In fact, you
need at least four measurements to characterize a microprocessor:
(1) external data-bus width, (2) arithmetic/logical unit width,
(3) register width, and (4) address-bus width.
     For each parameter, the general rule is "the bigger, the
better."  Increase any one of these numbers, and throughput,
measured in mips (million instructions per second), increases,
often with non-linear bonuses.  An inevitable corollary is "the
bigger, the more expensive."
```

Doc 1 Pg 1 Ln 12   Pos 43

Figure EWP.14 - Microprocessors

Step 2: **Moving Text**
WordPerfect implements the move and copy operations through a menu activated by **Ctrl+F4**. Nevertheless, we have found that the *easiest* way to implement these functions is through a delete and subsequent restore; i.e. we move text by first deleting it, then moving the cursor to the new location, and finally by restoring it. A copy operation is implemented in much the same way except that the deleted text is restored twice, at the original location, and again at the new location.

By way of illustration, we will take the first paragraph in the document just created, and place it at the end of the document. Move the cursor to the beginning of the first paragraph (before the tab), then press **Alt+F4** to begin marking a block of text. Use the arrow keys to highlight the first paragraph.

When the entire first paragraph is highlighted, press the **Del** key to delete the paragraph (responding **y** to the confirming prompt). Now move the cursor to where you what the deleted text to appear; i.e. to the end of the second paragraph (after the hard carriage return). Press the **F1** key and the deleted text will appear in reverse video; press **1** to restore the deleted text which in effect has moved the first paragraph from the beginning of the document to the end.

Step 3: **A Shortcut for Blocking Text**
You can use a convenient shortcut to highlight a word, a sentence, or a paragraph by pressing **Alt+F4** followed by a space, a period, or the enter key, respectively. This works because the block (Alt+F4) command highlights to the first occurrence of the indicated character; i.e. Alt+F4 followed by a period, highlights to the first occurrence of a period, which corresponds to the end of a sentence. In similar fashion Alt+F4 followed by the return key highlights to the first occurrence of a hard return; i.e. to the end of a paragraph, while Alt+F4 followed by a space highlights to the first occurrence of a space; i.e. to the next word.

Step 4: **Copying Text**
You can copy text by 1) highlighting the text to be copied, 2) deleting the highlighted text, 3) restoring the deleted text at the original location, and 4) moving the cursor to the new location and restoring the deleted text for a second time. Use this procedure to duplicate the first paragraph in the document of Figure EWP.14 at the end of the document. Remember to use the shortcut in step 3 for highlighting a paragraph. You can also press the **home, home, down arrow** to move directly to the end of the document.

Step 5: **Other Block Commands**
The block command (Alt+F4) was used in the previous step to highlight existing text for moving and/or copying. Realize, however, that once a block is highlighted you can perform other operations on that block. If, for example, you had pressed the **F6** or **F8** key, rather than the delete key, the highlighted block would have been boldfaced or underlined respectively. You could also press **Shift+F3** (followed by 1 or 2) to change the highlighted text to upper or lower case respectively.

Step 6: Search and Replace Operations

If the text in step 1 was copied exactly as it appeared, the acronym "mips" was entered in lower case letters. With the cursor positioned at the beginning of the document, type **Alt+F2** (WordPerfect's find and replace command). WordPerfect will respond with:

```
w/Confirm? (Y/N) N
```

asking in effect if it should obtain confirmation prior to performing the replace operation. Type **Y** (yes) to this prompt, as a search and replace operation without confirmation can lead to unexpected results. WordPerfect will follow with:

```
-->Srch:
```

Tell WordPerfect to find **mips**, and press **Alt+F2** again. You will then see

```
Replace with:
```

on the status line. Type **MIPS** and press **Alt+F2**. WordPerfect will then find all occurrences of *mips* in the document (there are two occurrences since the paragraph containing this entry was copied in step 4), asking for confirmation each time prior to making a replacement. Respond accordingly (Y or N) as you see fit.

Step 5: Print the document

Print the document and exit WordPerfect as in previous exercises.

New Commands - Exercise 5	
To center text	**Shift+F6**
Search and replace	**Alt+F2**
To move text	**Alt+F4** (highlight text) **Delete** highlighted text Move cursor to new location **F1** (restore deleted text)
To copy text	**Alt+F4** (highlight text) **Delete** highlighted text **F1** (restore deleted text) Move cursor to new location **F1** (restore deleted text)

Hands-On Exercise 6: Sending Form Letters

Objective: To produce a form letter in conjunction with WordPerfect's merge facility. The mail merge operation requires the creation of two documents; a *primary* file containing the form letter and a *secondary* file containing the list of names and addresses. Each file is created separately then merged together to create a third file which contains the form letters.

Step 1: **Clear the Screen**
It is imperative that you begin the exercise with a clear screen. This is automatically true when you load WordPerfect initially, but not necessarily true if you have been using WordPerfect for other exercises. Press **F7** to exit from the current document (if any), answer **Y** or **N** depending on whether or not you wish to save the current document, then **N** in response to whether you wish to exit WordPerfect.

Step 2: **Create the Form Letter (The Primary File)**
Create the form letter of Figure EWP.15a following the instructions below to enter the date, and the instructions in step 3 to enter the merge codes. Press **Shift+F5** to enter the Date/Outline Menu:

1 Insert Text; **2** Format; **3** Insert Function: **0**

Type **1** to insert the system date at the position of the cursor, then press the **return** key twice to position the cursor where the first merge code will be entered.

Step 3: **Merge Codes**
The information in carets, e.g. ^F1^, in the letter of Figure EWP.15a is known as a *merge code* and is entered in special fashion. Press **Alt+F9** to indicate a merge code. WordPerfect prompts with the menu:

^C; ^D; ^F; ^G; ^N; ^O; ^P; ^Q; ^S; ^T; ^U; ^V:

Type **F** (for field), and when the next prompt "Field Number?" appears, type **1** and press the enter key. You should see ^F1^ appear on the screen where the addressee's title will be placed. Continue in this manner, using the **Alt+F9** keys to define the fields, until your document looks exactly like the letter in Figure EWP.15a.

```
April 20, 1990

^F1^ ^F2^ ^F3^
^F4^
^F5^, ^F6^  ^F7^

Dear ^F2^,

Congratulations!  Your outstanding high school record has earned
you acceptance into the Computer Information Systems program at the
University of Miami.  This is an exciting time for you, and we wish
you every success in your college career.

We look forward to seeing you in September.

Sincerely,


Dr. Joel Stutz, Chairman
Computer Information Systems
```

(a) Form letter

```
Mr.^R
Alan^R
Moldof^R
2770 N.W. 115 Terrace^R
Coral Springs^R
Florida^R
33065^R
^E
Mr.^R
David^R
Grand^R
1380 Veteran Avenue^R
Los Angeles^R
California^R
90024^R
^E
Ms.^R
Marion^R
Milgrom^R
63-38 77 Place^R
Middle Village^R
New York^R
11379^R
^E
```

(b) Name and Address File

Figure EWP.15 - MailMerge

Step 4: **Save the Form Letter**
Press **F7** to save the form letter. Answer **Y** (Yes) to save the document, use **FORMLET** for the name of the document, and answer **N** (No) to exit WordPerfect. Check that you once again have a clear screen.

Step 5: **Create the Names and Addresses (The Secondary File)**
Create the file of names and addresses in Figure EWP.15b, using the instructions below to enter the merge codes following each field.

Type **Mr.** to enter the first field of the first record, then press **F9** to indicate the end of the field; WordPerfect will insert the merge code ^R as shown in the figure. Continue in this fashion until you come to the last field in the record (33065), then press **Shift+F9** which produces the code ^E as shown.

Step 6: **Save the Names and Addresses**
Press **F7** to save the data file. Answer **Y** (Yes) to save the document, use **NAMES** for the name of the document, and **N** (No) to exit WordPerfect. Check that you once again have a clear screen.

Step 7: **Verify Your Work**
Press **F5** followed by the return key to obtain a listing of the files in the default directory. Check that both FORMLET and NAMES appear in your directory. Press the F7 key to return to a clear screen.

Step 8: **Merge the files**
Be sure you have a clear screen then press **Ctrl+F9** to perform the actual merge. The following menu will appear on the status line:

```
1 Merge; 2 Sort; 3 Sorting Sequence:  0
```

Select option **1** and WordPerfect will prompt for the names of the primary and secondary files, **FORMLET** and **NAMES,** respectively. It will then merge the two files and produce a new document containing all three letters, with the individual fields inserted in their appropriate place. You can save this file if you choose.

Step 9: **Print the Merged Document**
Press **Shift+F7** to enter the print menu, then type **1** (Full Document). You should produce three letters, one for each student, with each letter on a separate page.

WordPerfect 4.2 Reference

Proficiency in WordPerfect comes with time; the more you use it, the better you will become. Try to learn a little every day, and take the approach that WordPerfect's many commands give it power and flexibility rather than making it difficult to learn. Don't try to memorize individual commands (that will come with practice) and do take advantage of the function key template.

This section is intended as a reference which we hope you will find useful. It was developed by extracting commands from the various help screens to create an alphabetical list of tasks you need to perform.

Task	Keystroke(s)
Block	Alt+F4
Bold	F6
Cancel	F1
Center	Shift+F6
Center Page (top to bottom)	Alt+F8
Change Default Directory	F5
Change Print Options	Shift+F7
Copy	Ctrl+F4
Cut	Ctrl+F4
Date	Shift+F5
Delete File	F5
Delete Left	Backspace
Delete Right	Del
Delete to End of Line	Ctrl+End
Delete to End of Page	Ctrl+PgDn
Delete Word	Ctrl+Backspace
Dictionary	Ctrl+F2
Display Disk Space	F5
Double Underline	Ctrl+F8
DOS File Conversion	Ctrl+F5
Dual Document Editing	Shift+F3
Exit	F7
File Management	F5
Flush Right	Alt+F6
Footers	Alt+F8
Forward Search	F2
Full Text Print	Shift+F7
Hard Page Break	Ctrl+Return
Headers	Alt+F8

Help (template)	F3
Insert/Replace	Ins
Justification	Ctrl+F8
List Files	F5
Macro (invoke)	Alt+F10
Macro Define	Ctrl+F10
Margin Release	Shift+Tab
Margins	Shift+F8
Merge	Ctrl+F9
Move	Ctrl+F4
New Current Page Number	Alt+F8
New Page	Ctrl+Return
Number of Copies	Shift+F7
Page Format	Alt+F8
Page Length	Alt+F8
Page Number Position	Alt+F8
Page Print	Shift+F7
Print	Shift+F7
Print Format	Ctrl+F8
Rename File	F5
Replace	Alt+F2
Retrieve	Shift+F10
Reveal Codes	Alt+F3
Save	F10
Search	F2
Spacing	Shift+F8
Spell	Ctrl+F2
Super/Subscript	Shift+F1
Switch Documents	Shift+F3
Tabs	Shift+F8
Thesaurus	Alt+F1
Top Margin	Alt+F8
Undelete	F1
Underline	F8
Word Count	Ctrl+F2
Word Delete	Ctrl+Backspace
Word Left (move)	Ctrl+Left Arrow
Word Right (move)	Ctrl+Right Arrow

WordPerfect 4.2 Self-Evaluation

By far the best way of judging how much you have learned about WordPerfect is to see how successful you are in using the program to do actual word processing. Nevertheless we have included a quiz, with answers immediately following, should you want to attempt it.

1. Explain how to load WordPerfect, distinguishing between a configuration with and without a hard disk.

2. Insertion and Deletion. Indicate how to delete the following:
   (a) A character
   (b) A word
   (c) A sentence
   (d) A paragraph
   (e) How do you restore the last deleted entry?
   (f) How does WordPerfect toggle between the insertion and typeover modes?
   (g) How do you know which mode (insertion or typeover) is active?

3. Command Structure.
   (a) How do you enter the print menu?
   (b) How do you enter the format menu?
   (c) How do you cancel a command?
   (d) How do you change the current directory (i.e. the directory where documents are saved)?
   (e) How do you initiate the dictionary?
   (f) How do you initiate the thesaurus?
   (g) How do you reveal hidden codes?
   (h) How do you force a hard page break?
   (i) How do you boldface existing text?
   (j) How do you boldface text as it is being entered?
   (k) How do you change margins?
   (l) How do you change line spacing?

4. Cursor control. How do you move
   (a) To the beginning of a document?
   (b) To the end of a document?
   (c) Left one word?
   (d) Right one word?
   (e) To the next page?
   (f) To the previous page?
   (g) To a specific page?

5. Online help.
   (a) What happens when you press the F3 key in the Educational version of WordPerfect?
   (b) What happens when you press the F3 key in the commercial version?

6. Saving files.
   (a) Differentiate between the F7 and F10 keys with respect to saving a file.
   (b) How do you obtain a clear screen?

7. Move and copy commands.
   (a) How do you move a sentence? a paragraph?
   (b) How do you copy a sentence? a paragraph?
   (c) What is the difference between the move and copy options?

8. Mail merge.
   (a) How many files are required for a mail merge operation?
   (b) What does the keystroke combination, Alt+F9 followed by the letter F, accomplish?
   (c) What does Shift+F9 do?
   (d) How do you invoke the actual merge operation, given the existence of the primary and secondary files?

9. Hidden codes.
   (a) How do you reveal hidden codes?
   (b) How do you return to a normal screen after hidden codes have been displayed?
   (c) What is the difference between the codes [HRt] and [SRt]?
   (d) What is the difference between the codes [B] and [b]?
   (e) What keystroke combination produces the hidden code [Spacing Set]?

Answers to WordPerfect 4.2 Self-Evaluation

1. The commands for a *hard disk* assume the existence of separate subdirectories for the program files and WordPerfect documents:
   ```
   C>  CD C:\WP42\PRACTICE
   C>  PATH C:\WP42
   C>  WP
   ```
   The commands for a *two drive floppy* configuration load WordPerfect in drive A and store the documents on drive B
   ```
   A>  B:
   A>  PATH A:
   A>  WP
   ```

2. (a) Move cursor under the character and press Del (or press the backspace key with the cursor immediately to the right of the character to be deleted).
   (b) Highlight the word (Alt+F4 followed by a space) and press Del; alternatively press Ctrl+Backspace
   (c) Highlight the sentence (Alt+F4 followed by a period) and press Del
   (d) Highlight the paragraph (Alt+F4 followed by enter) and press Del
   (e) F1 (cancel)
   (f) The Ins key
   (g) The status line displays the word *Typeover* when this mode is active.

3. (a) Shift+F7
   (b) Shift+F8
   (c) F1
   (d) F5 followed by an equal sign
   (e) Ctrl+F2
   (f) Alt+F1
   (g) Alt+F3
   (h) Ctrl+Return
   (i) Highlight text, then F6
   (j) F6 to begin, F6 to end
   (k) Shift+F8, 3
   (l) Shift+F8, 4

4. (a) Home, home, up arrow
   (b) Home, home, down arrow
   (c) Ctrl+left arrow
   (d) Ctrl+right arrow
   (e) PgDn
   (f) PgUp
   (g) Ctrl+Home, page number

5. (a) The WordPerfect Template is displayed on the screen
   (b) The help facility is entered

6. (a) The F10 key saves a file and continues editing the current document. The F7 key saves the document, then either returns to a clear screen or exits WordPerfect.
   (b) F7, Y/N to save the document, N to remain in WordPerfect.

7. (a) Highlight the sentence (Alt+F4 followed by a period), press the Del key to delete the sentence; move the cursor to new location, and press F1 to restore the deleted sentence. Follow the same procedure for a paragraph, except that you press Alt+F4 followed by return, to highlight the paragraph.
   (b) Identical to part (a) except you need to restore the deleted text in its original position, prior to moving the cursor to the new position.
   (c) The move operation changes the location of the block to elsewhere in the document; the copy operation duplicates the block in two places.

8. (a) Three
   (b) Produces a merge code for a field
   (c) Produces a merge code for end of record
   (d) Ctrl+F9

9. (a) Alt+F3
   (b) Alt+F3 (although many other keystrokes will also return you to a normal screen; e.g. the space bar)
   (c) They denote a hard and soft carriage return, respectively
   (d) The beginning and end of boldface
   (e) Shift+F8 followed by 4 (line space)

WordPerfect 5.0/5.1

Introduction

WordPerfect has become the acknowledged leader among full featured word processing programs, with annual sales estimates for the privately held company approaching $300 million (see Corporate Profile in Chapter 4). The success of WordPerfect is all the more remarkable in that the company was late in entering an already crowded market, with WordStar the then undisputed champion, and MultiMate, Volkswriter, IBM's DisplayWrite and Microsoft Word as formidable competition. Who would have thought that an obscure company based in Utah, with only two employees and no venture capital, could possibly succeed, let alone unseat the entrenched leaders of word processing? Yet it happened, and WordPerfect today is the standard against which other word processors are judged, with an estimated 60 percent share of the market.

WordPerfect is truly an incredible program and includes virtually every feature you could want in a word processor and/or low end desktop publishing program. (This manual was produced entirely with WordPerfect 5.1.) At the same time the program is remarkably simple to use, and you can learn the basics in a session or two. Our objective is not to teach you all of WordPerfect (we couldn't possibly), but only a subset of commands needed to do the hands-on exercises contained in the text. The exercises do, however, contain sufficient material to enable you to use WordPerfect productively for your work in your other courses.

Requirements

The manual assumes the availability of either WordPerfect 5.0 or WordPerfect 5.1, and further that the program has been installed on a hard disk in a separate WordPerfect directory. As you might expect, there are subtle differences between the two versions, and the latter does in fact contain additional capabilities not found in the earlier release. WordPerfect 5.0, however, is fully upwardly compatible with WordPerfect 5.1, meaning that all of the hands-on exercises in this manual will run under either release of the program. (All of the screens are from release 5.1.)

Unfortunately, a student version does not exist for either Wordperfect 5.0 or WordPerfect 5.1, and hence you must have access to the commercial version in order to do the exercises in this manual. Alternatively you can use the educational version of WordPerfect 4.2 which is shrinkwrapped with this manual, and described in the preceding pages.

Hands-On Exercise 1: Creating a Document

Objective: Load WordPerfect; create, save, and print a simple document. (Corresponds to Hands-on Exercise 1 in Chapter 3).

Step 1: Install WordPerfect

As indicated in the introduction, the manual requires the availability of either WordPerfect 5.0 or WordPerfect 5.1, and further assumes that these programs have been installed in accordance with the instructions provided by WordPerfect Corporation.

Step 2: Create a Subdirectory for Your Documents

We suggest you create a new subdirectory to store the documents that will be created in the various exercises. Accordingly, boot the system, then enter the command **MD C:\WP51\PRACTICE** (from the DOS prompt) to create the directory. All subsequent exercises assume the existence of this directory and follow the instructions to load WordPerfect in step 3.

Step 3: Load WordPerfect

Type the following commands to change directories and load WordPerfect:

CD \WP51\PRACTICE	Changes to the PRACTICE directory
PATH C:\WP51	Indicates to DOS where to find the WordPerfect program
WP	Loads WordPerfect

After typing the last command, the screen in Figure WP.1 will appear briefly on your screen, followed shortly by the clear screen of Figure WP.2. It is, however, possible to see another prompt prior to Figure WP.2,

```
Are other copies of WordPerfect currently running (Y/N)
```

Should this message appear, it means that you (or whoever used WordPerfect last), did not exit the program properly. Simply type **N** (to indicate that no other copies are running) and Figure WP.2 will appear.

Figure WP.2 is the basic WordPerfect editing screen and is clear except for the status line in the lower right indicating the document number (two separate documents may be created and/or edited at the same time), and the page, line, and cursor position for the current document.

```
              WordPerfect
                 5.1
```

```
            (C) Copyright 1982, 1989
               All Rights Reserved
              WordPerfect Corporation
                 Orem, Utah  USA
```

```
NOTE: The WP System is using C:\WP51

* Please wait *
```

Figure WP.1 - WordPerfect's Opening Message

```
                                              Doc 1 Pg 1 Ln 1" Pos 1"
```

Figure WP.2 - WordPerfect's Clear Screen

Step 4: Create the Document
You are now in a position to enter your document. Type as you would on a regular typewriter, but do not press the return (enter) key until you come to the end of a paragraph, as WordPerfect goes automatically from one line to the next (word wrap) as the document is entered. If you make a mistake, use the backspace key to erase the last letter(s) that were typed. Figure WP.3 shows the screen after we have entered a short one paragraph document.

```
              You should not attempt to develop a long document until you
          are confident of your ability to save and retrieve the documents
          you create.  Nothing is more frustrating than to spend an extended
          time entering text only to learn that you are unable to save or
          retrieve it._
```

                                              Doc 1 Pg 1 Ln 1.67" Pos 2.2"

Figure WP.3 - Creating a Document

Note how the status line in the lower right side of Figure WP.3 has changed to reflect the current position of the cursor (i.e. 1.67 inches from the top of the page and 2.2 inches from the left.)

Step 5: **Correct the Document (Insertion versus Replacement)**
Check your document to see that it is correct. Remember that WordPerfect, like all word processors, is always in one of two modes, insertion or replacement (typeover). In the insertion mode, new text is added to the document (to the left of the cursor), with existing text pushed to the right. The typeover mode, on the other hand, causes new text to replace existing text on a character by character basis.

The **Ins** key functions as a toggle switch which alternates between the two modes; i.e., pressing the Ins key switches from one mode to the other. Try it. Press the Ins key a few times, observing that the left side of the status line will contain the word *Typeover* whenever you are in the replacement mode. Practice entering text in each of these modes.

Step 6: **Save the Document**   *Alt = File Save*
Press the **F10** function key to save the document (and continue editing); the following message will appear in place of the status line at the bottom of the screen:

   Document to be saved:

Type **FIRST** (as the name of your document) and press the return key, after which you will be returned to your document. In other words pressing the F10 key is WordPerfect's equivalent of the *save and continue editing* command.

Step 7: **Print the Document**
Be sure that the printer is turned on and is on-line. (This can be verified by checking the indicator light(s) on the top or front of the printer.)

To initiate the printing process, press the shift key, and while holding the shift key down, press the F7 function key. We use the notation **Shift+F7** to indicate that the keys are pressed at the same time, and this combination will present you with the print menu of Figure WP.4. Type **1** or **F** (for Full Document) to print the document, after which you will be returned to the document screen.

```
Print

    1 - Full Document
    2 - Page
    3 - Document on Disk
    4 - Control Printer
    5 - Multiple Pages
    6 - View Document
    7 - Initialize Printer


Options

    S - Select Printer              HP LaserJet Series II
    B - Binding Offset              0"
    N - Number of Copies            1
    U - Multiple Copies Generated by   WordPerfect
    G - Graphics Quality            Medium
    T - Text Quality                High



Selection: 1
```

Figure WP.4 - WordPerfect Print Menu

Step 8: Exit WordPerfect

Press the **F7** key whereupon you will be presented with a series of messages to: 1) save the current document and exit WordPerfect, or 2) save the current document, clear the screen, and begin work on a different document. Either way you will see the prompt:

```
Save Document? Yes (No)                    (Text was not modified)
```

Type **N** (since the document has not been modified since the previous save operation (in Step 6). Next you will see:

```
Exit WP? No (Yes)                    (Cancel to return to document)
```

Type **Y** to exit WordPerfect and return to DOS. (Note, however, that were you to respond No to this prompt, *you would remain in WordPerfect with a clear screen* and hence could begin work on another document. The command sequence to clear a screen, and thus go from one document to another, is one of the most important, and most misunderstood, in all of WordPerfect.)

New Commands - Exercise 1	
To load WordPerfect	**CD\WP51\PRACTICE** **PATH C:\WP51** **WP**
To erase a letter	**Backspace**
Toggle between insertion and replacement (typeover)	**Ins**
To save and resume editing	**F10**
To exit WordPerfect	**F7** **Y/N** to save current document **Y** to exit WordPerfect
To clear the screen	**F7** **Y/N** to save current document **N** to remain in WordPerfect
To print a document	**Shift+F7** Full Document (1)

Hands-On Exercise 2: Retrieving a Document

Objective: Retrieve an existing document; revise it and save the revision; print the revision (corresponds to Hands-on Exercise 2 in Chapter 3).

Step 1: **Load WordPerfect**
Load WordPerfect as described in step 3 of the previous exercise. This is the procedure you will follow throughout the remainder of the manual.

File List Files

Step 2: **Retrieve an Existing Document**
To retrieve the document from the first exercise, press the **F5** key to list the files in the currently logged directory (C:\WP51\PRACTICE). You will see the message:

```
DIR C:\WP51\PRACTICE\*.*                    (Type = to change default Dir)
```

Press the enter key bring up the screen of Figure WP.5, then use the up and down arrow keys to highlight the FIRST file (*but do not press return*). Now type **R** (for **R**etrieve) to load the document.

```
06-16-90  09:12a            Directory C:\WP51\PRACTICE\*.*
Document size:        0   Free: 55,687,168 Used:       601      Files:       1

.    Current    <Dir>              | ..    Parent     <Dir>
FIRST      .          601  06-16-90 09:05a




1 Retrieve; 2 Delete; 3 Move/Rename; 4 Print; 5 Short/Long Display;
6 Look; 7 Other Directory; 8 Copy; 9 Find; N Name Search: 6
```

Figure WP.5 - List Files Display

An alternate way to retrieve a file (instead of the list files command) is to press **Shift+F10**, whereupon WordPerfect will prompt with the message:

Document to be retrieved:

Enter **FIRST** as the name of the document to be retrieved. The difference between the two techniques is that F5 (List Files) does not require the precise name of the file, as it lists the directory and enables you to select (highlight) the file for retrieval. Shift+F10, on the other hand, shortens the procedure by a keystroke or two, provided you know (in advance) the name of the file you wish to retrieve. Do not, however, use both methods in the same exercise or you will wind up with two copies of the document on the screen and in memory.

Step 3: **Editing (revising) a document**
The original document from Figure WP.3 should be displayed on the monitor. You will now edit this document to include an additional sentence at the end.

Use the arrow keys to move the cursor to the end of the document. [Alternatively you can press **Home, Home,** and the down arrow (↓) keys to move to the end of the document.] Now press the return key to end this paragraph and enter the following sentence in the next paragraph.

Success - I can save and retrieve documents with my word processor!

Step 4: Deletions and the Undelete Command

You can delete text within a document; for example, a letter, a word, or an entire line. To delete a letter, position the cursor under the letter and press the **Del** key. In similar fashion, a word is deleted by placing the cursor anywhere in the word, and pressing the Ctrl key and the Backspace key (**Ctrl+Backspace**). An entire line may be deleted by placing the cursor at the beginning of the line and pressing the Ctrl key and the End key (**Ctrl+End**).

WordPerfect also has an *undelete* (cancel) function which can restore your last three deletions, regardless of whether the deletion consists of a character, word, line, or a block. To illustrate this very useful capability, we will ask you to delete a line, then restore it. Accordingly move to the beginning of the document [you can press the **Home, Home,** and up arrow (↑) keys] and press **Ctrl+End** to delete the line. Now press the **F1** (cancel) key and the deleted text reappears in reverse video with the following prompt at the bottom of the screen:

```
Undelete  1 Restore; 2 Previous Deletion:
```

Type **1** or **R** to restore the deleted text.

Step 5: Save the Document

To save the document (and continue editing), press the **F10** function key as in the first exercise. This time, however, WordPerfect will not ask you for the name of the document, but instead will prompt you with the following message:

```
Document to be Saved: C:\WP51\PRACTICE\FIRST
```

Press the enter key to save the edited version as the document FIRST. WordPerfect will then prompt with a second message:

```
Replace C:\WP51\PRACTICE\FIRST? No (Yes)
```

In other words the document FIRST already exists because you saved it in the first exercise. WordPerfect wants to be certain that you intend for the edited version of the document (i.e., the document currently in memory) to overwrite the original file. Type **Y**, and WordPerfect will replace the file that was created in the first hands-on exercise with the edited version of the FIRST file.

Step 6: Backup

WordPerfect can be installed to automatically create a backup version of every document you create, using the same file name and appending the extension BK!. You can verify that the backup document was created by pressing the F5 function key to see the files on your directory. Press F5 and Figure WP.6 should come into view:

[handwritten margin note: just duplicate using Dos com. → no backup req'd]

```
06-16-90  11:32a              Directory C:\WP51\PRACTICE\*.*
Document size:         0   Free: 55,642,112  Used:      1,535    Files:      2

         Current     <Dir>                ..     Parent    <Dir>
    FIRST    .           917  06-16-90 11:31a | FIRST    .BK!       601  06-16-90 09:05a
```

```
1 Retrieve; 2 Delete; 3 Move/Rename; 4 Print; 5 Short/Long Display;
6 Look; 7 Other Directory; 8 Copy; 9 Find; N Name Search: 6
```

Figure WP.6 - Backup Documents

The directory in Figure WP.6 contains two files, FIRST and FIRST.BK!. Note too, the time associated with both files, and that FIRST was created after FIRST.BK!. In other words FIRST.BK! is the previous version (i.e., backup version) of the current FIRST file.

It is possible, however, that your version of WordPerfect was not installed to provide automatic backup in which case you have to enter the following commands to obtain the backup version. (You need not do this every time you use WordPerfect as the changes will stay in effect from one session to the next.) Press **Shift+F1** (to get to the WordPerfect Setup menu), **3** or **E** for Environment, **1** or **B** for Backup Options, and finally **2** or **O** for Original Document Backup. Save the FIRST document once again, press the F5 key to view the existing document files, and this time you will see the FIRST.BK! file.

Step 7: Print the Document

Press **Shift+F7** as in the previous exercise to initiate the printing process, then type **1** (or **F**) from the print screen to print the full document.

[handwritten margin note: File Print]

Step 8: Exit WordPerfect

(handwritten: File Exit)

Press the **F7** function key, answer N indicating that you do not wish to save the document (as it was previously saved in step 5), then answer Y to exit WordPerfect and return to DOS.

New Commands - Exercise 2	
To retrieve a document from a directory listing	**F5** (List Files) Retrieve
To retrieve a document when the file name is known	**Shift+F10**
To delete a word	**Ctrl+Backspace**
To delete to end of line	**Ctrl+End**
To restore previous deletion	**F1** Restore (1)

Hands-On Exercise 3: Reformatting a Document

Objective: Create a new document, then change its margins and line spacing; introduce underlining and boldface (corresponds to Hands-on exercise 3 in Chapter 3).

Step 1: Enter the Preamble to the Constitution

Load WordPerfect as in the previous exercises, then enter the Preamble to the Constitution as shown in Figure WP.7. Remember not to press the return key until you come to the end of the paragraph.

```
We, the people of the United States, in order to form a more
perfect Union, establish justice, insure domestic tranquility,
provide for the common defense, promote the general welfare, and
secure the blessings of liberty to ourselves and our posterity, do
ordain and establish this Constitution for the United States of
America.
```

                                                   Doc 1 Pg 1 Ln 1" Pos 1"

Figure WP.7 - The Preamble

Step 2: Cursor Movement

Check carefully that the preamble has been entered correctly. In so doing you may want to take advantage of WordPerfect's ability to move more rapidly than one character at a time, as shown in the table below. (Additional commands can be obtained through the online help facility which is explained in a subsequent section.)

Cursor Movement	
Left one word	**Ctrl+left arrow**
Right one word	**Ctrl+right arrow**
To beginning of paragraph	**Ctrl+up arrow**
To end of paragraph	**Ctrl+down arrow**
Beginning of document	**Home, Home, Up arrow**
End of document	**Home, Home, Down arrow**
To next page (large document)	**PgDn**
To previous page	**PgUp**
To page number nn	**Ctrl+Home** **nn** (desired page number)

There is one curious feature about cursor movement of which you should be aware, namely that the cursor may not be moved past the end of a document. In other words, when the cursor is positioned at the end of the preamble, after the period, the right and/or down arrow keys have no effect.

Step 3: Changing Margins

Be sure that the cursor is at the beginning of the preamble (pressing home, home, and the up arrow keys will move the cursor to the beginning of the document if it isn't already there). Press **Shift+F8** to enter the format menu of Figure WP.8.

The format menu is one of the more powerful in WordPerfect and leads to several other (subordinate) menus which control formatting of the document at various levels; e.g. for a line or a page. Search the menu in Figure WP.8, observing that margins (left/right) fall under Line.

Hence, to change margins, type **L** for Line (you can also type **1**) and you will be presented with the line format menu of Figure WP.9. Now type **M** for Margins. Type **1.5** to set the left margin at 1.5 inches and press return (the quotation sign for inches will appear automatically). Type **1.5** a second time to change the right margin to 1.5 inches as well and press return once more.

```
Format

     1 - Line
              Hyphenation                    Line Spacing
              Justification                  Margins Left/Right
              Line Height                    Tab Set
              Line Numbering                 Widow/Orphan Protection

     2 - Page
              Center Page (top to bottom)    Page Numbering
              Force Odd/Even Page            Paper Size/Type
              Headers and Footers            Suppress
              Margins Top/Bottom

     3 - Document
              Display Pitch                  Redline Method
              Initial Codes/Font             Summary

     4 - Other
              Advance                        Overstrike
              Conditional End of Page        Printer Functions
              Decimal Characters             Underline Spaces/Tabs
              Language                       Border Options

Selection: 1
```

Figure WP.8 - Format Menu

```
Format: Line

     1 - Hyphenation                         No

     2 - Hyphenation Zone      Left          10%
                               Right         4%

     3 - Justification                       Full

     4 - Line Height                         Auto

     5 - Line Numbering                      No

     6 - Line Spacing                        1

     7 - Margins - Left                      1.5"
                   Right                     1.5"

     8 - Tab Set                             Rel: -1", every 0.5"

     9 - Widow/Orphan Protection             No

Selection: 7
```

Figure WP.9 - Line Menu

Step 4: Double Spacing

The line format menu of Figure WP.9 should still be on the screen enabling you to enter additional formatting changes. (Should this not be the case press Shift+F8, as in the previous step.) Type **S** (for Line Spacing), type **2** (to double space), and press return. Press **F7** to return to the document screen.

Step 5: Underlining and Boldface

Any portion of a document may be underlined (boldfaced), but the procedure varies depending on whether a document is being created for the first time, or whether text in an existing document is to be underlined.

To underline text as the document is being created, press the **F8** key and continue typing; underlining of new text takes place as the text is being entered. (Note, however, that on a color monitor the underlined text will appear in a different color rather than with an underline. Note too, that the number indicating the cursor position at the bottom right of the screen is also underlined.) Press the **F8** key a second time to end the underline.

A different procedure is used to underline text that has been previously created, whereby you first highlight (block) the text to underline, then press the F8 underline key. Assume, for example that you wish to underline the words United States in the first line of the preamble. Move the cursor to the beginning of the intended underlining, the letter U in United States. Press **Alt+F4** to begin highlighting the text to underline; the words *Block On* will flash on and off at the bottom left of the screen. Use the right arrow key to move the cursor to the end of the block (i.e. after the lowercase s in States) and as you do so each character in the block will be highlighted in reverse video or a different color. Finally press the **F8** key and the block of text, i.e. the words United States, no longer appears in reverse video, but are underlined instead.

In similar fashion, you can boldface rather than underline by pressing the **F6** key before and after the text to be emphasized when entering a document for the first time, or by blocking existing text (Alt+F4) and pressing F6, as described above. (On color monitors, boldfaced text may appear in a different color.) Note too, that boldfaced text should be brighter, and if this is not the case, i.e. you can't distinguish between bold and regular text, you should adjust the contrast control on your monitor.

Step 6: The Block Command

The block command (Alt+F4) was used in the previous step to highlight existing text for underlining and/or boldfacing. Realize, however, that once a block is highlighted you can perform other operations on that block. If, for example, you had pressed the Del key, rather than the underline or boldface key, the highlighted block would have been deleted. Remember, too, that you can always press the F1 key to restore deleted text.

You can use the Alt+F4 command to quickly highlight a word, a sentence, or a paragraph, by pressing Alt+F4 followed by a space, a period, or the enter key, respectively. This works because the block command highlights to the first occurrence of the indicated character; i.e. Alt+F4 followed by a period, highlights to the first occurrence of a period, which corresponds to the end of a sentence.

Step 7: **Reveal Hidden Codes**

WordPerfect embeds special formatting codes (which are normally hidden from view) into a document, to instruct the printer as to how text is to appear in finished form. Position the cursor at the beginning of the preamble, then press **Alt+F3** to show the reveal the hidden codes. The following (seemingly unintelligible) display of Figure WP.10 will appear on the monitor:

```
       We, the people of the United States, in order to form a

       more perfect Union, establish justice, insure domestic

       tranquility, provide for the common defense, promote the

       general welfare, and secure the blessings of liberty to

       ourselves and our posterity, do ordain and establish this

       Constitution for the United States of America.
C:\WP51\PRACTICE\PREAMBLE                         Doc 1 Pg 1 Ln 1" Pos 1.5"
▲        {       ▲        ▲         ▲         ▲         ▲         ▲
[L/R Mar:1.5",1.5"][Ln Spacing:2]We, the people of the [UND]United States[und],
in order to form a[SRt]
more perfect Union, establish justice, insure domestic[Srt]
tranquility, provide for the common defense, promote the[SRt]
general welfare, and secure the blessings of liberty to[SRt]
ourselves and our posterity, do ordain and establish this[SRt]
Constitution for the [BOLD]United States of America[bold].[HRt]
```

Press **Reveal Codes** to restore screen

Figure WP.10 - WordPerfect's Reveal Codes Display

WordPerfect uses a split screen format when codes are revealed, with the text of the document on the upper half of the screen, and the text with the embedded codes displayed on the lower. Separating the two is a ruler line; the triangles represent tab settings, and the brackets { } indicate the left and right margins. Press **Alt+F3** (reveal codes) a second time to return to a normal screen.

Anything contained in square brackets is a WordPerfect hidden code. The first hidden code indicates the margins in effect, whereas the next code shows double spacing. The pair of codes [UND] and [und] indicate the beginning and ending of underlining. Recall also that WordPerfect automatically wraps words from one line to the next when the right margin is encountered; this is called a soft return, and is shown as [SRt] when codes are revealed. [HRt] indicates a hard carriage return which was produced by pressing the enter key.

The Reveal Codes command is useful because it shows the formatting commands in effect in a document. You can use the arrow keys as before to move within the document, and further you can delete any hidden code, and remove its effect, with the Del or Backspace key. (The Del key deletes the highlighted hidden code, while the Backspace key deletes the code to the left of the cursor.)

Step 8: **Print the Document**
Print the completed preamble by accessing the print menu (**Shift+F7**) and selecting option 1 (or **F** for **F**ull document). Press the **F7** key to exit WordPerfect, saving the document when prompted during the exit procedure.

New Commands - Exercise 3	
To highlight a block	**Alt+F4**
Reveal codes	**Alt+F3**
Underlining (new text)	**F8** (before and after)
Underline (existing text)	Highlight block (**Alt+F4**) **F8**
Boldface (new text)	**F6** (before and after)
Boldface (existing text)	Highlight block (**Alt+F4**) **F6**
To change margins	**Shift+F8**, Line, Margin
To change spacing	**Shift+F8**, Line, Spacing

Understanding WordPerfect 5.0/5.1

The exercises just completed illustrate the basics of WordPerfect and some of its many formatting capabilities. To the inexperienced beginner however, the various keystroke combinations, e.g. F10, Shift+F7, Alt+F3, etc., appear haphazard and/or difficult to remember. Fortunately however, there is a way around this in the form of the WordPerfect template, which as you will soon discover, is indispensable.

The WordPerfect Template

The WordPerfect template is designed to rest on your keyboard and serve as a convenient reference. WordPerfect makes two distinct templates, depending on whether your function keys are grouped together on the left side or whether they are located in the top row. (Note, too that if you have 12 function keys rather than 10, F11 is equivalent to Alt+F3, while F12 is equivalent to Alt+F4.)

Next to each function key is a color-coded description of what the key does, with black denoting that the key is pressed by itself, and red, green, and blue meaning the key is pressed in conjunction with the Ctrl, Shift, and Alt keys, respectively. A rough approximation of the template is shown in Figure WP.11 with different type styles substituting for the different colors:

```
          Shell            Spell
F1        SETUP            <-SEARCH        F2
          Thesaurus        Replace
          Cancel           ->Search
          Screen           Move
F3        SWITCH           ->INDENT<-      F4          Legend:
          Reveal Codes     Block
          Help             ->Indent                Ctrl + Function Key
          Text In/Out      Tab Align              SHIFT + FUNCTION KEY
F5        DATE/OUTLINE     CENTER          F6      Alt + Function Key
          Mark Text        Flush Right            Function Key alone
          List             Bold
          Footnote         Font
F7        PRINT            FORMAT          F8
          Columns/Table    Style
          Exit             Underline
          Merge/Sort       Macro Define
F9        MERGE CODES      RETRIEVE        F10
          Graphics         Macro
          End Field        Save
```

WP.11 - Function Key Template (WordPerfect 5.1)

You can see how the template helps in finding keystrokes to perform various functions in WordPerfect. Verify, for example, that the F6 and F8 function keys in isolation provide boldface and underlining respectively, that Alt+F3 reveals hidden codes, Shift+F10 retrieves a file, and so on.

The Help Facility

In addition to the template, WordPerfect provides an on-line help facility with additional information. The help facility can be entered at any time by pressing the **F3** function key, and is illustrated in Figure WP.12.

Figure WP.12a depicts the initial help screen which appears in response to pressing the F3 function key. Once in the help facility, you can type any letter and WordPerfect returns a list of functions beginning with that letter together with the required keystrokes (Figure WP.12b). You can also press any key, e.g. F7 (exit) to view a detailed explanation of its function (Figure WP.12c). Press the space bar or return key to exit help and return to your document.

The best way to master WordPerfect is not by memorizing all of the various keystrokes, but by effectively using the help facility. Assume, for example, that you want to change margins and don't know the necessary keystrokes. Simply press **F3** to enter help, than **M** for Margin whereupon you will see Figure WP.12b. Now scan the screen looking for the word margins and you will be presented with the identical keystrokes from the previous hands-on exercise.

Hidden codes

WordPerfect uses onscreen or *wysiwyg* (pronounced "wizzy-wig") formatting to the greatest extent possible, meaning that what you see (on the screen) is what you get (on the printer). It accomplishes its various formatting operations through the insertion of hidden codes within a document.

In general, you do not need to be concerned with these codes other than to know they exist. There are times, however, when the appearance of your document is not what you intend it to be, at which point you should reveal the hidden codes to see precisely which formatting commands are in effect. Recall that **Alt+F3** divides the screen in two and reveals the hidden codes (Figure WP.10), and pressing **Alt+F3** a second time restores the screen to normal. Once the hidden codes are visible, you can delete the existing codes or issue additional formatting commands to change the options in effect.

The WordPerfect Reference Manual contains over 100 hidden codes with the more common ones listed in an appendix. Remember too, that many of the codes have an on/off condition indicated by upper and lower case respectively; e.g. [BOLD] signifies the start of boldface whereas [bold] terminates boldface.

Different values can be associated with the same code in different portions of a document, as in the case of a document with different margins in different places. In other words you might see the hidden code [L/R Mar:1.5",1.5"] at the beginning of the document to indicate left and right margins of an inch and a half. These margins will stay in effect until another hidden code appears to change the margins; e.g. [L/R Mar: 1",1"] to change the margins back to one inch.

```
Help                                               WP 5.1    03/30/90

     Press any letter to get an alphabetical list of features.

          The list will include the features that start with that letter,
          along with the name of the key where the feature is found.  You
          can then press that key to get a description of how the feature
          works.

     Press any function key to get information about the use of the key.

          Some keys may let you choose from a menu to get more information
          about various options.  Press HELP again to display the template.

Selection: 0                                  (Press ENTER to exit Help)
```

(a) Initial Help Screen

```
Features [M]                     WordPerfect Key    Keystrokes
Macro Editor                     Macro Define       Ctrl-F10
Macro Commands                   Macro Commands     Ctrl-PgUp
Macro Commands, Help On          Macro Define       Ctrl-F10
Macros, Define                   Macro Define       Ctrl-F10
Macros, Execute                  Macro             Alt-F10
Macros, Keyboard Definition      Setup              Shft-F1,5
Mail Merge                       Merge/Sort         Ctrl-F9,1
Main Dictionary Location         Setup              Shft-F1,6,3
Manual Hyphenation               Format             Shft-F8,1,1
Map, Keyboard                    Setup              Shft-F1,5,8
Map Special Characters           Setup              Shft-F1,5
Margin Release                   Margin Release     Shft-Tab
Margins - Left and Right         Format             Shft-F8,1,7
Margins - Top and Bottom         Format             Shft-F8,2,5
Mark Text For Index (Block On)   Mark Text          Alt-F5,3
Mark Text For List (Block On)    Mark Text          Alt-F5,2
Mark Text For ToA (Block On)     Mark Text          Alt-F5,4
Mark Text For ToC (Block On)     Mark Text          Alt-F5,1
Master Document                  Mark Text          Alt-F5,2
Math                             Columns/Table      Alt-F7,3
More... Press m to continue.

Selection: 0                                  (Press ENTER to exit Help)
```

(b) Partial List of Functions Beginning with "M"

```
Exit

     Gives you the option to save your document and then allows you to either
     exit WordPerfect or clear the screen.

     Exit is also used to exit from editing headers, styles, footnotes, etc.

     When you are in screens other than editing screens, pressing Exit leaves
     menus and will normally take you back to the normal editing screen (you
     may need to press Exit more than once).

Selection: 0                                  (Press ENTER to exit Help)
```

(c) Explanation of the F7 (Exit) Key

Figure WP.12 - The Help Function

Pull-Down Menus

WordPerfect 5.1 introduces *pull-down* menus in addition to the traditional function-key interface. The menus can be accessed with or without a mouse, although the author finds them more effective with a mouse. Either way, the menus can be accessed only from the menu bar, which in turn is displayed by clicking the **right** button of the mouse or pressing **Alt=** on systems without a mouse.

Once the menu-bar has been brought to the screen, the way in which you select options again depends on whether or not you have a mouse. On systems with a mouse, move the mouse pointer to the menu name and click the **left** button; on systems without a mouse simply type the letter corresponding to the menu option such as L to select the Layout option; i.e. the keystroke sequence to display the Layout menu is **Alt=L**.

Figure WP.13 displays the pull-down menu of the Layout option. The menu pulls down on top of any existing text in the document (temporarily hiding that text). The menu disappears after the selection is made and the hidden text is again visible.

```
               File Edit Search Layout Mark Tools Font Graphics Help
                              | Line      Shft-F8 |
WordPerfect 5.1 i             | Page      Shft-F8 | menus in addition to the
traditional funct             | Document  Shft-F8 | The menus can be accessed with
or without a mous             | Other     Shft-F8 | or finds them more effective
with a mouse. Ei              |                   | an be accessed only from the
menu bar, which i             | Columns   Alt-F7 ►| by clicking the right button
of the mouse or p             | Tables    Alt-F7 ►| ems without a mouse.
                              | Math      Alt-F7 ►|
                              |                   |
                              | Footnote  Ctrl-F7►|
                              | Endnote   Ctrl-F7►|
                              |                   |
                              | Justify         ► |
                              | Align           ► |
                              |                   |
                              | Styles    Alt-F8  |

                                              Doc 1 Pg 1 Ln 1.33" Pos 1"
```

Figure WP.13 - Pull-Down Layout Menu

You make your next selection either by clicking with the **left** button on the option of choice, or by typing the highlighted letter of the associated option. Choosing the line option of Figure WP.13, for example, will display the line format menu shown earlier in Figure WP.8. Note too, that some of the choices in the pull-down menu contain a right arrow which implies an additional pull-down menu prior to making the final selection. The pull-down menu and menu bar will disappear after the last choice has been made.

Hands-On Exercise 4:
Using a Dictionary and Thesaurus

Objective: Use the WordPerfect Dictionary and Thesaurus.

Step 1: **Load WordPerfect**
Load WordPerfect and retrieve the PREAMBLE document.

Step 2: **The Thesaurus**
Position the cursor at any word within the document; e.g. common. Press **Alt+F1** to invoke the WordPerfect thesaurus, whereupon Figure WP.14 will appear on your monitor.

```
We, the people of the United States, in order to form a more
perfect Union, establish justice, insure domestic tranquility,
provide for the common defense, promote the general welfare, and
secure the blessings of liberty to ourselves and our posterity, do
ordain and establish this Constitution for the United States of
┌common-(a)─────────────┬─────────────────────┬─common-(n)──────────┐
│ 1 A ·collective       │   ·trite            │ 8   ·center         │
│   B  communal         │                     │     ·park           │
│   C ·public           │ 5 ·mere             │     ·plaza          │
│                       │   ·ordinary         │                     │
│ 2 D ·customary        │   ·simple           │ common-(ant)────────│
│   E ·familiar         │   ·typical          │ 9   ·private        │
│   F  frequent         │                     │     ·unusual        │
│   G ·routine          │ 6 ·insignificant    │     ·uncommon       │
│                       │   ·nondescript      │     ·original       │
│ 3 H ·average          │    undistinguished  │     ·exceptional    │
│   I ·conventional     │    unremarkable     │     ·important      │
│   J ·standard         │                     │     ·refined        │
│   K ·traditional      │ 7 ·cheap            │                     │
│                       │   ·crass            │                     │
│ 4 L ·banal            │   ·crude            │                     │
│   M ·hackneyed        │   ·vulgar           │                     │
│   N ·prosaic          │                     │                     │
│   O ·provincial       │                     │                     │
└───────────────────────┴─────────────────────┴─────────────────────┘
 1 Replace Word; 2 View Doc; 3 Look Up Word; 4 Clear Column: 0
```

Figure WP.14 - Illustration of WordPerfect Thesaurus

To replace *common* with any of the lettered synonyms, type **1** to indicate replacement, followed by the letter of the alternative word; e.g. **B** for communal. If the word you are looking for is in the second (or third) column, press the right arrow key to move to that column, whereupon the lettered choices will be associated with the words in that column. Finally if none of the choices are satisfactory, select option 3 to look up any of the bulleted words, whereupon you will be presented with yet another screen of synonyms.

Step 3: **The Dictionary** [handwritten: alt = Tools, Spell]
To demonstrate the dictionary, edit the document to deliberately misspell one or more words; e.g. *perfet*, rather than perfect. Press **Ctrl+F2** to initiate the dictionary whereupon Figure WP.15 will appear on your monitor.

```
We, the people of the United States, in order to form a more perfet
Union, establish justice, insure domestic tranquility, provide for
the common defense, promote the general welfare, and secure the
blessings of liberty to ourselves and our posterity, do ordain and
establish this Constitution for the United States of America.
```

Check: 1 Word; 2 Page; 3 Document; 4 New Sup. Dictionary; 5 Look Up; 6 Count: 0

Figure WP.15 - Initiating the Dictionary

Type **3** (or **D** for Document) to check the entire document. WordPerfect will scan the document, stopping at, and highlighting, each word it doesn't recognize. Figure WP.16 shows the first misspelling where perfet is highlighted within the document, and contains a *Not Found* message is at the bottom of the screen.

```
We, the people of the United States, in order to form a more perfet
Union, establish justice, insure domestic tranquility, provide for
the common defense, promote the general welfare, and secure the
blessings of liberty to ourselves and our posterity, do ordain and
establish this Constitution for the United States of America.
```

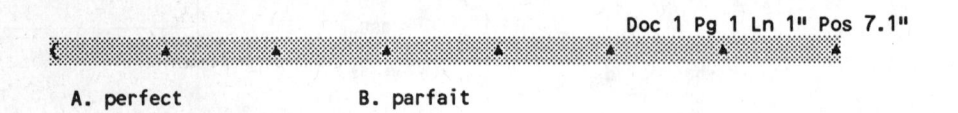

                                                    Doc 1 Pg 1 Ln 1" Pos 7.1"

A. perfect   B. parfait

Not Found: 1 Skip Once; 2 Skip; 3 Add; 4 Edit; 5 Look Up; 6 Ignore Numbers: 0

Figure WP.16 - Entering Corrections

Figure WP.16 also indicates the prompts displayed by the dictionary program upon flagging the word perfet, and shows the suggestions provided for correction. Type the letter associated with the correct spelling, **A** (in this example), and the substitution is made automatically. Alternatively, you can select one of the prompts at the bottom of the screen; **1** to skip the word this time only, **2** to skip it everywhere in the document, **3** to add a word to the auxiliary dictionary, and so on.

The dictionary continues to the end of the document, then displays the message:

```
Word count: 52                              Press any key to continue
```

Press any key to return to the document screen.

Step 4: **Help in Crossword Puzzles**
You can use the Look Up option of the dictionary to help in crossword puzzles. For example, what is a five letter word, meaning severe or firm with the pattern, *s _ _ r n*? If you answered stern, you don't need our help, but if not press **Ctrl+F2** to enter the dictionary, press **L** for Look Up, then type the pattern you want to check, substituting a question mark for each missing letter; i.e. type **s??rn** and press return. You will see the screen in Figure WP.17 and crosswords will never be the same.

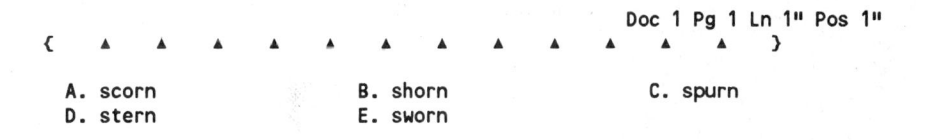

```
                                                    Doc 1 Pg 1 Ln 1" Pos 1"
{   ▲   ▲   ▲   ▲   ▲   ▲   ▲   ▲   ▲   ▲   ▲   }

    A. scorn            B. shorn              C. spurn
    D. stern            E. sworn




Word or word pattern: s??rn
```

Figure WP.17 - Help in Crossword Puzzles

Step 5: **Exit WordPerfect**
Press **F7** to save the document, exit WordPerfect, and return to DOS.

New Commands - Exercise 4	
To use the thesaurus	**Alt+F1**
To initiate the dictionary	**Ctrl+F2**

Hands-On Exercise 5: Block Commands and Other Operations

Objective: Move and copy text within a document; introduce the search and replace command (corresponds to Hands-on exercise 1 in Chapter 4).

Step 1: Create the Document

Enter the document in Figure WP.18. The creation of this document is straight forward, and should not pose a problem. We do, however, ask you to try the following as you enter the text:

[handwritten: alt = ┌ Layout, align, center]

a) Center the title by pressing **Shift+F6**, typing the text to be centered (Microprocessors), and then pressing the return key.
b) Press the **Tab** key to indent each paragraph.
c) Save the document at the end of each paragraph by pressing the **F10** function key. Saving a document repeatedly is a good habit to get into, due to the possibility of power fluctuations or other problems, to minimize the amount of work that would be lost.
d) Press the return key at the end of the second paragraph.

```
                            Microprocessors

     Microprocessors are often misleadingly described with a
single parameter, such as 8-bit, 16-bit or 32-bit.  In fact, you
need at least four measurements to characterize a microprocessor:
(1) external data-bus width, (2) arithmetic/logical unit width,
(3) register width, and (4) address-bus width.
     For each parameter, the general rule is "the bigger, the
better."  Increase any one of these numbers, and throughput,
measured in mips (million instructions per second), increases,
often with non-linear bonuses.  An inevitable corollary is "the
bigger, the more expensive."
```

Doc 1 Pg 1 Ln 2.83" Pos 3.8"

Figure WP.18 - Microprocessors

Step 2: The Search and Replace Command *[handwritten: alt = SEARCH, REPLACE]*

We will use the search and replace command to substitute MIPS for mips in the document of Figure WP.18. Given that the command takes effect from the position of the cursor, you must first move to the beginning of the document (press **home, home, up arrow**). Now press **Alt+F2** to initiate the search and replace command. WordPerfect responds with:

```
w/Confirm? No (Yes)
```

WordPerfect is asking if additional confirmation is necessary before doing the actual replacement; we urge you to always respond **Y** (yes) to avoid unintended substitutions. WordPerfect next asks for the search string:

`-->Srch:`

Type **mips,** and press **Alt+F2** a second time. (Do *not* press the return key after typing mips or WordPerfect will include a hard carriage return in the search string.) The next prompt is for the replacement string:

`Replace with:`

to which you respond **MIPS** and press **Alt+F2** once again. WordPerfect scans the entire document, asking for confirmation of the replacement whenever it locates "mips" in the document. Respond accordingly (Y or N) and the substitution is done or not according to your instructions.

Step 3: **Move Text**

To illustrate the move command we will take the first paragraph in the document just created, and place it after the second paragraph. The *easiest* way to perform this operation in WordPerfect 5.1 (it will not work in WordPerfect 5.0) is to proceed as follows:

[handwritten: Alt= ⌐ Edit, Block]

  a) Use the block (**Alt+F4**) command to indicate the text to be moved,
  b) Press **Ctrl+Del** to initiate the move operation,
  c) Move the cursor to the destination then press the **enter** key to complete the operation.

Accordingly to move the first paragraph do the following:

  a) Move to the beginning of the first paragraph and press **Alt+F4** to begin highlighting. You can use the arrow keys to move to the end of the paragraph, or you can immediately press the **return** (enter) key to extend the highlighting to the first occurrence of a hard carriage return; i.e. to the end of the first paragraph.
  b) Press **Ctrl+Del** to initiate the move operation; the paragraph will (temporarily) disappear in conjunction with the following prompt at the bottom of the screen:

`Move cursor; press Enter to retrieve`

  c) Move the cursor to the end of the second paragraph and press the **enter** (return) key as instructed.

The move operation is now complete. (Unfortunately, however, **Ctrl+Del** is not implemented in WordPerfect 5.0. Hence the easiest way to implement a move operation in the earlier release is to delete the highlighted text, move the cursor to the new location, then press the F1 key to restore the deleted text at the new destination.)

Step 4: **Copy Text**

The copy operation is implemented in similar fashion except that **Ctrl+Ins** is used rather than **Ctrl+Del**. To illustrate the copy command we will take the second paragraph and duplicate it at the beginning of the document. Accordingly:

[handwritten: alt = Edit, Block (r)]

a) Move to the beginning of the second paragraph and press **Alt+F4** to begin highlighting. Press the **return** (enter) key to extend the highlighting to the first occurrence of a hard carriage return which in effect marks the end of the paragraph.

b) Press **Ctrl+Ins** to initiate the copy operation at which point you will see the following prompt at the bottom of the screen:

```
Move cursor; press Enter to retrieve
```

c) Move the cursor to the beginning of the document and press the **enter** (return) key as instructed.

The copy operation is now complete. (Unfortunately, however, Ctrl+Ins is not implemented in WordPerfect 5.0. Hence the easiest way to implement a copy operation in the previous version is to delete the highlighted text, press the F1 key to restore the deleted text at the current position, move the cursor to the new destination and press F1 a second time to restore the text in the second location.)

New Commands - Exercise 5	
To center text	Shift+F6
Search and replace	Alt+F2
To move text (5.1 only)	Ctrl+Del
To copy text (5.1 only)	Ctrl+Ins

WordPerfect 5.0/5.1 Hands-On Exercises   97

Hands-On Exercise 6:
Sending Form Letters

Objective: To produce a form letter in conjunction with WordPerfect's merge facility. (Corresponds to hands-on exercise 2 in Chapter 5).

Step 1: **About Mail Merge**
The mail merge operation requires the creation of two documents; a *primary* file containing the form letter and a *secondary* file containing the list of names and addresses. Each file is created separately as described below, then merged together to create a third file in step nine which contains the actual form letters.

Note too that while the mail merge operation is essentially the same in WordPerfect 5.0 and WordPerfect 5.1, the merge codes (which will be described shortly) appear differently in the two releases. All of our illustrations are for the latter release, but you should be able to adapt the material to WordPerfect 5.0 with little difficulty.

Step 2: **Clear the Screen**
It is imperative that you begin the exercise with a clear screen. This is automatically true when you load WordPerfect initially, but not necessarily true if you have been using WordPerfect for other exercises. Accordingly we suggest you execute the following commands to make sure that you have a clear screen; i.e. that no document is currently in memory. Press F7 to exit from the current document (if any), answer **Y** or **N** depending on whether or not you wish to save the current document, then **N** in response to whether you wish to exit WordPerfect. Your monitor should now display the opening WordPerfect screen.

[handwritten margin note: alt= File Exit]

Step 3: **Create the Form Letter (The Primary File)**
Create the form letter of Figure WP.19a following the instructions below to enter the date, and the instructions in step 4 to enter the merge codes. Press **Shift+F5** to enter the Date/Outline Menu whereupon you will see the following prompt:

[handwritten margin note: alt= Tools]

    1 Date Text; 2 Date Code; 3 Date Format; 4 Outline; 5 Para Num; 6 Define: 0

Type **T** for **T**ext whereupon the system date will be entered at the position of the cursor. (The difference between Date Text and Date Code is that the former date remains constant if the file is retrieved at a later date; i.e.

the original date always appears no matter when the file is retrieved. Date Code, on the other hand inserts the current system date whenever the file is retrieved.

Step 4: **Merge Codes**
The bracketed information and field numbers in the form letter are known as *merge codes* and are entered in special fashion. Enter the date of the letter as described above, then press the **enter** key twice to position the cursor where the merge code will be entered. Press **Shift+F9** to indicate a merge code. WordPerfect will prompt you with the menu:

> 1 Field; 2 End Record; 3 Input; 4 Page Off; 5 Next Record; 6 More: 0

Type **F** for Field and WordPerfect prompts you to enter a field number:

> Enter field:

Enter **1** for the first field and {FIELD}1~ will be inserted in the document. Press the **space bar** because you want a space between the first and second fields, press **Shift+F9**, **F** for Field, **2** for the second field, and so on. Continue until you have completed the form letter.

Step 5: **Save the Form Letter**
Press **F7** to save the form letter. Answer **Y** (Yes) to save the document, **FORMLET** for the name of the document, and **N** (No) to exit WordPerfect. Check that you once again have a clear screen.

Step 6: **Create the Names and Addresses (The Secondary File)**
Create the file of names and addresses in Figure WP.19b, using the instructions below to enter the merge codes following each field. Type **Mr.** to enter the first field of the first record, then press **F9** to indicate the end of the field; WordPerfect will insert the merge code {END FIELD} as shown in the figure. Continue in this fashion until you come to the last field in the record, then press **Shift+F9** (for the merge codes menu) and **E** to End the record. *alt = Tools, Merge Codes*

Step 7: **Save the Names and Addresses**
Press **F7** to save the data file. Answer **Y** (Yes) to save the document, **NAMES** for the name of the document, and **N** (No) to exit WordPerfect. Check that you once again have a clear screen.

Step 8: **Verify Your Work**
Press **F5** to obtain a listing of the files in your directory. Check that both FORMLET and NAMES appear in your directory.

alt = File, list, File

June 20, 1990

{FIELD}1~ {FIELD}2~ {FIELD}3~
{FIELD}4~
{FIELD}5~, {FIELD}6~ {FIELD}7~

Dear {FIELD}2~,

Congratulations! Your outstanding high school record has earned you acceptance into the Computer Information Systems program at the University of Miami. This is an exciting time for you, and we wish you every success in your college career.

We look forward to seeing you in September.

Sincerely,

Dr. Joel Stutz, Chairman
Computer Information Systems

(a) Form letter

Mr.{END FIELD}
Alan{END FIELD}
Moldof{END FIELD}
2770 NW 115 Terrace{END FIELD}
Coral Springs{END FIELD}
FL{END FIELD}
33065{END FIELD}{END RECORD}
==
Mr.{END FIELD}
David{END FIELD}
Grand{END FIELD}
1380 Veterans Avenue{END FIELD}
Loss Angeles{END FIELD}
CA{END FIELD}
90024{END FIELD}{END RECORD}
==
Ms.{END FIELD}
Marion{END FIELD}
Milgrom{END FIELD}
63-38 77 Place{END FIELD}
Middle Village{END FIELD}
NY{END FIELD}
11379{END FIELD}{END RECORD}
==

(b) File of Names and Addresses

Figure WP.19 - WordPerfect Mail Merge

Step 9: Merge the files

Be sure you have a clear screen then press **Ctrl+F9** to perform the actual merge. The following menu will appear on the status line:

(handwritten: alt = Tools, Merge)

```
1 Merge; 2 Sort; 3 Convert Old Merge Codes: 0
```

Select **M** for (Merge) and you will be prompted for the names of the primary and secondary files. Answer **FORMLET** and **NAMES** as shown:

Primary file: **FORMLET**
Secondary file: **NAMES**

You should see a brief message, then the cursor will be positioned at the end of the merged file (the status line will indicate page 3, because there are three pages in the merged document, one for each student). WordPerfect automatically inserts a *hard page break* at the end of each letter to force the next letter to begin on a new page; press ALT+F3 to reveal the hidden code [HPg] for a hard page break. (You can explicitly insert a hard page break in any document by pressing **Ctrl+Return**.)

Step 10: Print the Merged Document

Press **Shift+F7** to enter the print menu, then press **F** for (Full Document). Your printer should produce three letters, one for each student, with each letter on a separate page.

(handwritten: alt = File, Print)

New Commands - Exercise 6	
To enter a date	**Shift+F5** Choose Text or Code

Merge codes:
   Enter field (primary file)
   End field (secondary file)
   End record (secondary file)
	
	 Shift+F9, Field, (field number)
	 F9
	 Shift+F9, End Record

To perform the actual merge	**Ctrl+F9**
To clear the screen	**F7** (begin exit) Y/N to save current document N to remain in WordPerfect
To insert a hard page break	**Ctrl+Return**

WordPerfect 5.0/5.1 Hands-On Exercises 101

Hands-On Exercise 7: Combining Text and Graphics

F5 – lists Graphics files

Objective: To combine text and graphics into a single document; to distinguish between the text and graphics modes of WordPerfect. The exercise assumes the availability of WordPerfect graphics figures.

Step 1: **A Look Ahead**
Figure WP.20 contains the finished document we will produce in this exercise and contains both text and graphics.

Software, rather than hardware, should govern the purchase of any computer. In other words you should first settle on the applications you intend to run, then determine which software is best for those applications, and finally determine the hardware necessary to run those applications. Only then should you begin to think about a specific computer.

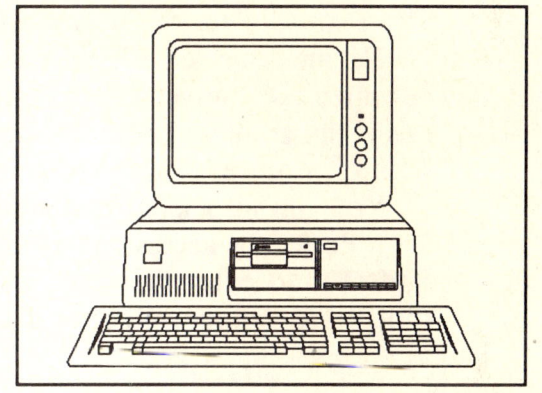

We suggest, too, that you pay for your computer with the **American Express Card** as the company will double the warranty of any item charged on its credit card for up to one additional year. All you need to do is send a copy of the credit card transaction together with a copy of the manufacturer's warranty to Buyer's Assurance, POB 6069, Torrance, CA, 90504-0069.

Figure WP.20 - Text With Graphics

Step 2: **Check for the Availability of Graphics Figures**
The computer in Figure WP.20 is one of several graphics included with WordPerfect 5.1. (WordPerfect 5.0 includes a different set of figures.) Realize, however, that to incorporate any of these figures within a WordPerfect document you must know their location on disk; i.e., the subdirectory where they are stored (which is determined during the WordPerfect installation procedure). The most common practice is to put the graphics files in their own subdirectory, for example, in the subdirectory C:\WP51\GRAPHICS. You need, however, to verify that the files are in fact in this subdirectory.

Boot the system ending at the DOS prompt. Now enter the command **DIR C:\WP51\GRAPHICS /W** to produce Figure WP.21. (The W in the DIR command produces a wide directory, listing the file names and extensions but omitting the file size, date, and time the file was created.

```
Directory of  C:\WP51\GRAPHICS

.                  ..               ARROW-22 WPG    BALLOONS WPG    BANNER-3 WPG
BICYCLE  WPG    BKGRND-1 WPG    BORDER-8 WPG    BULB     WPG    BURST-1  WPG
BUTTRFLY WPG    CALENDAR WPG    CERTIF   WPG    CHKBOX-1 WPG    CLOCK    WPG
CNTRCT-2 WPG    DEVICE-2 WPG    DIPLOMA  WPG    FLOPPY-2 WPG    GAVEL    WPG
GLOBE2-M WPG    HANDS-3  WPG    MAGNIF   WPG    MAILBAG  WPG    NEWS     WPG
PC-1     WPG    PRESNT-1 WPG    PRINTR-3 WPG    SCALE    WPG    STAR-5   WPG
TELPHONE WPG    TROPHY   WPG
```

Figure WP.21 - WordPerfect Graphics Files

There are a total of 30 graphics (WPG) files, each with the extension WPG, any one of which can be incorporated into a WordPerfect document. Observe also that the file PC-1.WPG is highlighted because this is the graphics file we will use later in step 4 of the exercise. Go to step 3 if you were successful in locating the graphics files.

You can also identify the location of the graphics files from within WordPerfect by accessing the setup menu. Load WordPerfect, then press **Shift+F1** to enter the setup menu, then L for Location of files. You should see the equivalent of Figure WP.22 on your monitor:

alt= File, Setup

```
Setup: Location of Files

    1 - Backup Files                    C:\WP51\BACKUP

    2 - Keyboard/Macro Files            C:\WP51\MACROS

    3 - Thesaurus/Spell/Hyphenation
                    Main                C:\WP51
                    Supplementary       C:\WP51

    4 - Printer Files                   C:\WP51

    5 - Style Files                     C:\WP51
                Library Filename        C:\WP51\LIBRARY.STY

    6 - Graphic Files                   C:\WP51\GRAPHICS

    7 - Documents

Selection: 0
```

Figure WP.22 - Location of WordPerfect Files

The setup menu identifies the location of the various files needed by the WordPerfect program. As you can see from Figure WP.22 the graphics files have been installed on our system in the directory C:\WP51\GRAPHICS (corresponding to the entry in our DIR command).

Your system may reflect a different subdirectory, which in turn is the location of the graphics files on your system. If, however, there is no entry for the graphics files, you must return to the installation procedure in order to copy the files from the WordPerfect disks to your system.

Step 3: **Enter the Graphics Menu**
Now that you know where to find the computer graphic, you can begin to create the document shown earlier at the beginning of the exercise. Load WordPerfect (if you haven't already done so), and clear the screen as well. Be sure you are at the beginning of the document (**Home, home, up arrow**), then press **Alt+F9** to enter the graphics menu:

[handwritten: L alt = File, graphics]

```
1 Figure; 2 Table Box; 3 Text Box; 4 User Box; 5 Line; 6 Equation: 0
```

Press **F** to enter the Figure menu:

```
Figure: 1 Create; 2 Edit; 3 New Number; 4 Options: 0
```

Press **C** (for Create) whereupon the menu in Figure WP.23 should appear on your monitor. You are now ready to bring the computer graphic into your WordPerfect document.

```
Definition: Figure

     1 - Filename
     2 - Contents              Empty
     3 - Caption
     4 - Anchor Type           Paragraph
     5 - Vertical Position     0"
     6 - Horizontal Position   Right
     7 - Size                  3.25" wide x 3.25" (high)
     8 - Wrap Text Around Box  Yes
     9 - Edit


Selection: 0
```

Figure WP.23 - Figure Definition Menu

Step 4: **Create the Figure**
Type **F** (for filename) and WordPerfect will prompt you to enter the name of the file containing the computer graphic; i.e. you will see the prompt:

```
Enter filename:                                          (List files)
```

Enter the name of the file containing the computer graphic, which in our example is **C:\WP51\GRAPHICS\PC-1.WPG**. Alternatively, you can take advantage of the prompt to list the available graphic files by pressing the **F5** key; you can then use the arrow keys to highlight the desired graphics file, then press **R** to retrieve the highlighted file.

There will be a brief message, "Please wait - loading WP Graphics file", after which you will be returned to the figure definition menu of Figure WP.23. You should notice that the menu has been modified to reflect *PC-1.WPG* and *graphics*, corresponding to the Filename and Contents entries. Press **F7** to return to the document screen and begin entering text.

Step 5: **Enter Text**

You will not see the computer picture per se, but only a single horizontal line containing the label FIG 1; do not be concerned, however, because everything is going well. Enter the text as indicated in Figure WP.20 at the beginning of the exercise. Figure WP.24 shows the document as text is being entered with hidden codes revealed.

```
Software, rather than hardware,    ┌FIG 1──────────────┐
should govern the purchase of      │                   │
any computer.  In other words      │                   │
you should first settle on the     │                   │
applications you intend to run,    │                   │
then determine which software      │                   │
                                   │                   │
                                   └───────────────────┘

                                         Doc 1 Pg 1 Ln 1.67" Pos 4.1"
░░░░▲░░░▲░░░▲░░░▲░░░▲░░░▲░░░▲░░░▲░░░▲░░░▲░░░▲░░)░░▲░░░▲
[Fig Box:1;;]Software, rather than hardware,[SRt]
should govern the purchase of[SRt]
any computer.  In other words[SRt]
you should first settle on the[SRt]
applications you intend to run,[SRt]
then determine which software[SRt]




Press Reveal Codes to restore screen
```

Figure WP.24 - Combining Text and Graphics (Text Mode)

Step 6: **View the Document**

WordPerfect is a character based word processor which means you enter (edit) a document in the text mode, but preview it in the graphics mode. To see the document as it will appear on paper, press **Shift+F7** to enter the print menu, then **V** (View Document) to see the document. Figure WP.25 will appear on your monitor:

alt = File, Print

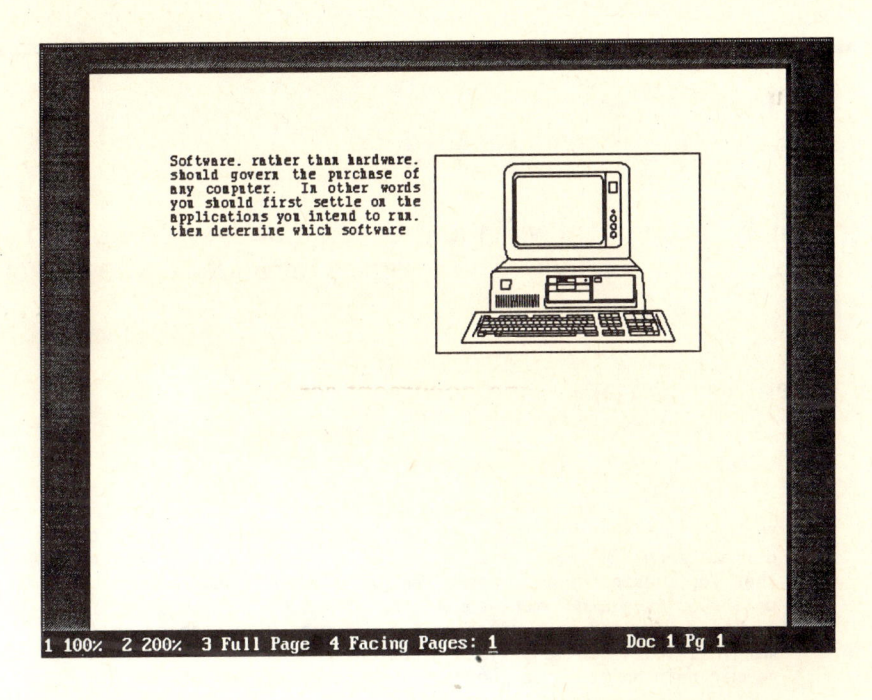

Figure WP.25 - Text and Graphics (Graphics Mode)

Step 7:   **Complete the Document**   *alt = ~~File~~, graphics*
Press **F7** to exit the graphics mode and return to the edit screen. Complete the document as shown earlier in Figure WP.20. Should you wish to change the graphic, press **Alt+F9** to enter the graphics menu, press **F** for Figure, and **E** for Edit. Type **1** in response to the prompt requesting a figure number (your document contains only one figure) and you will be returned to the figure definition menu of Figure WP.23. Change any of the options, e.g. change the position of the graphic from right to left, then view the revised document.
   Save the completed document, then print it in the usual manner.

New Commands - Exercise 7	
To locate graphic files	**Shift+F1**, Location of Files
To create a figure	**Alt+F9**, Figure, Create, Filename, **F5** (list), Retrieve
To view a document	**Shift+F7**, View

Hands-On Exercise 8:
Introduction to Desktop Publishing

Objective: To experiment with the rudiments of desktop publishing within the context of WordPerfect. The exercise introduces type selection and newspaper columns.

Step 1: Prepare the Copy
Load WordPerfect as in the previous exercises then create a document with the text in Figure WP.26.

```
The best way to learn about desktop publishing is to implement
different designs for the same document.  We suggest, therefore,
that you create a sample paragraph, then copy it several times
until you have a document consisting of two or three pages.  You
can then vary the appearance of the document with respect to
margins, justification, type selection, and so on, and in this
manner gain an appreciation for basic typography.




                                           Doc 1 Pg 1 Ln 1" Pos 1"
```

Figure WP.26 - Text for Desktop Publishing Exercise

Step 2: Initialize the Printer
Press **Shift+F7** for the print menu, then press **I** to Initialize the printer. You will then be prompted with a second message,

```
Proceed with Printer Initialization No (Yes)?
```

Respond **Y** to continue the initialization. This process should be done at the beginning of every session to download soft fonts from disk into the printer's memory. This step is not necessary, however, when the fonts are built into the printer (as is the case with the HP LaserJet Series III) or with other printers which use cartridge rather than soft fonts.

Step 3: Font Selection
Move to the beginning of the document (**Home, Home, Up Arrow**) so that the font change takes effect for the entire document. Press **Ctrl+F8** to enter the font selection menu:

[handwritten: alt= Font]

1 Size; 2 Appearance; 3 Normal; 4 Base Font; 5 Print Color: 0

Select **F** (for Base Font) and the fonts available on your printer will come into view. Your screen will resemble Figure WP.27, but the exact fonts will depend on your configuration. The highlighted font, Courier 10 cpi in the figure, is the default font on our system.

```
Base Font

* Courier 10cpi
  Courier 10cpi Bold
  Helv  8pt (AC)
  Helv 10pt (AC)
  Helv 10pt Bold (AC)
  Helv 10pt Italic (AC)
  Helv 12pt (AC)
  Helv 12pt Bold (AC)
  Helv 12pt Italic (AC)
  Helv 18pt Bold (AC)
  Helv 24pt Bold (AC)
  Line Draw 10cpi (Full)
  Line Printer 16.67cpi
  TmsRmn  8pt (AC)
  TmsRmn 10pt (AC)
  TmsRmn 10pt Bold (AC)
  TmsRmn 10pt Italic (AC)
  TmsRmn 12pt (AC)
  TmsRmn 12pt Bold (AC)
  TmsRmn 12pt Italic (AC)
  TmsRmn 18pt Bold (AC)
  TmsRmn 24pt Bold (AC)

1 Select; N Name search: 1
```

Figure WP.27 - Font Menu

To change to a different font, e.g., 12 Point Times Roman, use the arrow keys to highlight the desired font and press the **enter** key to select the new font. You will not see any immediate change in your document; you can, however, press **Alt+F3** to reveal the hidden codes to confirm the font change has taken place; i.e. you should see a code approximating [Font:TmsRmn 12pt (AC)] for 12 Point Times Roman.

[handwritten: alt = Edit reveal codes]

Step 4: View the Document
Press **Shift+F7** for the print menu, then press **V** (for View Document). The document will appear in *graphics mode*, which as you know from the previous exercise, is very different from the *text mode*. The distinction between the two modes is important; WordPerfect is a character based word processor, meaning that you edit the document in the text mode, but preview it in the graphics mode.

[handwritten: alt = File, Print]

Step 5: Print the Document *[handwritten: = Cancel Key]*
Press **F1** to return to the print menu, then print the document with the same procedure as in previous exercises; i.e. by pressing **F** for (Full Document).

Step 6: Newspaper Columns

Newspaper columns are implemented in two steps. You first define the column specification (as described in step 8) by indicating the number of columns and the space between columns. Then, after the columns have been defined, you activate the column feature at the particular place in the document where columns are to take effect, as described in step 9.

Step 7: Enter the Additional Text

Move to the beginning of the document, then press **Ctrl+F8** to enter the font menu in order to select a new font; e.g. 8 Point Times Roman. Now enter the additional text in Figure WP.28 corresponding to the document we will create in the remainder of the exercise.

Note too that before you enter the new text, you must press **Ctrl+Return** at the end of the first paragraph, in order to produce a hard page (column) break. This will take you to a new page when the columns feature is not in effect (which is presently the case), and to a new column after columns have been activated.

[alt = Font]

The best way to learn about desktop publishing is to implement different designs for the same document. We suggest, therefore, that you create a sample paragraph, then copy it several times until you have a document consisting of two or three pages. You can then vary the appearance of the document with respect to margins, justification, type selection, and so on, and in this manner gain an appreciation for basic typography.

There is a definite relationship between type size and column width; the smaller the type size the shorter the line, or conversely the larger the type size the longer the line. This makes perfect sense given that smaller type accommodates more letters in a fixed amount of space, and hence requires a shorter line to display the same number of characters. Your are, of course, referred to Chapter 5 in the text for additional information.

Figure WP.28 - Newspaper Columns

Step 8: Define the Newspaper Columns

Move to the beginning of the document, then press **Alt+F7** to enter the column menu:

[alt = layout, Columns]

    1 Columns; 2 Tables; 3 Math: 0

Type **C** for Columns (Tables and Math are useful features, but beyond the scope of this manual.) Next you will be confronted with a second menu:

    Columns: 1 On; 2 Off; 3 Define: 0

Press **D** to define columns and Figure WP.29 comes into view. The default column arrangement is two newspaper columns with the indicated margins (parallel columns are another type of column which are beyond the scope of this discussion).

```
Text Column Definition

     1 - Type                              Newspaper

     2 - Number of Columns                 2

     3 - Distance Between Columns

     4 - Margins

        Column   Left    Right    Column   Left    Right
         1:       1"      4"       13:
         2:       4.5"    7.5"     14:
         3:                        15:
         4:                        16:
         5:                        17:
         6:                        18:
         7:                        19:
         8:                        20:

Selection: 0
```

Figure WP.29 - Definition of Newspaper Columns

You could, if you wanted, change any of these parameters to implement other designs. For example, to get three columns rather than two, you would type **N**, then **3**, then press the return key. WordPerfect will automatically change the margins in effect for each column to reflect the new specifications. You could also change the distance between columns which is currently set at one half an inch, by typing **D** (for Distance between columns), then **.25** (to change to one quarter of an inch) and finally pressing return. Once again the column boundaries will change automatically. Alternatively you could type **M** for (Margins) and enter the column boundaries explicitly (as in the case of different size columns).

Step 9: **Turn Newspaper Columns On**
Press **F7** to exit the column definition menu at which point you should see the earlier menu shown below.

```
Columns: 1 On; 2 Off; 3 Define: 0
```
alt = Layout

If this is not the case, press **Alt+F7** followed by **C** for Columns, being sure you are at the beginning of the document. Now press **O** (for **On**) and the column feature is in effect. You will not, however, see the actual columns, until you move to the end of your document.

Step 10: **View and Print the Document**
Press **Shift+F7** to enter the print menu. Press **V** (for View) to view the document in graphics mode. If you are satisfied with the appearance of the finished document, press **F1** to return to the print menu, then press **F**

alt = File, Print

to print the Full Document; if not press F7 to return to the text screen and make the appropriate changes.

Step 11: Experiment
Experiment with different designs by repeating any or all of the previous steps. You will find, however, that the revision of a document in column mode takes some getting used to because the cursor moves down to the last row in the first column before coming to the first row in the second column. You can simplify the process and move immediately to the next column, by pressing ~~Ctrl+right arrow~~ to move right one column, and **Ctrl+left** arrow to move left one column.

[handwritten: Ctrl + Home (let go) right arrow]

Step 12: Hidden Codes
Hidden codes assume special importance because so many different options are in effect. Hence if you are not satisfied with your document, press **Alt+F3** to reveal the hidden codes currently in effect, then change the document as necessary. At first glance the codes may appear rather complex, but given some thought, they make perfect sense. Consider:

[handwritten: alt = EDIT Reveal Codes]

```
[Col Def:Newspaper;2;1.25",4";4.5",7.25"][Col On][Font:TmsRmn 8pt (AC)]
```

This set of codes reflects the definition and subsequent activation of the column feature, shown as [Col Def] and [Col On] respectively. The third (and last) code shows the font in effect at that position in the document.

Step 13: Exit WordPerfect
Press **F7** to save the document and exit WordPerfect.

New Commands - Exercise 8	
To change fonts	Ctrl+F8, F (Font)
To initialize the printer	Shift+F7, Initialize
To view a document	Shift+F7, View Document
To define columns	Alt+F7, Columns, Define
To activate columns	Alt+F7, On
To move left one column	Ctrl+left arrow
To move right one column	Ctrl+right arrow

WordPerfect 5.0/5.1 Reference

Proficiency in WordPerfect comes with time; the more you use it, the better you will become. Try to learn a little every day, and take the approach that WordPerfect's many commands give it power and flexibility rather than making it difficult to learn. Don't try to memorize individual commands (that will come with practice) and do take advantage of the function key template.

This section is intended as a reference which we hope you will find useful. It was developed by extracting commands from the various help screens to create an alphabetical list of tasks you need to perform. The list of commands also implies the existence of capabilities you may not have thought existed; for example, the ability to *add a password*, to *convert documents* to other releases, to invoke a *DOS command*, and so on.

In conclusion WordPerfect is an extremely powerful word processor, capable of virtually anything you might imagine. The key to being successful is a willingness to experiment coupled with knowing where to look in the help facility.

Features [A]	WordPerfect Key	Keystrokes
Add Password	Text In/Out	Ctrl-F5,2
Additional Printers	Print	Shft-F7,s,2
Advance (To Position, Line, etc.)	Format	Shft-F8,4,1
Advanced Merge Codes	Merge Codes	Shft-F9,6
Alphabetize Text	Merge/Sort	Ctrl-F9,2
ASCII Text File	Text In/Out	Ctrl-F5,1
Auxiliary Files Location	Setup	Shft-F1,6
Backup Options	Setup	Shft-F1,3,1
Backward Search	<-Search	Shft-F2
Base Font	Font	Ctrl-F8,4
Block	Block	Alt-F4
Block, Center (Block On)	Center	Shft-F6
Block Copy (Block On)	Block Copy	Ctrl-Ins
Block, Delete (Block On)	Del	Del
Block Move (Block On)	Block Move	Ctrl-Del
Block, Print (Block On)	Print	Shft-F7
Block Protect (Block On)	Format	Shft-F8
Bold Print	Bold	F6
Bottom Margin	Format	Shft-F8,2,5
Cancel	Cancel	F1
Cancel Print Job(s)	Print	Shft-F7,4,1
Capitalize Block (Block On)	Switch	Shft-F3,1
Cartridges and Fonts	Print	Shft-F7,s,3,4

Feature	Menu	Keystrokes
Case Conversion (Block On)	Switch	Shft-F3
Center Block (Block On)	Center	Shft-F6
Center Justification	Format	Shft-F8,1,3,2
Center Page (Top to Bottom)	Format	Shft-F8,2,1
Center Text	Center	Shft-F6
Change Default Directory	List	F5,=,Dir name, Enter
Change Font	Font	Ctrl-F8
Clear Screen	Exit	or y,n
Columns	Columns/Table	Alt-F7,1
Columns, Define	Columns/Table	Alt-F7,1,3
Columns, Move Through	Go To	Ctrl-Home,arrow
Conditional End of Page	Format	Shft-F8,4,2
Control Characters	Merge Codes	Shft-F9
Control Printer	Print	Shft-F7,4
Convert Documents (5.1 to 5.0/4.2)	Text In/Out	Ctrl-F5,3,2 or 3
Copy Block (Block On)	Move	Ctrl-F4,1,2
Copy Block (Block On)	Block Copy	Ctrl-Ins
Count Words	Spell	Ctrl-F2,6
Cursor Movement	Home and Arrow keys	Arrow keys
Cursor Speed	Setup	Shft-F1,3,3
Date/Time	Date/Outline	Shft-F5
Default Directory	List	F5
Default Settings	Setup	Shft-F1
Define Macros	Macro Define	Ctrl-F10
Define Printer	Print	Shft-F7,s
Delete	Delete	Backspace or Delete
Delete Block (Block On)	Block Delete	Backspace or Delete
Delete to End of Page	Delete End of Page	Ctrl-PgDn
Delete to End of Line	Delete End of Line	Ctrl-End
Delete to Word Boundary	Delete	Ctrl,Del or Bksp
Delete Word	Delete	Ctrl-Bksp
Dictionary	Spell	Ctrl-F2
Directories	List	F5,Enter
DOS Command	Shell	Ctrl-F1,5
DOS Text File	Text In/Out	Ctrl-F5,1
Download Fonts to Printer	Print	Shft-F7,7
Draw Lines	Screen	Ctrl-F3,2
Dual Document Editing	Switch	Shft-F3
End of Field	End Field	F9
End of Record	Merge Codes	Shft-F9,2
Environment	Setup	Shft-F1,3
Equation Editor	Graphics	Alt-F9,6,1,9
Execute Macro	Macro	Alt-F10
Exit WordPerfect	Exit	F7,n or y,y
Extended Replace	Replace	Home,Alt-F2
Extended Search	Search	Home,F2
Extra Large Print	Font	Ctrl-F8,1,7

Field	Merge Codes	Shft-F9,1
File Management	List	F5,Enter
Find	List	F5,Enter,9
Flush Right	Flush Right	Alt-F6
Font Base	Font	Ctrl-F8,4
Font Size	Font	Ctrl-F8,1
Fonts Directory	Print	Shft-F7,s,3,6
Fonts, Download to Printer	Print	Shft-F7,7
Footers	Format	Shft-F8,2,4
Footnote	Footnote	Ctrl-F7,1
Format Line/Page/Document/Other	Format	Shft-F8
Forms, Define	Format	Shft-F8,2,7
Forward Search	->Search	F2
Full Justification	Format	Shft-F8,1,3,4
Global Search and Replace	Replace	Home,Alt-F2,Replace
Go To	GoTo	Ctrl-Home
Graphics	Graphics	Alt-F9
Graphics Files Directory	Setup	Shft-F1,6,6
H-Zone	Format	Shft-F8,1,2
Hanging Indent	Indent	F4,Shft-Tab
Hard Hyphen	Hard Hyphen	Home,-
Hard Page Break	Hard Page	Ctrl-Enter
Headers	Format	Shft-F8,2,3
Help	Help	F3
Hidden Codes	Reveal Codes	Alt-F3
Hyphenation	Format	Shft-F8,1,1
Inches (Units of Measure)	Setup	Shft-F1,3,8
Indent Left and Right	->Indent<-	Shft-F4
Indent Left Only	->Indent	F4
Initialize Printer	Print	Shft-F7,7
Input (Merge)	Merge Codes	Shft-F9,3
Insert/Replace Mode	Insert	Ins
International Characters	Compose	Ctrl-v or Ctrl-2
Interrupt Print Job	Print	Shft-F7,4,5
Italics Print	Font	Ctrl-F8,2,4
Justification	Format	Shft-F8,1,3
Justification Limits	Format	Shft-F8,4,6,4
Keep Lines Together	Format	Shft-F8,4,2
Kerning	Format	Shft-F8,4,6,1
Labels	Format	Shft-F8,2,7,5,8
Landscape Paper Size/Type	Format	Shft-F8,2,7
Large Print	Font	Ctrl-F8,1,5
Leading	Format	Shft-F8,4,6,6

Left and Right Margins	Format	Shft-F8,1,7
Left Justification	Format	Shft-F8,1,3,1
Line Draw	Screen	Ctrl-F3,2
Line Height	Format	Shft-F8,1,4
Line Spacing	Format	Shft-F8,1,6
List Files	List	F5,Enter
Location of Backup Files	Setup	Shft-F1,6,1
Location of Files	Setup	Shft-F1,6
Lower/Upper Case (Block On)	Switch	Shft-F3
Macro Editor	Macro Define	Ctrl-F10
Mail Merge	Merge/Sort	Ctrl-F9,1
Margin Release	Margin Release	Shft-Tab
Margins - Left and Right	Format	Shft-F8,1,7
Margins - Top and Bottom	Format	Shft-F8,2,5
Math	Columns/Table	Alt-F7,3
Menu Bar	Menu Bar	Alt-=
Merge	Merge/Sort	Ctrl-F9,1
Merge Codes	Merge Codes	Shft-F9
Merge Codes (Convert Old Codes)	Merge/Sort	Ctrl-F9,3
Merge Codes Display	Setup	Shft-F1,2,6,5
Merge Options	Setup	Shft-F1,4,1
Mouse	Setup	Shft-F1,1
Move Block (Block On)	Block Move	Ctrl-Del
Move Down One Paragraph	Paragraph Down	Ctrl-Down
Move One Word Right	Word Right	Ctrl-Right
Move One Word Left	Word Left	Ctrl-Left
Move/Rename File	List	F5,Enter,3
Move Up One Paragraph	Paragraph Up	Ctrl-Up
Multiple Copies	Print	Shft-F7,5
New Page	Hard Page	Ctrl-Enter
New Page Number	Format	Shft-F8,2,6,1
Newspaper Columns	Columns/Table	Alt-F7,1,3,1
Number of Copies	Print	Shft-F7,n
Number Pages	Format	Shft-F8,2,6,4
Orientation, Paper Size/Type	Format	Shft-F8,2,7
Original Document Backup	Setup	Shft-F1,3,1,2
Orphan/Widow	Format	Shft-F8,1,9
Outline	Date/Outline	Shft-F5,4
Overstrike	Format	Shft-F8,4,5
Page Break, Hard	Hard Page	Ctrl-Enter
Page Down	Page Down	PgDn
Page Format	Format	Shft-F8,2
Page Length	Format	Shft-F8,2,7
Page Number, Go To	Go To	Ctrl-Home, page#
Page Number, New	Format	Shft-F8,2,6,1

Page Number Style	Format	Shft-F8,2,6,2
Page Numbering	Format	Shft-F8,2,6,4
Page Up	Page Up	PgUp
Page View	Print	Shft-F7,6
Paper Size/Type	Format	Shft-F8,2,7
Paragraph Down	Paragraph Down	Ctrl-Down
Paragraph Up	Paragraph Up	Ctrl-Up
Password	Text In/Out	Ctrl-F5,2
Path for Downloadable Fonts	Print	Shft-F7,s,3,6
Preview	Print	Shft-F7,6
Primary File, Merge	Merge/Sort	Ctrl-F9,1
Print	Print	Shft-F7
Print (Cancel,Rush,Display,Stop)	Print	Shft-F7,4,1-3 or 5
Print Block (Block On)	Print	Shft-F7
Print Document on Disk	Print	Shft-F7,3
Print From Disk	Print	Shft-F7,3
Print From Disk	List	F5,Enter,4
Print Full Document	Print	Shft-F7,1
Print Multiple Pages	Print	Shft-F7,5
Print Page	Print	Shft-F7,2
Printer Control	Print	Shft-F7,4
Printer, Initialize	Print	Shft-F7,7
Protect a Document	Text In/Out	Ctrl-F5,2
Protect Block (Block On)	Format	Shft-F8
Quit WordPerfect	Exit	F7,y or n,y
Recover Text	Cancel	F1,1
Rectangle, Move/Copy (Block On)	Move	Ctrl-F4,3
Redline Print	Font	Ctrl-F8,2,8
Relative Tab Settings	Format	Shft-F8,1,8,t,2
Rename/Move File	List	F5,Enter,3
Repetition Number (n)	Repeat Value	Esc
Replace	Replace	Alt-F2
Replace, Extended	Replace	Home,Alt-F2,
Report Printer Status	Print	Shft-F7,4
Restore Deleted Text	Cancel	F1,1
Retrieve Document	List	F5,Enter,1
Retrieve Document	Retrieve	Shft-F10
Retrieve DOS Text File	Text In/Out	Ctrl-F5,1,2 or 3
Reveal Codes	Reveal Codes	Alt-F3
Reverse Search	<-Search	Shft-F2
Right Justification	Format	Shft-F8,1,3,3
Right Margin	Format	Shft-F8,1,7
Right Tab Setting	Format	Shft-F8,1,8,r
Save Text	Save	F10
Screen Down	Screen Down	+(NumPad)
Screen Up	Screen Up	-(NumPad)

Scrolling Speed	Setup	Shft-F1,3,3
Search	Search	F2
Search and Replace	Replace	Alt-F2
Secondary File, Merge	Merge/Sort	Ctrl-F9,1
Select Printer	Print	Shft-F7,s
Set Tabs	Format	Shft-F8,1,8
Setup	Setup	Shft-F1
Small Capitalized Print	Font	Ctrl-F8,2,7
Small Print	Font	Ctrl-F8,1,4
Sort	Merge/Sort	Ctrl-F9,2
Spacing, Lines	Format	Shft-F8,1,6
Spell	Spell	Ctrl-F2
Split Screen	Screen	Ctrl-F3,1
Status Line Display	Setup	Shft-F1,2,6,3
Stop Printer	Print	Shft-F7,4,5
Strikeout	Font	Ctrl-F8,2,9
Subscript Print	Font	Ctrl-F8,1,2
Superscript Print	Font	Ctrl-F8,1,1
Switch Documents	Switch	Shft-F3
Tab Set	Format	Shft-F8,1,8
Table	Columns/Table	Alt-F7,2
Text Box	Graphics	Alt-F9,3
Text Columns	Columns/Table	Alt-F7,1
Text In/Out	Text In/Out	Ctrl-F5
Time/Date	Date/Outline	Shft-F5
Timed Document Backup	Setup	Shft-F1,3,1,1
Top Margin	Format	Shft-F8,2,5
Typeover Mode	Insert	Ins
Undelete	Cancel	F1,1
Underline Spaces and Tabs	Format	Shft-F8,4,7
Underline Text	Underline	F8
Units of Measure	Setup	Shft-F1,3,8
Upper/Lower Case (Block On)	Switch	Shft-F3
Very Large Print	Font	Ctrl-F8,1,6
View Codes	Reveal Codes	Alt-F3
View Document	Print	Shft-F7,6
Widow/Orphan Protection	Format	Shft-F8,1,9
Word Count	Spell	Ctrl-F2,6
Word Left, Cursor Movement	Word Left	Ctrl-Left
Word Look Up	Spell	Ctrl-F2,5
Word Right, Cursor Movement	Word Right	Ctrl-Right
Word Spacing, Justification Limits	Format	Shft-F8,4,6,4

WordPerfect 5.0/5.1 Self-Evaluation

By far the best way of judging how much you have learned about WordPerfect is to see how successful you are in using the program to do actual word processing. Nevertheless we have included a quiz, with answers immediately following, should you want to attempt it.

1. Explain how to load WordPerfect.

2. Insertion and Deletion. Indicate how to delete the following:
   (a) A character
   (b) A word
   (c) A sentence
   (d) A paragraph
   (e) How do you restore the last deleted entry?
   (f) How does WordPerfect toggle between the insertion and typeover modes?
   (g) How do you know which mode (insertion or typeover) is active?

3. Command Structure.
   (a) How do you enter the print menu?
   (b) How do you enter the font menu?
   (d) How do you enter the format menu?
   (d) How do you enter the graphics menu?
   (e) How do you enter the setup menu?
   (f) How do you cancel a command?
   (g) How do you switch to a second document?
   (h) How do you change the current directory (i.e. the directory where documents are saved)?
   (i) How do you activate the pull-down menus?
   (j) How do you initiate the dictionary?
   (k) How do you initiate the thesaurus?
   (l) How do you reveal hidden codes?
   (m) How do you force a hard page break?
   (n) How do you boldface existing text?
   (o) How do you boldface text as it is being entered?
   (p) How do you change margins?
   (q) How do you change line spacing?

4. Cursor control. How do you move
   (a) To the beginning of a document?
   (b) To the end of a document?
   (c) Left one word?
   (d) Right one word?
   (e) To the next page?
   (f) To the previous page?
   (g) To a specific page?

5. Online help.
   (a) How do you enter the online help facility?
   (b) What is the effect of typing the letter "D" after entering the help facility?
   (c) What is the effect of pressing Ctrl+F8 after entering the help facility?
   (d) Explain the meaning of context-sensitive help
   (e) How do you exit help?

6. Saving files.
   (a) Differentiate between the F7 and F10 keys with respect to saving a file.
   (b) How do you obtain a clear screen?

7. Move and copy commands.
   (a) How do you move a sentence? a paragraph?
   (b) How do you copy a sentence? a paragraph?
   (c) What is the difference between the move and copy options?

8. Columns.
   (a) Differentiate between defining and activating newspaper columns
   (b) How do you define a column?
   (c) How do you activate columns?
   (d) How do you deactivate the column feature?
   (d) How do you produce a hard column break?
   (e) How can you move directly from one column to the next?

Answers to WordPerfect 5.0/5.1 Self-Evaluation

1. Exit to the DOS prompt. Enter the following commands to load WordPerfect from a PRACTICE subdirectory, which will save (retrieve) documents to this directory:
   C> CD\WP51\PRACTICE
   C> PATH C:\WP51
   C> WP

2. (a) Move cursor under the character and press Del (or press the backspace key with the cursor immediately to the right of the character to be deleted).
   (b) Highlight the word (Alt+F4 followed by a space) and press Del; alternatively press Ctrl+Backspace
   (c) Highlight the sentence (Alt+F4 followed by a period) and press Del
   (d) Highlight the paragraph (Alt+F4 followed by enter) and press Del
   (e) F1 (cancel)
   (f) The Ins key
   (g) The status line displays the word *Typeover* when this mode is active.

3. (a) Shift+F7
   (b) Ctrl+F8
   (c) Shift+F8
   (d) Alt+F9
   (e) Shift+F1
   (f) F1
   (g) Shift+F3
   (h) F5 followed by =
   (i) Alt= (or right mouse button)
   (j) Ctrl+F2
   (k) Alt+F1
   (l) Alt+F3 (also F11)
   (m) Ctrl+Return
   (n) Highlight text, then F6
   (o) F6 to begin, F6 to end
   (p) Shift+F8, L, M
   (q) Shift+F8, L, S

4. (a) Home, home, up arrow
   (b) Home, home, down arrow
   (c) Ctrl+left arrow
   (d) Ctrl+right arrow
   (e) PgDn
   (f) PgUp
   (g) Ctrl+Home+page number

5. (a) F3
   (b) Lists all functions beginning with the letter D
   (c) Explains the result of pressing Ctrl+F8
   (d) The displayed help screen depends on the command being executed
   (e) Press space or enter

6. (a) The F10 key saves a file and continues editing the current document. The F7 key saves the document, then either returns to a clear screen or exits WordPerfect.
   (b) F7, Y/N to save the document, N to remain in WordPerfect.

7. (a) Highlight the sentence (Alt+F4 followed by a period); Press Ctrl+Del; move the cursor to new location and press return. Follow the same procedure for a paragraph, except that you press Alt+F4 followed by return, to highlight the paragraph.
   (b) Identical to part (a) except press Ctrl+Ins to copy the highlighted text.
   (c) The move operation changes the location of the block to elsewhere in the document; the copy operation duplicates the block in two places.

8. (a) Defining a column provides information about the columns; (number, margins, etc.) but does not implement them; activating a column implements columns according to the last column definition.
   (b) Alt+F7, C, D
   (c) Alt+F7, C, O (after columns have been defined)
   (d) Alt+F7, C, F
   (e) Ctrl+Return
   (f) Ctrl+right (left) arrow once columns are active

Lotus/VP Planner Plus

Introduction

Lotus 1-2-3 by Lotus Development Corporation (see corporate profile in Chapter 7) continues as the dominant spreadsheet program in the PC marketplace and the most successful program ever. It has sold several million copies and spurred the introduction of numerous "Lotus clones" in the process. At the high end of the scale are programs such as Microsoft's Excel or Borland's Quattro Pro, which include capabilities beyond those found in Lotus. Opposite these are lower priced, less powerful spreadsheets, such as Paperback Software's VP Planner Plus, which also maintain the "look and feel" of Lotus while retaining its essential capabilities.

The next several pages take you through the hands-on exercises from Chapters 6 through 10 in the text, as they are implemented in Lotus and/or the student version of VP Planner Plus (which is provided in conjunction with this manual). Follow the instructions carefully and enjoy your time at the computer. We begin with a hands-on exercise to install and load the spreadsheet program.

Hands-On Exercise 1: Installation and Loading

Objective: Install and load the spreadsheet program. The instructions will vary considerably depending on whether or not you are using a hard disk, and to a lesser extent depending on the program you are using.

Step 1a: Installation (VP Planner Plus with Two Floppy Drives)
There are no special installation requirements for VP Planner Plus on a system with two floppy drives. Go to step 2a for information on loading.

Step 1b: Installation (VP Planner Plus with a Hard Disk)
The installation procedure creates a subdirectory on the hard disk, then copies the VP Planner files from the floppy disk to the hard disk. Thus:
(a) Boot the system. Place the VP Planner disk in drive A.
(b) Type **C:** to make drive C the default drive. Type **MD \VPPLUS** to create a subdirectory called VPPLUS to hold the VP Planner program files. Type **MD\VPPLUS\SPRDSHTS** to create a second subdirectory to hold the spreadsheets themselves.

(c) Type **CD \VPPLUS** to change to the newly created VP Planner Plus subdirectory. Now type **COPY A:*.* C:** to copy the VP Planner files to this subdirectory.

Step 1c: Installation (Lotus with Two Floppy Drives)
Follow the instructions in the Lotus manual for installation, then skip to step 2c for information on loading.

Step 1d: Installation (Lotus with a Hard Disk)
Follow the instructions in the Lotus manual for installation. Type **MD C:\LOTUS\SPRDSHTS** (assuming that LOTUS is the name of the subdirectory containing the Lotus program files) to create a subdirectory to hold the spreadsheets themselves. Skip to step 2d.

Step 2a: Load VP Planner Plus (Two Floppy Drives)
Boot the system ending at the A prompt. Place the VP Planner Plus program disk in drive A and a formatted data disk in drive B. Type **VPP** to load VP Planner Plus at which point you should the screen in Figure VP.1a. Press any of the arrow keys and the message in the middle of the screen will disappear leaving you with the empty spreadsheet of Figure VP.1b.

Step 2b: Load VP Planner Plus (with a Hard Disk)
Type **CD C:\VPPLUS** to change to the VP Planner Plus directory, then type **VPP** to load VP Planner Plus at which point you should see the screen in Figure VP.1a. Press any of the arrow keys and the message in the middle of the screen will disappear leaving you with the empty spreadsheet of Figure VP.1b.

Step 2c: Load Lotus (Two Floppy Drives)
Boot the system ending at the A prompt. Place the Lotus program disk in drive A and a formatted data disk in drive B. Type **LOTUS** to display the opening Lotus menu of VP.2a. Use the arrow keys to highlight **1-2-3** and press return. You should then see the empty spreadsheet of Figure VP.2b.

Step 2d: Load Lotus (with a Hard Disk)
Type **CD C:\LOTUS** to change to the Lotus directory, then type **LOTUS** and you will see the opening Lotus menu of VP.2a. Use the arrow keys to highlight **1-2-3** and press return. You should then see the empty spreadsheet of Figure VP.2b.

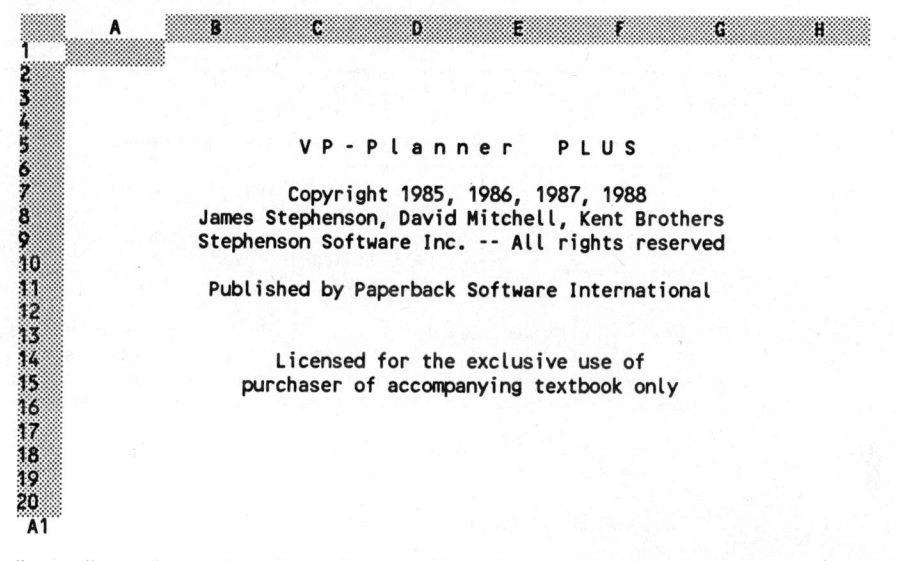

```
         A         B         C         D         E         F         G         H
  1
  2
  3
  4
  5                         V P - P l a n n e r     P L U S
  6
  7                         Copyright 1985, 1986, 1987, 1988
  8                   James Stephenson, David Mitchell, Kent Brothers
  9                   Stephenson Software Inc. -- All rights reserved
 10
 11                     Published by Paperback Software International
 12
 13
 14                          Licensed for the exclusive use of
 15                        purchaser of accompanying textbook only
 16
 17
 18
 19
 20
 A1
```

1help 2edit 3name 4abs 5goto 6window 7data 8table 9recalculate 0graph
187K   12:10   READY

(a) Opening Screen

```
         A         B         C         D         E         F         G         H
  1
  2
  3
  4
  5
  6
  7
  8
  9
 10
 11
 12
 13
 14
 15
 16
 17
 18
 19
 20
 A1
```

1help 2edit 3name 4abs 5goto 6window 7data 8table 9recalculate 0graph
187K   12:10   READY

(b) Empty Spreadsheet

Figure VP.1 - Loading VP Planner Plus

122 Lotus/VP Planner Plus Hands-On Exercises

```
1-2-3   PrintGraph   Translate   Install   Exit
Use 1-2-3
```

```
                     1-2-3 Access System
                   Copyright   1986, 1989
                  Lotus Development Corporation
                      All Rights Reserved
                         Release 2.2

The Access system lets you choose 1-2-3, PrintGraph, the Translate utility,
and the Install program, from the menu at the top of this screen.  If
you're using a two-diskette system, the Access system may prompt you to
change disks.  Follow the instructions below to start a program.

o  Use → or ← to move the menu pointer (the highlighted rectangle
   at the top of the screen) to the program you want to use.

o  Press ENTER to start the program.

You can also start a program by typing the first character of its name.

Press HELP (F1) for more information.
```

(a) Opening Menu

```
A1:                                                                    READY

           A      B      C      D      E      F      G      H
     1
     2
     3
     4
     5
     6
     7
     8
     9
    10
    11
    12
    13
    14
    15
    16
    17
    18
    19
    20
09-Jul-90   03:10 PM
```

(b) Empty Spreadsheet

Figure VP.2 - Loading Lotus

Lotus/VP Planner Plus Hands-On Exercises   123

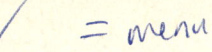

(handwritten annotation at top: / = menu)

Step 3: **The Opening Screen**
Regardless of whether you have a hard disk, or whether you are using Lotus or VP Planner Plus, you should be positioned in cell A1 of an empty spreadsheet, and further the spreadsheet should reflect that you are in the READY mode. You will find subtle differences in the screens for Lotus and VP Planner Plus (the READY prompt appears in different places, for example) but the two programs are otherwise quite similar to one another. Accordingly we provide a single set of instructions for all exercises.

Step 4: **Optional - Change the Default Directory**

(handwritten annotation in margin: Worksheet Global Default Directory (A:\))

Just as with word processing, we suggest that you keep the spreadsheet program (i.e., Lotus or VP Planner) and its data (i.e., the spreadsheets themselves) in separate places. This means that on systems with a hard disk you will store the program in one directory (e.g., \VPPLUS) and the data in another directory (e.g., \VPPLUS\SPRDSHTS), whereas on a system with two floppy drives you will use drive A for the program disk and drive B for the data disk.

The command sequence we are about to describe is best understood after you have been introduced to the command mode in the spreadsheet program. Nevertheless we present the instructions now as they are in fact part of the installation procedure. Accordingly be sure you are at the opening screen of the spreadsheet program as described in step 3, then type **/WGDD** (Worksheet Global Default Directory). You will then be asked for the name (path) of the default directory. Respond as follows:

On systems with a hard disk: Type **C:\VPPLUS\SPRDSHTS** or **C:\LOTUS\SPRDSHTS**, depending on whether you are using VP Planner Plus or Lotus. (Notice how the directory names correspond to the directories created earlier in steps 1b and 1d respectively.) Press return after you have entered the directory name.

On systems with two flopy drives: Type **B:** since the spreadsheets will be stored on the disk in drive B and press return.

You are not yet finished. On either system type **UQ** (Update Quit) to make this change permanent and exit from the default menu.

Step 5: **Exit the Spreadsheet Program**
Type **/Q** to invoke the Quit command and exit the spreadsheet program. You will see a second message, prompting you for a Yes or No response, asking whether you do in fact wish to exit. Answer Y to exit.

Hands-On Exercise 2: Creating a Simple Spreadsheet

Objective: Create a spreadsheet corresponding to the professor's grade book of Figure 6.4 in the text; the commands which generated the spreadsheet appear in Figure 6.8 in the text and are reproduced in the Laboratory Manual as Figures VP.3a and VP.3b respectively. (Corresponds to Hands-on Exercise 1 in Chapter 6.)

Step 1: **Load Lotus (VP Planner Plus)**

Load Lotus/VP Planner Plus as described in the previous exercise. The cursor should be in cell A1 of an empty spreadsheet and you should be in the READY mode.

Step 2: **Cursor Movement**

Move the cursor (cell pointer) with the arrow keys, observing how the cell address in the display panel changes. (The current cell address appears at the top of the screen in Lotus and at the bottom in VP Planner Plus.) Note too how the current cell is highlighted within the spreadsheet.

Move the cell pointer to any cell in column A and press the left arrow key. You should hear a beep, indicating that the cell pointer cannot move further left. In similar fashion, pressing the up arrow key when the cell pointer is in row 1 will also produce a beep.

Move the cell pointer to column A, then press the right arrow continually until you observe a scrolling effect (as the leftmost columns disappear from the screen). Position the cell pointer in row 1 and press the down arrow continually until scrolling is observed in this direction. Finally press the Home key and watch the cell pointer jump to cell A1.

Step 3: **Enter Row 4**

Move the cursor to cell **A4**. Type **Adams**. Press the right arrow key to complete the entry and position the cursor in cell B4. Type **100**. Press the right arrow key again to move to cell C4 and type **90**, then move to cell D4 and type **81**.

When you reach cell E4, you must enter the mathematical expression, **(B4+C4+2*D4)/4** to obtain the weighted average. Remember to begin the formula with a left parenthesis to differentiate the expression from a label (as well as to ensure the proper sequence of operations). Press the return key after you have entered the formula. The control panel indicates cell E4 and displays the expression you just entered; however the entry displayed in cell E4 is 88, the result of the expression.

```
         A         B        C        D        E
1
2    Student     Test 1   Test 2   Final   Wt Avg
3    ==========================================
4    Adams        100       90       81       88
5    Baker         90       76       87       85
6    Brown         92       80       78       82
7    Class Avg    ---      ---      ---
8                  94       82       82
9
```

(a) Professor's Grade Book

```
A2:  'Student              B5:  90
B2:  "Test 1               C5:  76
C2:  "Test 2               D5:  87
D2:  "Final                E5:  (B5+C5+2*D5)/4
E2:  "Wt Avg               A6:  'Brown
A3:  \=                    B6:  92
B3:  \=                    C6:  80
C3:  \=                    D6:  78
D3:  \=                    E6:  (B6+C6+2*D6)/4
E3:  \=                    A7:  'Class Avg
A4:  'Adams                B7:  "---
B4:  100                   C7:  "---
C4:  90                    D7:  "---
D4:  81                    B8:  @AVG(B4..B6)
E4:  (B4+C4+2*D4)/4        C8:  @AVG(C4..C6)
A5:  'Baker                D8:  @AVG(D4..D6)
```

(b) Cell Contents

Figure VP.3 - Professor's Grade Book

Step 4: **Complete the Spreadsheet**

Complete the spreadsheet using Figure VP.3b as a guide. Enter data for Baker and Brown in rows 5 and 6 as in the previous step, then complete rows 2 and 3, and rows 7 and 8. Check your spreadsheet, making sure it matches Figure VP.3a. Fix any errors by first moving the cell pointer to the cell containing the error, and then retyping the entry in that cell.

Step 5: **Experiment (What if?)**

Now that the spreadsheet is finished, you can experiment with changes. Imagine that a grading error was made in Baker's second test which is contained in cell C5. Move the cursor to cell C5 and enter the correct grade, say 86 instead of the previous entry of 76.

The effects of this change ripple through the spreadsheet automatically changing any cells whose formulas depend on Baker's second test (cells E5 and C8 in the example). Try making additional changes to the spreadsheet and note the speed with which these corrections are made.

Step 6: Save the Spreadsheet

Although the command mode has not yet been covered, we ask that you save the spreadsheet just created. The next paragraph should make intuitive sense now, and we promise that everything will be explained in detail in the next exercise.

To save the spreadsheet, press the slash / key to enter the command mode, type **F** (to specify the File command), and **S** (to indicate the Save option of the file command). Type **GRADES** (or any other name you desire) then press the return key, to save the spreadsheet. You should see the light on the disk drive come on as the file GRADES.WK1 is written to the disk.

Step 7: Exit the Spreadsheet Program

Type **/Q** to invoke the Quit command and exit the spreadsheet program. You will see a second message, prompting you for a Yes or No response, asking whether you do in fact wish to exit. Answer **Y** to exit the spreadsheet program.

Hands-On Exercise 3: Basic Spreadsheet Commands

Objective: Introduce the command mode in conjunction with menus to load, save, and print a spreadsheet. The exercise will modify the professor's grade book from the previous exercise to develop the revised spreadsheet shown in VP.4. (Corresponds to Hands-On Exercise 2 in Chapter 6.)

	A	B	C	D	E
1					
2	Student	Test 1	Test 2	Final	Wt Avg
3	===
4	Adams	100	90	81	88
5	Adamson	90	90	90	90
6	Baldwin	82	84	87	85
7	Brown	92	80	78	82
8	Class Avg	---	---	---	
9		91	86	84	
10					

Figure VP.4 - Modified Grade Book

Step 1: Enter the Command Mode

Load Lotus or VP Planner Plus as in the previous exercise. Press the **slash (/) key** to enter the **command mode** and **display the menus** in Figure

VP.5. At first glance the menus appear to differ greatly; upon closer examination, however, they will be shown to be almost identical.

Consider, for example, the Lotus menu in Figure VP.5a. The main menu appears in the first row of the control panel and contains the choices Worksheet, Range, Copy, and so on. The second row of the control panel contains a submenu corresponding to the highlighted option on the first row; i.e. Global, Insert, Delete, and so on, are choices associated with the Worksheet option.

Now look at the VP Planner Plus menu in Figure VP.5b which displays essentially the same choices (there are minor variations beyond the scope of this manual), but arranged differently. Nevertheless the concepts are identical, in that the box on the right displays the choices associated with the highlighted Worksheet option.

Regardless of which program you have, use the arrow keys to move from one command to another, observing how a different command is highlighted each time an arrow key is pressed, and further how a different submenu is displayed with each new highlighted command. Alternatively, you can select a command by typing its first letter, as each command begins with a different letter; i.e. type **W for Worksheet**, **R for Range**, and so on. (In addition, with VP Planner Plus only, you can press the indicated function key to select a command, for example, the F2 key for Worksheet, the F3 key for Range, etc.)

Step 2: **Retrieve the Existing Spreadsheet**
Select the **File** command from the main menu, by moving the arrow keys and pressing return, or by typing the letter F. This in turn produces a second menu listing the options of the File command, the appearance of which will depend on whether you are using Lotus or VP Planner Plus. For ease of explanation we will display this (and all subsequent menus) as they appear in Lotus Version 2.2; realize, however, that all of the menu choices in this and all future exercises are available in both Lotus and VP Planner Plus. Thus:

```
Retrieve  Save  Combine  Xtract  Erase  List  Import  Directory  Admin
Erase the current worksheet from memory and display the selected worksheet
```

Once again you can use the arrow keys to highlight the different options associated with the File command, observing that the submenu row changes as different options are highlighted. Select **Retrieve** which in turn prompts you for the name of the spreadsheet. Type **GRADES** (corresponding to the name in step six of the previous exercise), and press the **return key**. The spreadsheet will reappear on your monitor.

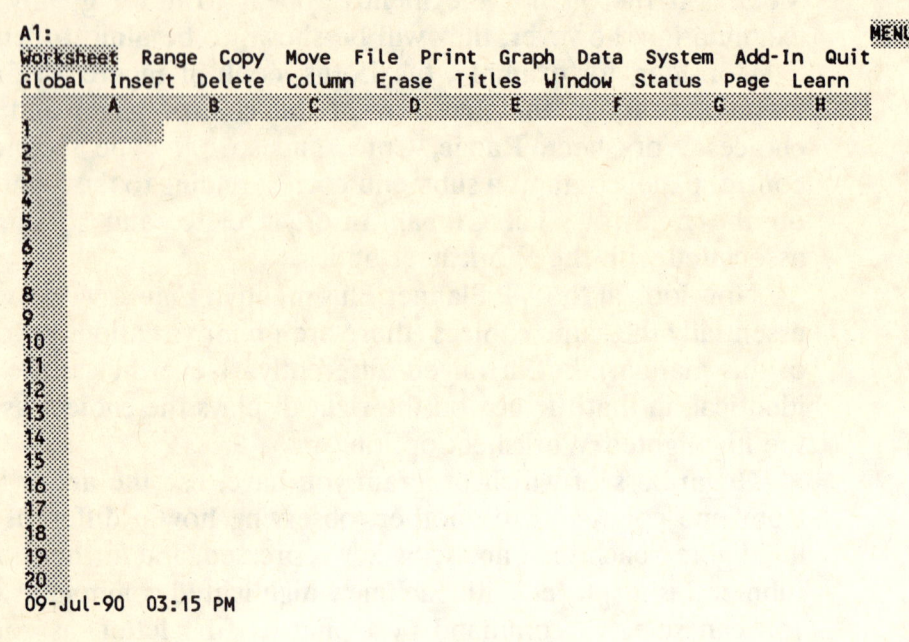

```
A1:                                                                    MENU
Worksheet  Range   Copy    Move    File    Print   Graph   Data    System  Add-In  Quit
Global     Insert  Delete  Column  Erase   Titles  Window  Status  Page    Learn
           A           B           C           D           E           F           G           H
  1
  2
  3
  4
  5
  6
  7
  8
  9
 10
 11
 12
 13
 14
 15
 16
 17
 18
 19
 20
09-Jul-90  03:15 PM
```

(a) Lotus

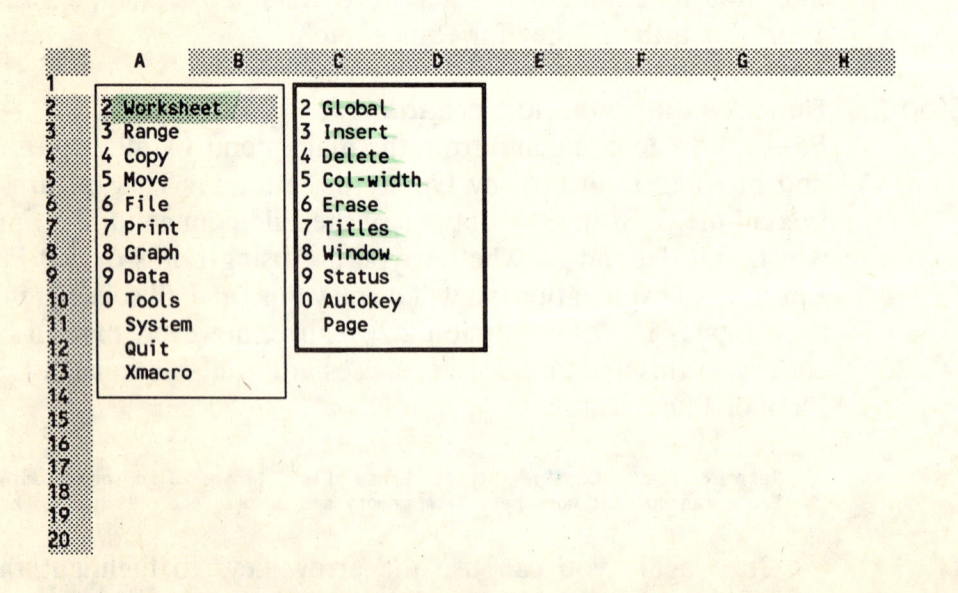

```
           A           B           C           D           E           F           G           H
  1
  2    ┌─────────────────┬─────────────────┐
  3    │ 2 Worksheet     │ 2 Global        │
  4    │ 3 Range         │ 3 Insert        │
  5    │ 4 Copy          │ 4 Delete        │
  6    │ 5 Move          │ 5 Col-width     │
  7    │ 6 File          │ 6 Erase         │
  8    │ 7 Print         │ 7 Titles        │
  9    │ 8 Graph         │ 8 Window        │
 10    │ 9 Data          │ 9 Status        │
 11    │ 0 Tools         │ 0 Autokey       │
 12    │   System        │   Page          │
 13    │   Quit          │                 │
 14    │   Xmacro        │                 │
 15    └─────────────────┴─────────────────┘
 16
 17
 18
 19
 20

1help 2edit 3name 4abs 5goto 6window 7data 8table 9recalculate 0graph
187K                           12:11                                    MENU
```

(b) VP Planner Plus

Figure VP.5 - Command Menus

Lotus/VP Planner Plus Hands-On Exercises

Step 3: **Delete a Row (Baker)**
Position the cursor anywhere in row 5 (the row containing Baker's data). Type **/WDR** (to enter the command mode and select **W**orksheet, **D**elete, and **R**ow) whereupon you will be prompted for the range to delete. Press the return key to indicate that row 5 (Baker) is to be deleted, and Baker will disappear. Note how the class averages are changed automatically.

Step 4: **Insert a Row (Adamson)**
Type **/WIR** (to enter the command mode and select **W**orksheet, **I**nsert, and **R**ow), whereupon you will be prompted for the range to insert. Press return and a new row 5 (since the cursor is in row 5) will be inserted.

The new row 5 is now blank (the other students have been dropped a row). Enter data for Adamson (as shown in Figure VP.4) in the appropriate columns; i.e. enter the name in column A, the test grades in columns B, C, and D respectively, and the formula to compute a weighted average in cell E5. Note that as each test grade is entered, the class average for that test is updated automatically.

Step 5: **Insert a Second Row (Baldwin)**
Move the cursor to row 6 then repeat the commands in step 4 to add Baldwin. Observe again how class averages are automatically updated with the insertion of new students.

Step 6: **Save the Modified Spreadsheet**
Execute the **F**ile **S**ave (**/FS**) command to save the modified spreadsheet. GRADES will already be entered as the name of the file to be saved (as GRADES is the name of the worksheet retrieved originally). Press the return key to save the revised worksheet as GRADES (it is also possible to enter a new name, saving the revised worksheet under the new name; e.g. NEWGRADE).

You will then see another menu, asking you whether you wish to **C**ancel, **R**eplace, or **B**ackup. Cancel aborts the save operation as it prevents the version on disk from being overwritten, whereas replace overwrites the existing version with the spreadsheet currently in memory. Backup effectively combines the two, saving the spreadsheet currently in memory as GRADES, and renaming the previous version GRADES.BAK. Make your selection accordingly.

Step 7: **Print the Spreadsheet**
The spreadsheet is printed by returning to the main menu and selecting the print command; i.e. by typing **/P**. A series of additional submenus will appear which require the following responses in the sequence shown:

Printer - to direct output to the printer (as opposed to a disk file where it can be subsequently pulled into a word processor)

Range - to indicate the portion of the spreadsheet that is to be printed; type **A1..E9** (you can enter one or two dots) to specify the upper left and lower right corners of the spreadsheet.

Align - to set the line counter to 1 and thus prevent unintended gaps from appearing in the middle of a printed spreadsheet; in addition you must physically align the paper in the printer.

Go - to initiate the actual printing

As you may have guessed, the print command is one of the more involved commands in terms of the number of required responses and corresponding menus.

Step 8: Print the Cell Contents

A spreadsheet may be printed in several formats; e.g. Figures VP.3a and VP.3b, depict the spreadsheet and the cell entries which created it. You can print the latter by following the same procedure as in step 7, but including additional responses prior to specification of the Go command. Accordingly type /PP to enter the print command and designate output going to the printer. Type **O for Options, O for Other**, and **C for Cell formulas**. Press **Q** to Quit the options menu, **A** for Align, and **G** for Go and the cell formulas will be printed.

Execution of the print command takes place within the context of an informational screen. Figure VP.6, for example, displays the print selections in effect after cell formulas have been specified and prior to execution of the final Go command. Although the screen may be intimidating at first, it is an invaluable aid once you understand the various menu options. Note too, that Figure VP.6 displays the screen as it would appear in Lotus; the same information is also displayed in VP Planner Plus, albeit in a different format.

Step 9: Exit the Spreadsheet

Type **/QY** to exit Lotus and return to DOS. Note, however, that if you made additional changes to the spreadsheet after the last save command, both Lotus and VP Planner will caution you about exiting the spreadsheet without the changes having being saved. You can cancel the exit operation by typing N (for No), save the changes in the normal fashion, then exit for good.

```
E4: (B4+C4+2*D4)/4                                              MENU
Range  Line  Page  Options  Clear  Align  Go  Quit
Print the specified range
                    ┌─────── Print Settings ───────┐
     Destination:  Printer

     Range:        A1..E9

     Header:
     Footer:

     Margins:
       Left 4     Right 76    Top 2    Bottom 2

     Borders:
       Columns
       Rows

     Setup string:

     Page length:  66

     Output:       Cell-Formulas (Formatted)

09-Jul-90  03:30 PM
```

Figure VP.6 - Print Settings (Lotus Implementation)

New Commands - Exercises 2 and 3	
/Worksheet	
WIR	Inserts a row
WDR	Deletes a row
/File	
FS	Saves the current spreadsheet
FR	Retrieves a spreadsheet
/Print	
Printer	Directs output to the printer
Range	Specifies range to be printed
Align	Prevents unintended blank lines
Options	Enables options such as cell formulas
Go	Initiates actual printing
Useful keys	
Home	Moves cursor to cell A1
Esc	Returns to previous menu

Hands-On Exercise 4:
Variable-Rate Mortgages

Objective: Develop the variable-rate mortgage analysis using Figure VP.7 as a guide. Figure VP.7a depicts the spreadsheet as it would appear on the screen; Figure VP.7b contains the various cell entries. The shaded entries represent formatting specifications and are **not** part of the formulas per se, but are entered with the Range Format command. (Corresponds to Hands-On Exercise 1 in Chapter 7.)

```
            A         B         C
    1          Variable Rate Mortgage
    2
    3    Amount borrowed:     $100,000
    4    Starting interest:      7.00%
    5    Term (years):              30
    6
    7                Interest   Payment
    8                ======================
    9                  7.00%    $665.30
   10                  8.00%    $733.76
   11                  9.00%    $804.62
   12                 10.00%    $877.57
   13                 11.00%    $952.32
   14                 12.00%  $1,028.61
   15                 13.00%  $1,106.20
```

(a) The Spreadsheet

```
A1:  PR '    Variable Rate Mortgage         B10: (P2) PR [W9]  +B9+0.01
A3:  PR 'Amount borrowed:                   C10: (C2) PR [W12] @PMT($C$3,B10/12,$C$5*12)
C3:  (C0) U [W12] 100000                    B11: (P2) PR [W9]  +B10+0.01
A4:  PR 'Starting interest:                 C11: (C2) PR [W12] @PMT($C$3,B11/12,$C$5*12)
C4:  (P2) U [W12] 0.07                      B12: (P2) PR [W9]  +B11+0.01
A5:  PR 'Term (years):                      C12: (C2) PR [W12] @PMT($C$3,B12/12,$C$5*12)
C5:  U [W12]  30                            B13: (P2) PR [W9]  +B12+0.01
B7:  PR [W9]  ' Interest                    C13: (C2) PR [W12] @PMT($C$3,B13/12,$C$5*12)
C7:  PR [W12] '    Payment                  B14: (P2) PR [W9]  +B13+0.01
B8:  PR [W9]  \=                            C14: (C2) PR [W12] @PMT($C$3,B14/12,$C$5*12)
C8:  PR [W12] \=                            B15: (P2) PR [W9]  +B14+0.01
B9:  (P2) PR [W9]  +C4                      C15: (C2) PR [W12] @PMT($C$3,B15/12,$C$5*12)
C9:  (C2) PR [W12] @PMT($C$3,B9/12,$C$5*12)
```

(b) Cell Contents

Figure VP.7 - Variable Rate Mortgage Analysis

Step 1:   Load the Spreadsheet Program

Load your spreadsheet program following the steps from the earlier exercises. You should have a blank spreadsheet on the screen, ready to build the mortgage template.

Lotus/VP Planner Plus Hands-On Exercises 133

Step 2: Change the Default Directory
Spreadsheets (i.e., the WK1 files) should be stored a different subdirectory than the one containing the spreadsheet program itself. We suggest, therefore, that you implement steps 5 and 6 from the installation procedure (if you haven't already) to establish this subdirectory.

Step 3: Create the Mortgage Template
Enter the labels shown below. The apostrophes which precede the various entries indicate left justification. Note, however, that since left justification is the default, you needn't enter the apostrophe explicitly; you must, however begin an entry with quotation marks for right justification.

```
A1: '    Variable Rate Mortgage
A3: 'Amount borrowed:
A4: 'Starting interest:
A5: 'Term (years):
B7: '  Interest
C7: '     Payment
B8: \=
C8: \=
```

A label may exceed the width of the cell in which it is entered, yet still appear in its entirety if the cell(s) to its immediate right is empty. The entry in cell A1, for example, is longer than nine characters (the default width of column A), yet the entire label is displayed because the adjacent cells (B1 and C1) are empty.

Step 4: Use the Edit Capability
This is a good time to experiment with the editing capability, which avoids retyping an entire label if only a single character is in error. Imagine that you made a spelling error in entering the label for cell A3, e.g., you typed "Amount Burrowed". The error can be corrected by retyping the entire cell, or more simply with the edit capability. Move the cursor to cell A3 and press the **F2 function key**; the following will appear in the control panel:

```
A3: 'Amount Burrowed
Amount Burrowed
```

The cursor appears on the second line in the control panel, after the last character in the entry. It can be moved to any position within the entry using the right and left arrow keys, at which point you can insert and/or delete the appropriate characters. (The **Ins key** toggles between the insertion and replacement modes, whereas the **Del key** deletes one or more characters.) Make the necessary changes, then end the edit operation by pressing the return key.

Step 5: **Supply Initial Values**

Enter the initial values for the amount borrowed, starting interest rate, and term of the loan, in cells C3 C4, and C5, respectively. Be sure to enter these numbers as **100000, .07,** and **30**. In other words, do not enter a dollar sign, comma, or percent sign, as these are illegal characters. Formatting will be accomplished in step eight of the exercise.

Step 6: **Compute Monthly Payments at the Starting Interest Rate**

Enter the formulas for cells B9 and C9, corresponding to the starting interest rate and monthly payment as follows:

```
B9: +C4
C9: @PMT($C$3,B9/12,$C$5*12)
```

Your spreadsheet should now contain numerical values in cells B9 and C9 matching those in Figure VP.7a. Their appearance, however, will be different because the computations on your spreadsheet are carried out beyond two decimal places and, further, a dollar sign is not present.

Step 7: **Compute the Remaining Payments**

The similarities between the formulas in rows 10 through 15 enable you to use a copy command to generate the cell formulas for the remaining monthly payments. You must, however, explicitly enter the formulas for row 10 because the entry in cell B10 is significantly different from that in cell B9. Accordingly, enter the following:

```
B10: +B9+0.01
C10: @PMT($C$3,B10/12,$C$5*12)
```

You are now in a position to copy row 10 to the remaining rows in the spreadsheet. Type **/C** to invoke the **Copy** command which in turn will prompt for the source and destination ranges. Enter **B10..C10** as the source range and **B11..C15** as the destination range. (You can type either one or two periods when entering the ranges. Pointing, as a means of range specification will be illustrated in step 9.) The remaining interest rates and monthly payments should now appear in your spreadsheet, but will not yet be formatted.

Step 8: **Change to Percent Format**

Examine once again the entries in Figure VP.7b, noting that many cell formulas are preceded by a set of parentheses; for example, the cell contents of cells B9 through B15 each begin with the entry P2 enclosed in parentheses to denote percentage format with two decimal places. The formatting specifications are implemented through the **Range Format** command as described below. Type **/RFP2** (**Range Format Percent** with **2 decimal places**), then enter **B9..B15** as the range to format. For illustrative purposes, however, we will take you through the commands one at a time.

Press the slash key to enter the command mode and highlight (select) the **Range** command.

```
Worksheet Range  Copy  Move    File    Print   Graph  Data   System  Add-In  Quit
Format    Label  Erase Name    Justify Prot    Unprot Input  Value   Trans   Search
```

Highlight the **Format** option of the range command:

```
Format Label Erase   Name    Justify Prot    Unprot  Input Value   Trans    Search
Fixed  Sci   Currency ,      General +/-     Percent Date  Text    Hidden   Reset
```

Choose the **Percent** format:

```
Fixed  Sci  Currency ,  General  +/-  Percent  Date  Text  Hidden  Reset
Percent format (x.xx%)
```

Finally enter the number of decimal places (2) and the range to format (B9..B15).

```
Enter number of decimal places (0..15): 2
Enter range to format: B9..B15
```

Practice what you have learned by moving to cell C4 and typing **/RFP2** to change this cell to **percent format** as well. You're finished and the appearance of the spreadsheet has improved considerably.

Step 9: **Change to Currency Format**

Type **/RFC2** to establish **currency format** for the monthly payments in column C. This time, however, you will use pointing to indicate the range to be formatted; i.e. do not type C9..C15 explicitly (when asked for the range to format), but proceed as follows:

a) Press the **backspace** (or **Esc**) **key to free the cell pointer**
b) Move the cell pointer to cell C9 (the first cell in the range) and press the **period to anchor the beginning of the range.**
c) Move the cell pointer to cell C15 (the last cell in the range) observing how the range is continually highlighted and expanded. Press the **return** key when you reach cell C15 to complete the range.

Practice what you have learned by moving to cell C3 and typing **/RFC0** to change this cell to **currency format** as well.

136 Lotus/VP Planner Plus Hands-On Exercises

Step 10: Adjust Column Widths

Some of the cells in column C contain asterisks (rather than numbers) which indicates that these cells are not wide enough to display the computed value in the current format. Move the cursor to any cell in column C, then type **/WCS** (**W**orksheet **C**olumn **S**et). Type **12** as the new column width and press return. [Alternatively you can use the right and left arrow keys to increase (decrease) the column width one space at a time until you are satisfied with the new width.]

Step 11: Cell Protection

The concept of cell protection makes it possible to prevent the accidental alteration of the protected cells. In this example we will globally protect the entire spreadsheet, then unprotect cells C3 through C5 so that the user can vary the parameters of the mortgage.

Type **/WGPE** (**W**orksheet **G**lobal **P**rotection **E**nable). Now type **/RU** (**R**ange **U**nprotect) then use pointing to indicate cells C3 through C5 as the appropriate range.

Step 12: Save the Spreadsheet

Type **/FS** (**F**ile **S**ave) to save the completed spreadsheet. (In the future, however, you should save the spreadsheet periodically as you complete individual steps as opposed to waiting until the very end.)

Step 13: Print the Spreadsheet

Print the spreadsheet in both as displayed and cell formula formats corresponding to Figures VP.7a and VP.7b; the latter is obtained with the command sequence **/PPOOC** (**P**rint **P**rinter **O**ptions **O**ther **C**ell formulas), followed by **QAG** (**Q**uit **A**lign **G**o). Use pointing to specify the range to print (cells A1 through C15).

Hands-On Exercise 5: A Financial Forecast

*[handwritten note: **** in a cell = cell not wide enough for info put in]*

Objective: Develop the spreadsheet for Get Rich Quick Enterprises, using Figure VP.8 as a reference. (The shaded entries in Figure VP.8b represent formatting specifications and are not part of the cell formulas.) Completion of this exercise reinforces the copy and formatting commands from the previous exercise, and should go far toward establishing your proficiency with spreadsheets. (Corresponds to Hands-On Exercise 2 in Chapter 7.)

	A	B	C	D	E	F
1			GET RICH	QUICK	ENTERPRISES	
2		1991	1992	1993	1994	1995
3	Income:					
4	Projected unit sales	10,000	11,800	13,924	16,430	19,388
5	Unit price	$2.00	$2.10	$2.21	$2.32	$2.43
6	Gross revenue	$20,000	$24,780	$30,702	$38,040	$47,132
7						
8	Expenses:					
9	Variable cost per unit	$1.00	$1.08	$1.17	$1.26	$1.36
10	Total variable cost	$10,000	$12,744	$16,241	$20,697	$26,377
11	Overhead	$5,000	$5,500	$6,050	$6,655	$7,321
12	Total expenses	$15,000	$18,244	$22,291	$27,352	$33,697
13						
14	Earnings before taxes:	$5,000	$6,536	$8,411	$10,688	$13,435
15						
16	Assumed rates of increase:					
17	Unit sales	18.00%				
18	Selling price	5.00%				
19	Variable cost	8.00%				
20	Overhead	10.00%				

(a) Completed Spreadsheet

```
C1:  PR  '    GET RICH QUICK ENTERPRISES      B10: (C0) PR +B4*B9
B2:  PR  1991                                  C10: (C0) PR +C4*C9
C2:  PR  1992                                  D10: (C0) PR +D4*D9
D2:  PR  1993                                  E10: (C0) PR +E4*E9
E2:  PR  1994                                  F10: (C0) PR +F4*F9
F2:  PR  1995                                  A11: PR [W26] '  Overhead
A3:  PR [W26] 'Income:                         B11: (C0) PR 5000
A4:  PR [W26] '  Projected unit sales          C11: (C0) PR (1+$B$20)*B11
B4:  (,0) PR 10000                             D11: (C0) PR (1+$B$20)*C11
C4:  (,0) PR (1+$B$17)*B4                      E11: (C0) PR (1+$B$20)*D11
D4:  (,0) PR (1+$B$17)*C4                      F11: (C0) PR (1+$B$20)*E11
E4:  (,0) PR (1+$B$17)*D4                      A12: PR [W26] '  Total expenses
F4:  (,0) PR (1+$B$17)*E4                      B12: (C0) PR +B10+B11
A5:  PR [W26] '  Unit price                    C12: (C0) PR +C10+C11
B5:  (C2) PR 2                                 D12: (C0) PR +D10+D11
C5:  (C2) PR (1+$B$18)*B5                      E12: (C0) PR +E10+E11
D5:  (C2) PR (1+$B$18)*C5                      F12: (C0) PR +F10+F11
E5:  (C2) PR (1+$B$18)*D5                      A14: PR [W26] 'Earnings before taxes:
F5:  (C2) PR (1+$B$18)*E5                      B14: (C0) PR +B6-B12
A6:  PR [W26] '  Gross revenue                 C14: (C0) PR +C6-C12
B6:  (C0) PR +B5*B4                            D14: (C0) PR +D6-D12
C6:  (C0) PR +C5*C4                            E14: (C0) PR +E6-E12
D6:  (C0) PR +D5*D4                            F14: (C0) PR +F6-F12
E6:  (C0) PR +E5*E4                            A16: PR [W26] 'Assumed rates of increase:
F6:  (C0) PR +F5*F4                            A17: PR [W26] '  Unit sales
A8:  PR [W26] 'Expenses:                       B17: (P2) U 0.18
A9:  PR [W26] '  Variable cost per unit        A18: PR [W26] '  Selling price
B9:  (C2) PR 1                                 B18: (P2) U 0.05
C9:  (C2) PR (1+$B$19)*B9                      A19: PR [W26] '  Variable cost
D9:  (C2) PR (1+$B$19)*C9                      B19: (P2) U 0.08
E9:  (C2) PR (1+$B$19)*D9                      A20: PR [W26] '  Overhead
F9:  (C2) PR (1+$B$19)*E9                      B20: (P2) U 0.1
A10: PR [W26] '  Total variable cost
```

(b) - Cell Formulas

Figure VP.8 - Get Rich Quick Enterprises

Step 1: The Data Fill Command

The **Data Fill command** is a convenient way to enter a sequence of numbers with a specified increment or decrement. In the financial forecast, for example, you can use the command to enter the column headings 1991 through 1995, rather than entering each value individually. Type **/DF** (**Data Fill**) whereupon you will be prompted for additional responses as shown below. The numbers 1991 through 1995 will appear in columns B2 through F2 after you press the return key in response to the last prompt.

```
Enter fill range: B2..F2
Start: 1991
Step: 1
Stop: press return
```

Step 2: Enter the Row and Column Headings and Assumptions

Move the cursor to any cell in column A, then type **/WCS** (**Worksheet Column Set**) to change the column width. Type **26** as the new width for column A and press return. Enter the indicated labels for cells A3 through A20 as shown in Figure VP.8. Type **GET RICH QUICK ENTERPRISES** as the title of the spreadsheet in cell C1. Finally enter the assumed rates of increase in cells B17 through B20, being sure to use decimals rather than percentages; e.g., **.18**, rather than 18.00% in cell B17.

Step 3: Enter Formulas For Year One

Complete the entries for 1991 (which appear in column B) as shown below. **Do not**, however, enter commas, dollar signs, or percent signs with the numeric values.

```
B4: 10000          B10: +B4*B9
B5: 2              B11: 5000
B6: +B5*B4         B12: +B10+B11
B9: 1              B14: +B6-B12
```

Step 4: Enter Formulas For Year Two

Enter the formulas for 1992 which are based on the entries for 1991 and the assumptions at the bottom of the spreadsheet. You may find it easiest to first copy cells B4..B14 to C4..C14, then modify cells C4, C5, C9, and C11, or alternatively you can enter the cell contents directly. Regardless of how you proceed, column C should match the entries below which contain a combination of *relative* and *absolute* addresses.

```
C4: (1+$B$17)*B4        C10: +C4*C9
C5: (1+$B$18)*B5        C11: (1+$B$20)*B11
C6: +C5*C4              C12: +C10+C11
C9: (1+$B$19)*B9        C14: +C6-C12
```

Step 5: Enter Formulas For Years Three Through Five

Type **/C** to invoke the **Copy command** which in turn will prompt for the source and destination ranges. Enter **C4..C14** as the source range and **D4..F14** as the destination range. You can enter the addresses directly (typing either one or two periods in the range specification) or more easily through pointing.

Check the accuracy of your work by moving the cell pointer to cell F14, and verifying that it contains projected earnings of $13,435 in 1995 (although the number will not yet be formatted).

Step 6: The Help Facility

Lotus and VP Planner Plus have extensive help facilities which provide on-line information for all commands. The facilities are *context sensitive* which means the information displayed is a function of the command being executed. Type **/C** to initiate the copy command then press the **F1** function key to activate help. Figure VP.9 will appear on the monitor:

```
/Copy -- Copies data and cell formats from one area to another area in the
   same worksheet.

   CAUTION   If you copy data to a range that already contains data, 1-2-3
   writes over the existing data with the copied data.

   1. Select /Copy.
   2. Specify the range you want to copy FROM.
   3. Specify the range you want to copy TO.
        If the TO range is larger than one cell, 1-2-3 can make multiple
        copies of the same data.  For example, if you copy data from A1 to A2..A5,
        1-2-3 copies the data in A1 to A2, A3, A4, and A5, making four copies.

   NOTE   Formulas can contain three types of cell or range references:
   relative, absolute, and mixed.  When you copy a formula, 1-2-3 adjusts the
   copied formula if it contains relative or mixed references.  1-2-3 does not
   adjust the copied formula if it contains absolute references.


Help Index
```

Figure VP.9 - Help Screen (Lotus 2.2)

Step 7: Format the Spreadsheet

Type **/RF** to initiate the **Range Format** command whereupon you will be prompted for the specific format and associated range. Note, however, that the spreadsheet contains multiple formats, and hence you will have to execute this command several times. Implement the following formats:

Currency (two decimals):	Cells B5..F5 and B9..F9
Currency (no decimals):	Cells B6..F6 and B10..F14
Comma (no decimals):	Cells B4..F4
Percentage (two decimals):	Cells B17..B20

Step 8: Protect the Spreadsheet
Type **/WGPE** (**W**orksheet **G**lobal **P**rotection **E**nable). Now type **/RU** (**R**ange **U**nprotect) then use pointing to unprotect cells B17 through B20. The entire spreadsheet is protected except for the assumed rates of increase; i.e., a user can change any of these assumptions but cannot alter the contents of any other cell.

Step 9: Save and Print the Spreadsheet
Type **/FS** (**F**ile **S**ave) to save the spreadsheet supplying any name you deem appropriate. Type **/P** to invoke the **Print command**, then print the spreadsheet twice (as is and with cell formulas). Type **/QY** to exit the spreadsheet and return to DOS.

New Commands - Exercises 4 and 5	
/Worksheet	
WCS	Changes column width
WGPE	Enables global protection
WGPD	Disables global protection
/Copy	Initiates Copy command (absolute addresses are indicated with a $)
/Move	Initiates Move command
/Data Fill	Initiates Data Fill command
/Range	
Format	Formats the designated range (formats include currency, fixed, and percent with variable number of decimals)
Protect	Protects a designated range
Unprotect	Unprotects a designated range
Useful keys	
F1	Help key
F2	Edit key

Lotus/VP Planner Plus Hands-On Exercises 141

Hands-On Exercise 6
Extended Grade book

[handwritten notes: F2 - Edit key; Offset Column Number; @VLOOKUP (H17, $H$21..$J$25); offset column #]

Objective: Create the expanded grade book of Figure VP.10 using the cell formulas of Figure VP.11 (on the next page) as a guide. The exercise illustrates the Data Sort command, the @IF, @VLOOKUP, and @DATE functions, and various capabilities associated with large spreadsheets (Windows, Titles, and printing considerations.) Corresponds to Hands-On Exercise 1 in Chapter 8.

	A	B	C	D	E	F	G	H	I	J
1	24-Nov-90				Professor's Grade Book					
2										
3	Name	Home	Test 1	Test 2	Test 3	Test 4	Test	Final	Grade	
4		Work					Avg	Avg		
5	==									
6	Adams, John	Poor	80	71	70	84	78.3	78.3	C	*good*
7	Barber, Maryann	OK	96	98	97	90	97.0	99.0	A	
8	Boone, Dan	OK	78	78	60	78	78.0	80.0	B	
9	Borow, Jeff	OK	65	65	65	60	65.0	67.0	D	
10	Brown, James	OK	92	95	79	80	89.0	91.0	A	
11	Carson, Kit	OK	90	90	90	70	90.0	92.0	A	
12	Coulter, Sara	OK	48	50	40	79	59.0	61.0	D	
13	Glassman, Kris	OK	82	78	62	77	79.0	81.0	B	
14	Goodman, Neil	OK	92	88	65	78	86.0	88.0	B	
15	Milgrom, Marion	OK	94	92	86	84	90.7	92.7	A	
16	Moldof, Adam	OK	92	78	65	84	84.7	86.7	B	
17	Smith, Adam	Poor	60	50	65	80	68.3	68.3	D	
18										
19					Test Statistics			Grading Criteria		
20								(Minimum Req'd)		*2 offset col #*
21			Average	80.8	77.8	70.3	78.7		F	*Fail*
22			High	96	98	97	90	60	D	*Pass*
23			Low	48	50	40	60	70	C	*good*
24			Range	48	48	57	30	80	B	
25			Std Dev	15	16	15	7	90	A	*excellent*

Figure VP.10 - Completed Spreadsheet

Step 1: Enter Row and Column labels

Load your spreadsheet program as you have done throughout the text. Use the **Worksheet Column Set (/WCS)** command to change the width of column A to 15 characters, the width of column B to 7, the widths of columns D through H to 8, the width of column I to 3 characters, and the width of column J to 5. Enter column headings for rows 1 through 5 as indicated in Figure VP.10, and the student names in rows 6 through 17.

Enter the labels **Test Statistics** and **Grading Criteria** in row 19, the label **Minimum Req'd** in row 20, and finally the labels for test statistics (Average, high, and so on) in cells B21 through B25.

142 Lotus/VP Planner Plus Hands-On Exercises

```
A1:  (D1) [W15] @DATE(90,11,24)        D21: (F1) [W8] @AVG(TEST2)
E1:  [W8] 'Professor's Grade Book      E21: (F1) [W8] @AVG(TEST3)
A3:  [W15] ^Name                       F21: (F1) [W8] @AVG(TEST4)
B3:  [W7] ^Home                        I21: [W3] 'F
C3:  [W8] "Test 1                      B22: [W7] 'High
D3:  [W8] "Test 2                      C22: [W8] @MAX(TEST1)
E3:  [W8] "Test 3                      D22: [W8] @MAX(TEST2)
F3:  [W8] "Test 4                      E22: [W8] @MAX(TEST3)
G3:  [W8] ^Test                        F22: [W8] @MAX(TEST4)
H3:  [W8] ^Final                       H22: [W8] 60
I3:  [W3] "Grade                       I22: [W3] 'D
B4:  [W7] ^Work                        B23: [W7] 'Low
G4:  [W8] ^Avg                         C23: [W8] @MIN(TEST1)
H4:  [W8] ^Avg                         D23: [W8] @MIN(TEST2)
A5:  [W15] \=                          E23: [W8] @MIN(TEST3)
A6:  [W15] 'Adams, John                F23: [W8] @MIN(TEST4)
B6:  [W7] ^Poor                        H23: [W8] 70
C6:  [W8] 80                           I23: [W3] 'C
D6:  [W8] 71                           B24: [W7] 'Range
E6:  [W8] 70                           C24: [W8] +C22-C23
F6:  [W8] 84                           D24: [W8] +D22-D23
G6:  (F1) [W8] (@SUM(C6..F6)-@MIN(C6..F6))/3   E24: [W8] +E22-E23
H6:  (F1) [W8] @IF(B6="OK",+G6+2,G6)   F24: [W8] +F22-F23
J6:  [W5] @VLOOKUP(H6,$H$21..$I$25,1)  H24: [W8] 80
                                       I24: [W3] 'B
                                       B25: [W7] 'Std Dev
D19: [W8] '   Test Statistics          C25: [W8] @STD(TEST1)
G19: [W8] '   Grading Criteria         D25: [W8] @STD(TEST2)
G20: [W8] '     (Minimum Req'd)        E25: [W8] @STD(TEST3)
B21: [W7] 'Average                     F25: [W8] @STD(TEST4)
C21: (F1) [W8] @AVG(TEST1)             H25: [W8] 90
                                       I25: [W3] 'A
```

Figure VP.11 - Partial List of Cell Contents

Step 2: **Enter the Date**
Move the cursor to cell A1 (press the **Home** key) then enter the function @DATE(yy,mm,dd) using appropriate values [e.g., **@DATE(90,11,24)** for November 24, 1990]. You will not, however, see the date in the expected format as it is displayed initially as an integer equal to the number of days that have elapsed between January 1, 1900 and the date in question (33,201 for November 24, 1990). Accordingly, you must change the format of the entry in cell A1 as follows.

Type **/RFD** (**R**ange **F**ormat **D**ate) then select the desired format; e.g. **DD-MMM-YY**. Type A1 as the range to format then press return, and the more familiar date form (24-Nov-90) will be displayed.

Step 3: **Enter Student Data**
Enter all test grades and homework results in cells B6 through F17 as shown in Figure VP.10. Move to cell G6 and enter the formula to compute the average for the first student **(@SUM(C6..F6)-@MIN(C6..F6))/3** reflecting the professor's policy of dropping the lowest test grade. Now move the cursor to cell H6 and enter the function

@IF(E12=2043.52,@ABS(@INT(E13)),6+N) *[handwritten at top]*

Lotus/VP Planner Plus Hands-On Exercises 143

@IF(B6="OK",+G6+2,G6)   which awards a conditional two point bonus to students whose home work is "OK".

Copy the entries in cells G6 and H6 for the other students, then format both columns so that computed averages are displayed with one decimal place. Be sure that the calculations are correct.

Step 4: Compute the Test Statistics

Invoke the **Range Name Create (/RNC)** command to create the **range name TEST1,** consisting of the cells from C6 through C17. **Define range** names for **TEST2, TEST3,** and **TEST4** in similar fashion. Move to cell C21 and enter the function **@AVG(TEST1)** to compute the class average for the first test. Use Figure VP.11 to enter the functions to compute the other statistics for test 1, then copy the entries in cells C21 through C25 to calculate the statistics for the other three exams.

@VLOOKUP(*[handwritten]*

Step 5: Enter the Table Lookup Function

Use Figure VP.11 to enter the table containing the break points for each letter grade in cells H22 through H25 (cell H21 is left blank) remembering that the **break points are entered** in ascending order. Enter the associated letter grades in cells I21 through I25.

Now enter the function **@VLOOKUP(H6,$H$21..$I$25,1)** in cell J6 to obtain the letter grade for the first student, checking that Adams does in fact receive a C. Copy the @VLOOKUP function to the remaining cells in column J to obtain the letter grades for the other students. Your spreadsheet should now match Figure VP.10. Save your work to this point.

Step 6: Print the Spreadsheet

Print the spreadsheet using the same procedure as in previous exercises. Realize, however, that in order for the entire spreadsheet to fit on a single piece of 8 1/2 X 11 paper, you must use compressed print as well as increase the right margin. This, in turn, requires additional options within the print sequence.

To increase the right margin, type **/PPOMR** (**Print Printer Options Margin Right**) then enter **136.** To obtain compressed print you can either use the external switch on your printer (if one is available) or enter the appropriate setup string within the print sequence. Type **/PPOS** (**Print Printer Options Setup**) followed by the particular setup string for your printer. (**\015** is the setup string for an IBM dot matrix printer.)

Your spreadsheet should match Figure 8.1, and is effectively finished. The exercise is far from complete, however, as the next several steps direct you to try the other features discussed in the text.

Step 7: **Sort the Students**
Type **/DS** to invoke the **Data Sort command** which produces the following menu:

```
Data-Range  Primary-Key  Secondary-Key  Reset  Go  Quit
Select records to be sorted
```

We will use the command to rearrange the students according to their final average, with the student having the highest average listed first. The **Data-range** consists of all data for all students (**A6..J17**), but **does not** include headings or blank rows. The **Primary-key** is any cell in column H (e.g., **H6**) and the sort is **Descending**. There is **no secondary-key**. After you have made these selections type **G (for Go)** and the students will be listed in their new order.

Step 8: **Establish Manual Recalculation**
Type **/WGRM** (Worksheet Global Recalculation Manual) to change the recalculation mode to manual, then change Milgrom's grade on her first test from 94 to 74. A CALC indicator will appear in the lower right portion of the monitor, as a reminder to explicitly (that is, manually) recalculate the spreadsheet. In other words, Milgrom's test average is still 90.7 despite the fact that her grade was changed, because automatic recalculation no longer takes place.

Press the **F9** function key to recalculate the spreadsheet, which changes Milgrom's test average to 87.3, and causes the **CALC indicator to disappear**. Type **/WGRA** (Worksheet Global Recalculation Automatic) to restore automatic recalculation.

Step 9: **Freeze Titles**
The change in Milgrom's average produces a change in grade (from A to B), but the new grade is not immediately visible. In other words you have to move the cell pointer one or two columns to the right to bring the new grade into view, which in turn causes column A (containing the student name) to scroll off the screen. The Titles command fixes the problem.

Move the cell pointer to cell B6, then type **/WTB** (**Worksheet Titles Both**) to freeze titles in both horizontal and vertical directions. Now move the cell pointer once more to bring cell J15 into view (the cell containing Milgrom's grade). This time you will see both the grade (B) and name (Milgrom) as column A remains on the screen.

Titles can be implemented horizontally, vertically, or in both directions as was done here. Type **/WTC** (Worksheet Titles Clear) to **clear titles** and return to normal.

Step 10: Divide the Spreadsheet into Windows
Move the cell pointer to any cell in column D, then type invoke **/WWV** (Worksheet Windows Vertical) to implement windows in a vertical direction. The screen will divide itself in two presenting two views (windows) of the spreadsheet, each view with its own set of row numbers.

Position the cell pointer so that test 1 is visible in the window on your left. Now press **F6** key to move the cell pointer to the other window and bring the final grade into view. Press the **F6** key once more to return to the first window and change Milgrom's test grade back to 94. The grade change will be visible immediately in the second window, *without* having to move the cell pointer.

Save the completed spreadsheet, then exit and return to DOS.

New Commands - Exercise 6

/Worksheet
  WTB   Freezes titles in both directions
  WTC   Clears titles
  WWV   Implements windows in vertical direction
  WWC   Clears windows
  WGRM   Changes to manual recalculation
  WGRA   Changes to automatic recalculation

/DS   Initiates the Data Sort command

/Print
  PPOMR   Changes the right margin
  PPOS   Indicates a setup string

/RFD   Formats the designated range according to one of several date formats

@TODAY   Enters the system date
@DATE(yy,mm,dd)   Enters a specific date

Useful keys
  F6   Moves cell pointer to alternate window
  F9   Recalculates the spreadsheet

146 Lotus/VP Planner Plus Hands-On Exercises

Hands-On Exercise 7
Combining Spreadsheets

Objective: Combine data from three individual spreadsheets into a consolidated spreadsheet through the file combine command. The consolidated spreadsheet (the objective of the exercise) is shown in Figure VP.12 and the detailed spreadsheets are shown in Figure VP.13. Corresponds to Hands-On Exercise 1 in Chapter 9.

```
              A              B           C           D           E
1                                Any Business Enterprise
2                              Quarterly Results - All Stores
3
4                              Q1          Q2          Q3          Q4
5                              ------------------------------------------------
6          Store 1             $5,000      $11,500     $6,000      ($500)
7          Store 2             $7,500      $14,500     $22,000     $29,000
8          Store 3             $8,500      ($5,000)    $13,000     $26,000
9                              ------------------------------------------------
10         Gross Profit        $21,000     $21,000     $41,000     $54,500
```

Figure VP.12 - Completed Consolidated Spreadsheet
(Detailed spreadsheets appear in Figure VP.13)

Step 1: Create the Spreadsheet for Store 1
Create the spreadsheet for store 1 using Figure VP.13a as a guide. Enter the indicated row and column labels as well as the appropriate sales and expense data in cells B6 through E11. Enter the necessary **@SUM** function in cell B13 (**@SUM(B9..B11)**) and the formula to compute profit in cell B15 (**+B6-B13**). Copy these formulas to cells C13 to E15.

Step 2: The Range Name Command
Although the necessity for a range name is not immediately apparent, range names are required given the nature of the file combine command (and also the subsequent exercise on macros). Thus, type **/RNC** (to invoke the **R**ange **N**ame **C**reate command), indicate **QUARTERS** as the range name, and **B15..E15** as the range to be named. Type **/FS** (File Save) to save the completed spreadsheet as **STORE1**.

Step 3: Create the Remaining Spreadsheets
Save the existing spreadsheet twice more as **STORE2** and **STORE3**, then retrieve each of these spreadsheets, changing the title and data as appropriate. You should wind up with three separate spreadsheets, one for each store, as shown in Figures VP.13a, VP.13b and VP.13c.

(a) Store 1

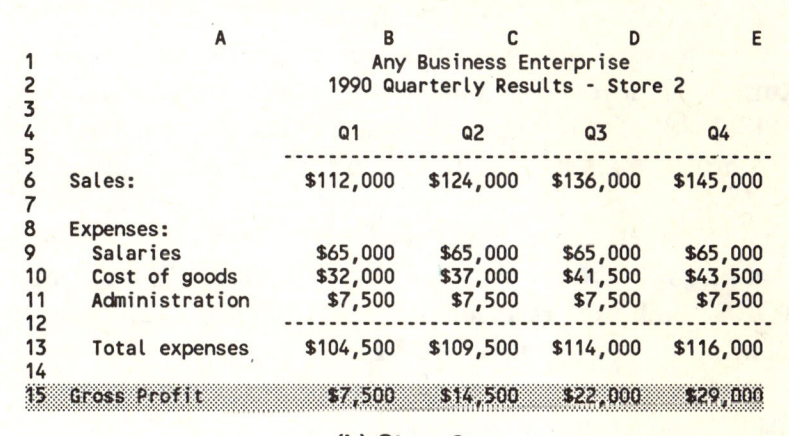

	A	B	C	D	E
1		\multicolumn{4}{c}{Any Business Enterprise}			
2		1990 Quarterly Results - Store 1			
3					
4		Q1	Q2	Q3	Q4
5		--------	--------	--------	--------
6	Sales:	$84,000	$92,000	$110,000	$102,500
7					
8	Expenses:				
9	Salaries	$48,000	$48,000	$68,000	$68,000
10	Cost of goods	$26,000	$27,500	$31,000	$30,000
11	Administration	$5,000	$5,000	$5,000	$5,000
12		--------	--------	--------	--------
13	Total expenses	$79,000	$80,500	$104,000	$103,000
14					
15	**Gross Profit**	**$5,000**	**$11,500**	**$6,000**	**($500)**

(b) Store 2

	A	B	C	D	E
1		\multicolumn{4}{c}{Any Business Enterprise}			
2		1990 Quarterly Results - Store 2			
3					
4		Q1	Q2	Q3	Q4
5		--------	--------	--------	--------
6	Sales:	$112,000	$124,000	$136,000	$145,000
7					
8	Expenses:				
9	Salaries	$65,000	$65,000	$65,000	$65,000
10	Cost of goods	$32,000	$37,000	$41,500	$43,500
11	Administration	$7,500	$7,500	$7,500	$7,500
12		--------	--------	--------	--------
13	Total expenses	$104,500	$109,500	$114,000	$116,000
14					
15	**Gross Profit**	**$7,500**	**$14,500**	**$22,000**	**$29,000**

(c) Store 3

	A	B	C	D	E
1		\multicolumn{4}{c}{Any Business Enterprise}			
2		1990 Quarterly Results - Store 3			
3					
4		Q1	Q2	Q3	Q4
5		--------	--------	--------	--------
6	Sales:	$104,500	$92,500	$114,000	$160,000
7					
8	Expenses:				
9	Salaries	$65,000	$65,000	$65,000	$80,000
10	Cost of goods	$26,000	$27,500	$31,000	$49,000
11	Administration	$5,000	$5,000	$5,000	$5,000
12		--------	--------	--------	--------
13	Total expenses	$96,000	$97,500	$101,000	$134,000
14					
15	**Gross Profit**	**$8,500**	**($5,000)**	**$13,000**	**$26,000**

Figure VP.13 - Spreadsheets for Individual Stores
(Shaded rows indicate data for the consolidated spreadsheet)

Step 4: **Create the Empty Consolidated Spreadsheet**
Create the template for the consolidated spreadsheet containing the row and column labels as shown in Figure VP.14a. The entries in row 10 consist of formatted @SUM functions [e.g. @SUM(B6..B9) in cell B10], and currently display zero values as the spreadsheet does not yet contain sales data from the individual stores. Save the spreadsheet as **CONSOL**.

Step 5: **The File Combine Command**
Move the cell pointer to cell B6 in the consolidated spreadsheet. One easy way to do this is to press the **F5 (goto)** function key, and answer **B6** when prompted for the destination.

Type **/FC** to initiate the **File Combine** command, answer **A** (to Add data), and **N** (for a Named-range as opposed to an entire spreadsheet). Type **QUARTERS** (this was the named ranged created in step 2) and press the **return** key. Type **STORE1** (the name of the spreadsheet) and press **return** once more. The quarterly sales data from store 1 (row 15 in Figure VP.13a) should now appear in row 6 of the consolidated spreadsheet; the gross profit totals in row 10 have also changed to reflect these numbers.

Move the cell pointer to cell **B7** of the consolidated spreadsheet in order to combine the data from the second store. Type **/FCAN** (**File Combine Add Named-range**). Type **QUARTERS** and press **return**, type **STORE2** and press **return** once more. The quarterly sales data from the second store (row 15 in Figure VP.13b) should now appear in row 7 of the consolidated spreadsheet; the gross profit totals in row 10 of the consolidated spreadsheet have also been updated.

Move the cell pointer to cell **B8** and repeat the entire process once again to obtain the data for the third store. The File Combine operation is depicted in Figure VP.14. Save the completed spreadsheet.

Step 6: **File Linking (Lotus 2.2 Only)**
The File Combine command is a static operation in that it uses values from the individual spreadsheets at the time the command is executed. In other words subsequent changes (if any) to the detailed spreadsheets will *not* be reflected in the consolidated spreadsheet unless the entire file combine process is repeated. Lotus 2.2 (but not VP Planner) provides for file linking whereby the changes are dynamic; i.e. done automatically.

Type **/RE** to initiate the **Range Erase** command and erase cells **B6..E8** (the cells containing the values from the individual stores). Now enter the following cell formulas exactly as they appear:

```
B6:  +<<C:\LOTUS\SPRDSHTS\STORE1.WK1>>B15
B7:  +<<C:\LOTUS\SPRDSHTS\STORE2.WK1>>B15
B8:  +<<C:\LOTUS\SPRDSHTS\STORE3.WK1>>B15
```

Lotus/VP Planner Plus Hands-On Exercises 149

```
              A           B           C           D           E
1                             Any Business Enterprise
2                           Quarterly Results - All Stores
3
4                          Q1          Q2          Q3          Q4
5                         ----------------------------------------
6      Store 1
7      Store 2
8      Store 3
9                         ----------------------------------------
10     Gross Profit        $0          $0          $0          $0
```

(a) Empty consolidated spreadsheet

```
              A           B           C           D           E
1                             Any Business Enterprise
2                           Quarterly Results - All Stores
3
4                          Q1          Q2          Q3          Q4
5                         ----------------------------------------
6      Store 1          $5,000      $11,500      $6,000      ($500)
7      Store 2
8      Store 3
9                         ----------------------------------------
10     Gross Profit     $5,000      $11,500      $6,000      ($500)
```

(b) Consolidated spreadsheet with one store

```
              A           B           C           D           E
1                             Any Business Enterprise
2                           Quarterly Results - All Stores
3
4                          Q1          Q2          Q3          Q4
5                         ----------------------------------------
6      Store 1          $5,000      $11,500      $6,000      ($500)
7      Store 2          $7,500      $14,500     $22,000     $29,000
8      Store 3
9                         ----------------------------------------
10     Gross Profit    $12,500      $26,000     $28,000     $28,500
```

(c) Consolidated spreadsheet with two stores

```
              A           B           C           D           E
1                             Any Business Enterprise
2                           Quarterly Results - All Stores
3
4                          Q1          Q2          Q3          Q4
5                         ----------------------------------------
6      Store 1          $5,000      $11,500      $6,000      ($500)
7      Store 2          $7,500      $14,500     $22,000     $29,000
8      Store 3          $8,500     ($5,000)     $13,000     $26,000
9                         ----------------------------------------
10     Gross Profit    $21,000      $21,000     $41,000     $54,500
```

(d) Completed consolidated spreadsheet

Figure VP.14 - The File Combine Command

The entry enclosed in << >> is the Lotus convention to indicate a cell from another spreadsheet. In other words the value in cell B6 which appears as +<<C:\LOTUS\SPRDSHTS\STORE1.WK1>>B15, is to be taken from cell B15 in the spreadsheet STORE1.WK1 (which is found in the LOTUS\SPRDSHTS subdirectory on drive C). You should have no trouble recognizing STORE1 as the name of the spreadsheet, but perhaps are perplexed at the sudden appearance of the subdirectory. Recall, however, our initial suggestion to create a separate subdirectory for the WK1 files (see pages 95 and 105) for additional information. Realize too, that if you are using a two drive floppy system and/or have not created the specific subdirectory to which we refer, you will have to modify the cell contents accordingly.

Type **/C** to invoke the Copy command, then copy cells **B6..B8** to cells **C6..E8**. The consolidated spreadsheet should once again reflect the values from the detailed spreadsheet but this time the values were obtained through dynamic linking. Type **/FS** to save the completed spreadsheet.

Step 7: **File Linking Continued (Lotus 2.2 Only)**
Retrieve one or more of the detailed spreadsheets and change any amounts you wish. Save the detailed spreadsheets with the changes you made. Retrieve the consolidated spreadsheet and verify that it contains your changes.

Macros

A *macro* is a set of keystrokes which is saved under a *macro name* for future recall. In other words, you can store as a macro the keystrokes that make up the file combine process, then subsequently invoke the macro to execute the stored commands. The advantages are significant in terms of saved time and reduced error; other macro commands extend the capabilities of a spreadsheet beyond what you can do from the keyboard.

The process of creating a macro is similar to writing a program in a computer language. We will describe the process in general terms, then apply it in the Hands-On Exercise which follows. Thus, you:

1. Define the task the macro is to perform, for example, combining data from the individual stores into the consolidated spreadsheet.

2. Determine the commands (keystrokes) needed to complete the task. This, in turn, requires you to execute the commands, keystroke by keystroke, so that

you can be sure the macro will work as intended. The keystrokes contained within a macro are for the most part identical to those typed in from the keyboard. Some, however, have special symbols such as the ~ which represents the return key, while others are contained in a pair of braces. The F5 function key, for example, is used to position the cell pointer and is represented as {GOTO}. Other frequently used keys are as follows:

Symbol	Key
~	Return key
{BS}	Backspace key
{CALC}	F9 (Calculate) key
{DEL}	Del key
{DOWN}	Down arrow key
{EDIT}	F2 (Edit) key
{END}	End key
{ESC}	Escape key
{GOTO}	F5 (Go to) key
{HOME}	Home key
{INSERT}	Insert key
{LEFT}	Left arrow key
{PGDN}	Page Down key
{PGUP}	Page Up key
{RIGHT}	Right arrow key
{UP}	Up arrow key

3. Enter the keystrokes determined in step two as a label in a cell *below and to the right of the main body of the spreadsheet*. Macros should be stored in this area so that they are unaffected by subsequent insertions and/or deletions of rows and/or columns in the main body of the spreadsheet.

4. Execute a **R**ange **N**ame command to name the macro (the set of keystrokes entered in step 3), after which it can be executed. *A macro name consists of a backward slash followed by a letter of the alphabet*, for example \C or \E, and pronounced "Alt C" or "Alt E" respectively. (There is also a special macro, \0, pronounced "Alt zero", known as an autoexec macro which is beyond the scope of this discussion.) The macro name (for purposes of documentation) appears in the cell immediately to the left of the cell to which it refers. *A macro is executed by pressing the **Alt** key and the associated letter*, e.g., the keystrokes *Alt C* activates the series of keystrokes in the \C macro.

Hands-On Exercise 8 should clarify this discussion.

Hands-On Exercise 8: Macros

Objective: Develop a macro equivalent to the file combine process from the previous exercise; extend the macro concept to include user-defined menus. The (empty) consolidated spreadsheet and the associated file combine macro are shown in Figure VP.15.

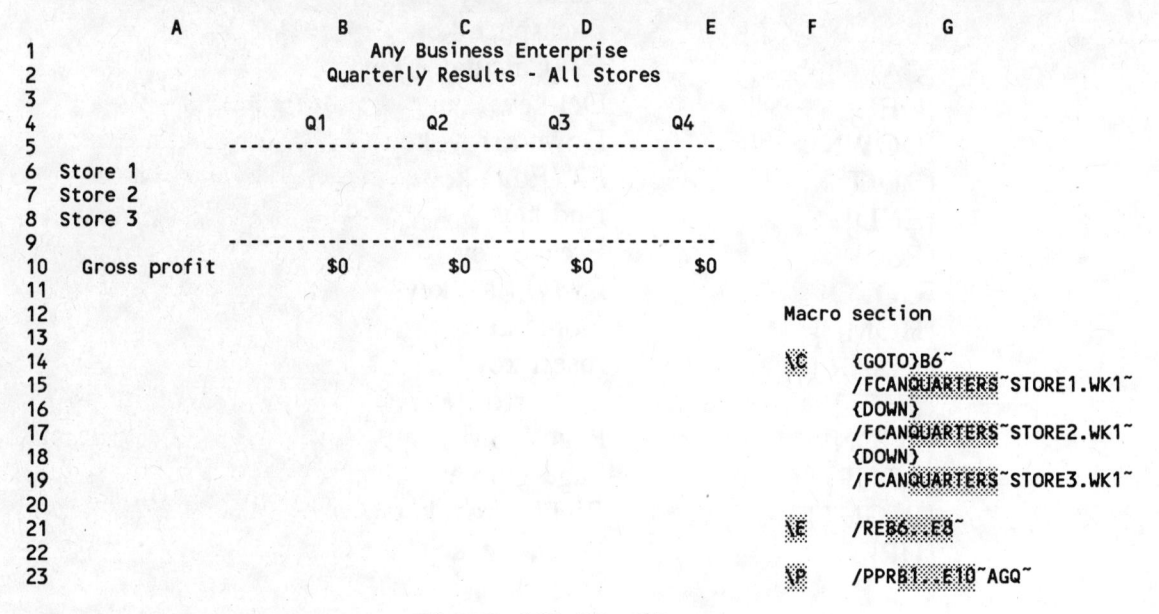

```
         A              B           C           D           E           F              G
 1                         Any Business Enterprise
 2                        Quarterly Results - All Stores
 3
 4                         Q1          Q2          Q3          Q4
 5                      ------------------------------------------
 6   Store 1
 7   Store 2
 8   Store 3
 9                      ------------------------------------------
10   Gross profit      $0          $0          $0          $0
11
12                                                              Macro section
13
14                                                              \C    {GOTO}B6~
15                                                                    /FCANQUARTERS~STORE1.WK1~
16                                                                    {DOWN}
17                                                                    /FCANQUARTERS~STORE2.WK1~
18                                                                    {DOWN}
19                                                                    /FCANQUARTERS~STORE3.WK1~
20
21                                                              \E    /REB6..E8~
22
23                                                              \P    /PPRB1..E10~AGQ~
```

Figure VP.15 - Macros

Step 1: **Retrieve the Consolidated Spreadsheet**
Retrieve the consolidated spreadsheet from the previous exercise. Use the **Range Erase (/RE)** command to erase values which may appear in cells **B6..E8**, so that you begin with an empty consolidated spreadsheet.

Step 2: **Determine the Necessary Keystrokes**
The first step in creating a macro is to define the task the macro is to perform, which in this case will duplicate the file combination process of the previous exercise. Next you have to determine the keystrokes needed to accomplish this task, which requires you to execute the Lotus commands, write down exactly what you are doing on a piece of paper, and finally translate your notes to the appropriate syntax. The results of that effort (which duplicates step 5 of the previous exercise) are shown on the next page with an accompanying explanation.

Lotus/VP Planner Plus Hands-On Exercises 153

Keystrokes	Explanation
{GOTO}B6~	Moves the cursor to cell B6
/FCANQUARTERS~STORE1.WK1~	Combines the named range QUARTERS from the spreadsheet STORE1.WK1
{DOWN}	Moves the cursor down one row (to B7)
/FCANQUARTERS~STORE2.WK1~	Combines the named range QUARTERS from the spreadsheet STORE2.WK1
{DOWN}	Moves the cursor down one row (to B8)
/FCANQUARTERS~STORE3.WK1~	Combines the named range QUARTERS from the spreadsheet STORE3.WK1

Step 3: **Enter the Macro**

The commands in a macro are stored in the spreadsheet itself; ideally below and to the right of the main area of the spreadsheet so that any insertion or deletion of rows or columns will not affect the macro.

Position the cell pointer in cell **G14** of the consolidated spreadsheet, then enter the keystrokes which constitute the macro, as they appear in Figure VP.15. Follow the rules below as you enter the individual commands:

a) Precede the macro keystrokes in each cell with a label prefix, preferably the apostrophe. The entry in cell G15, for example, begins '/FC rather than /FC. (Failing to begin with the apostrophe would cause the spreadsheet to enter the command mode upon encountering the slash.)

b) Avoid blank spaces in the macro - the keystrokes must be entered *without* any spaces (for example, '/FC is correct whereas ' / F C is incorrect and results in an error).

c) A macro may span several lines (rows) in the spreadsheet, but it must appear in a single column; a macro executes, beginning in the first cell by reading and executing keystrokes from left to right until all keystrokes in that cell have been read, and then continuing down to the next cell in the same column to continue execution, again reading from left to right; it continues in this manner until it encounters a blank cell, which terminates the macro.

Step 4: **Name the Macro**

Every macro has a name, consisting of the backslash followed by a letter, e.g., \C. (A macro may also be named with the backslash and a 0, \0, in which case it becomes an autoexec macro and executes automatically each time the spreadsheet in which it is stored is retrieved). The name of the macro should be placed in the cell immediately to the left of the first cell containing the macro.

Move to cell **F14** and enter '\C as the name of the macro (observing that the entry begins with an apostrophe). Type the command **/RNLR** (Range Name Label Right) to assign the label (i.e., the macro name) in cell F14 to the macro whose first entry appears in cell G14. Save the spreadsheet.

Step 5: **Execute the Macro**
The macro has been created and named. To execute the macro, press the **Alt** key, and while pressing this key and type **C**, the letter assigned as the macro name. If all goes well, you will see the spreadsheet repeat the command sequence contained within the macro, as it rebuilds the consolidated spreadsheet from the previous exercise.

Step 6: **Test and Debug the Macro**
You can interrupt execution of a macro at any time by pressing the **Ctrl** and **Break** keys at the same time. (You may, however, have to subsequently press the **Esc** key to return to the READY mode.)

You may also find it convenient to test the macro in *single step mode* which executes the macro one step at a time. Press **Alt+F2** (**Alt+F1** in VP Planner Plus) to activate the single step mode which in turn requires that a key be pressed between each step to continue execution. Note, too, that the **Alt+F2** (**Alt+F1** in VP Planner Plus) combination acts as a toggle switch; i.e. pressing these keys a second time returns the macro to normal execution.

The easiest way to change (correct) any of the entries within a macro is to use the **F2** key to edit the cell in question. The most common error is the presence of unintentional blanks at the end of a cell which terminates execution of the macro. (You can test for blanks at the end of a cell by pressing the F2 key and seeing whether the cursor is immediately to the right of the last character on the line; if it is not, blanks are present and must be deleted.)

Step 7: **Learn Mode (Lotus 2.2 Only)**
Lotus 2.2 facilitates the development of a macro by including a learn mode whereby the keystrokes in a macro are recorded automatically as they are executed. In other words it is no longer necessary to record (on paper) the keystrokes in the macro, only to subsequently re-enter them by hand as was done in the exercise. Type **/RE** to initiate the **Range Erase** command, then indicate cells **G14..G19** as the range to erase. This erases

the keystrokes in the Alt C macro which will be recreated through the learn mode as described below.

Type **/WLR** (**W**orksheet **L**earn **R**ange) to indicate the range where the recorded key strokes will be stored, then type **G14..G19** as these are the cells which will contain the macro. (In general, however, you will not know the precise range in which case you simply guess as to the number of cells required. Just remember the keystrokes within a macro are stored one cell under another.)

Type **Alt+F5** to beginning recording the keystrokes (which produces a LEARN indicator in the bottom of your monitor), then repeat the file combination process from step 5 in the previous exercise (page 148). Begin by pressing the **F5** (go to key) to move the cell pointer to cell **B6**, type **/FC** to initiate the File Combine command and so on. You will see the file combination process take place as the commands are executed, and in addition you will see the keystrokes recorded in cells G14 through G19. Press **Alt+F5** a second time to end the recording process. Test the macro by erasing the contents of cells B6..E8, then pressing **Alt+C** to execute the macro.

Step 8: **Creating Additional Macros**

Create two additional macros, \E (to erase the consolidated data) and \P (print the completed spreadsheet) as shown in Figure VP.16. Use the Learn Mode if it is available to you or else enter the keystrokes explicitly. Remember to name the macros after the keystrokes have been entered; the latter is accomplished with the **/RNLR** (**R**ange **N**ame **L**abel **R**ight) command as described earlier.

Test the macros to be sure they work as intended, then save the completed spreadsheet. Your spreadsheet now contains three macros, \C, \E, and \P which will be combined in a *user-defined menu* as depicted in Figure VP.16.

Step 9: **User-defined Menus**

Figure VP.16a contains the empty consolidated spreadsheet with which you are well acquainted, and in addition, a menu with four choices. The menu resembles a Lotus menu except that the choices (Combine, Erase, Print, and Quit) were defined by the user for this particular application. The options are selected in the normal fashion, i.e. by moving the (left and right) arrow keys to highlight an option and pressing the enter key, or by typing the first letter of the desired menu option.

The menu name, **usermenu** in the example, appears in the cell to the left of the menu. The menu itself extends over three rows in Figure VP.16b. Implementation of the menu is described in step 10.

```
Combine  Erase  Print  Quit
Combine store data
             A            B           C           D           E
 1                            Any Business Enterprise
 2                          Quarterly Results - All Stores
 3
 4                           Q1          Q2          Q3          Q4
 5                       ---------------------------------------------
 6       Store 1
 7       Store 2
 8       Store 3
 9                       ---------------------------------------------
10       Gross Profit       $0          $0          $0          $0
```

(a) Combine Choice Highlighted

```
          F            G                    H                I                  J
12  Macro section
13
14  \C           {GOTO}B6~
15               /FCANQUARTERS~STORE1.WK1~
16               {DOWN}
17               /FCANQUARTERS~STORE2.WK1~
18               {DOWN}
19               /FCANQUARTERS~STORE3.WK1~
20
21  \E           /REB6..E8~
22
23  \P           /PPB1..E10~AGQ~
24
25  USERMENU     COMBINE              ERASE            PRINT              QUIT
26               Combine store data   Erase combined data  Print spreadsheet   Return to ready mode
27               {BRANCH \C}          {BRANCH \E}      {BRANCH \P}        {QUIT}
28
29  \M           {HOME}
30               {MENUCALL USERMENU}
31               {BRANCH \M}
```

(b) Implementation

Figure VP.16 - User Defined Menus

Step 10: Creating the User-defined Menu

As indicated the menu consists of three rows and extends from cells G25 through J27. Thus:

Row 1 (row 25 in Figure VP.16b) contains the four choices, Combine, Erase, Print, and Quit, each of which begins with a different letter.

Row 2 (row 26 in Figure VP.16b) contains the explanations

Row 3 (row 27 in Figure VP.16b) contains a branch instruction to implement the previously defined macro. Cell G27, for example, contains the instruction to branch to (execute) the macro called \C.

Lotus/VP Planner Plus Hands-On Exercises

Enter the contents of cells G25 through J27 exactly as they appear in the figure. Move the cursor to cell **F25** and type **usermenu** as the name of the menu. Type **/RNLR** (Range Name Label Right) to associate the menu name in cell F25 with the menu beginning in cell G25.

Step 10: Invoking the User-defined Menu

You must create one last macro (shown in cells G29 through G31) to invoke the user-defined menu just created. Type **\M** in cell F29 and execute the **Range Name Label Right** command a final time. Press **Alt+M** to invoke the macro which in turn should produce the user-defined menu. Save the completed spreadsheet.

New Commands - Exercise 8

Creating a Macro

Step 1	Define the task
Step 2	Determine the keystrokes
Step 3	Enter the keystrokes below and to the right of the main part of the spreadsheet
Step 4	Enter the macro name, then use **/RNLR** to tie the name to the keystrokes
Alt+F2 (Lotus)	Toggles step mode on and off; useful in
Alt+F1 (VPP)	testing and debugging a macro

Learn Mode

/WLR	Defines the range where macro is stored
Alt+F5	Toggle switch to begin (and end) recording keystrokes

User-Defined Menus

Row 1	Contains the menu options, each of which begins with a different letter
Row 2	Contains the explanation
Row 3	Contains a {branch} or other instruction to implement the option

158 Lotus/VP Planner Plus Hands-On Exercises

Hands-On Exercise 9: Business Graphics

Objective: Use the graphics component of a spreadsheet program to produce various types of business graphs. *The exercise requires that your computer have graphics capability.* The graphs are based on the spreadsheet of Figure VP.17.

```
              A          B          C          D          E          F
 1                       Ralph Cordell Sporting Goods
 2                          Quarterly Sales Figures
 3
 4       Sales Rep       1st        2nd        3rd        4th       Total
 5       -----------------------------------------------------------------
 6       Friedel       $50,000    $55,000    $62,500    $95,400    $262,900
 7       Davis         $34,000    $48,500    $52,000    $62,000    $196,500
 8       McGrath       $49,000    $44,000    $42,500    $41,000    $176,500
 9       -----------------------------------------------------------------
10                    $133,000   $147,500   $157,000   $198,400    $635,900
```

Figure VP.17 - Ralph Cordell Spreadsheet

Step 1: **For Users of VP Planner and Hercules Graphics**
Do this step only if you are using VP Planner *and* have a Hercules graphics card (or a compatible computer which uses Hercules; e.g., a Leading Edge). Type **/WGDHVH** (**W**orksheet **G**lobal **D**efault **H**ardware **V**ideo **H**ercules) to change the default hardware configuration so that your graphs will be visible on the screen. Type **Q** (**Q**uit) to exit from this menu and return to the ready mode.

Step 2: **Create the Spreadsheet**
Create the spreadsheet for Ralph Cordell Sporting Goods, as shown in Figure VP.17. The spreadsheet is straight forward and should not pose any difficulty. Save the completed spreadsheet as **CORDELL.WK1**.

Step 3: **Enter the Graph Menu**
Type a slash to enter the command mode, then highlight the Graph command to view the menu options. The menus for Lotus and VP Planner Plus are essentially the same, although there are subtle differences as explained in the exercise. The menu below is that of Lotus 2.2:

```
Worksheet Range Copy Move File Print Graph Data System Add-In Quit
Type X A B C D E F Reset View Save Options Name Group Quit
```

Graphing is easy once you understand how the various menu options are used to develop a graph. Every graph, however, is created in more or less the same way, through specification of the following:

1) The category (type) of graph; the **Type** command indicates the nature of the graph (bar, line, pie, and so on).

2) The data to be plotted; the **A range** specifies the first, sometimes only, quantitative variable; up to five additional quantitative variables can be specified as the **B, C, D, E,** and **F ranges**.

3) A description of the data (which appears as labels on the x-axis); the **X range** specifies the cells containing the descriptive labels.

and 4) Options to enhance the appearance of the graph; the **Options** command and its submenus provides titles for the graph and/or the x and y axes; legends, scaling, and so on.

Other selections from the graph command allow you to View the graph on the monitor and to Save the graph in a special type of file for subsequent printing. All of these options are common to *both* Lotus and VP Planner.

VP Planner Plus contains a Print option (not found in the Lotus menu on the previous page) which facilitates the printing process and which is described in step 5. Lotus, on the other hand, contains a Group option not available in VP Planner, described in step 11.

Step 4: **Create a Bar graph (Figure VP.18a)**
The first graph you will create is the Bar Graph of Figure VP.18a which plots the quarterly sales totals in cells B10 through E10 of Figure VP.17.

Be sure that you are in the graph menu (i.e. you typed /G from the ready mode). Type **T (for Type)** then **B (to indicate a Bar graph)**. Next type **A to specify the A range**, which in this case consists of cells **B10..E10**. Type **X to specify the X range**, containing the descriptive information in cells **B4..E4**.

Type **V (to View)** the graph and a bar graph should be visible on your monitor; the graph is not complete, however, as it does not contain any title information. Press the **Esc key** to remove the graph from the monitor and return to the Graph menu. Note too, that as you specify the various graph parameters you will continually see a screen similar to Figure VP.18b depicting the various options currently in effect. (VP Planner displays the same information, albeit in a different format.)

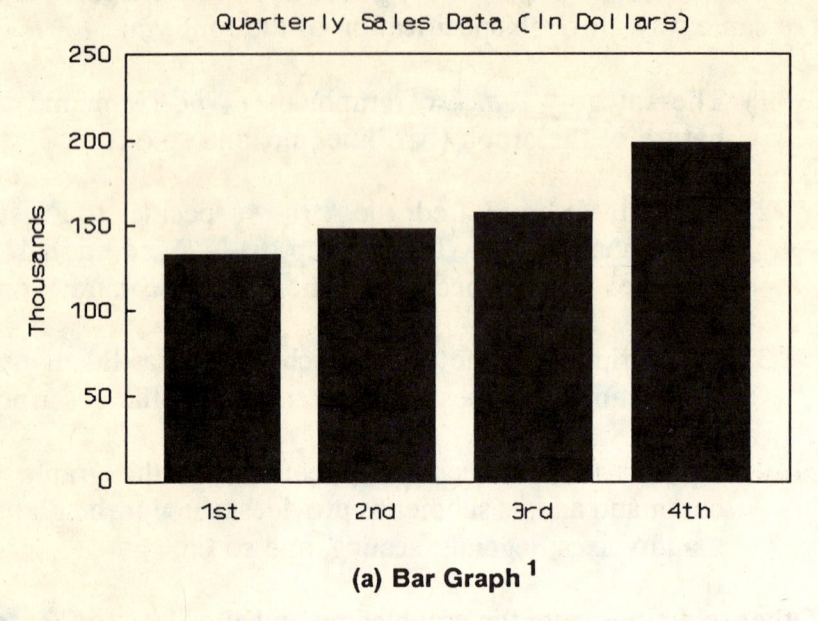

Ralph Cordell Sporting Goods
Quarterly Sales Data (In Dollars)

(a) Bar Graph [1]

```
Type  X  A  B  C  D  E  F  Reset  View  Save  Options  Name  Group  Quit
Add graph titles or axis titles to graph
```

Graph Settings			
Type: Bar	Titles: First Ralph Cordell Sporting Goods		
	Second Quarterly Sales Data (In Do...		
X: B4..E4	X axis		
A: B10..E10	Y axis		
B:			
C:		Y scale:	X scale:
D:	Scaling	Automatic	Automatic
E:	Lower		
F:	Upper		
	Format	(G)	(G)
Grid: None	Color: No	Indicator Yes	Yes
Legend:	Format:	Data labels:	Skip: 1
A	Both		
B	Both		
C	Both		
D	Both		
E	Both		
F	Both		

(b) Graph Settings

Figure VP.18 - A Graph and its Settings

---

[1] The appearance of the scale on the Y axis will differ according to the spreadsheet you are using; i.e. Lotus indicates thousands whereas VP Planner Plus indicates millions.

Type **O** (for **Options**) then **T** (to select the **Titles** submenu). Type **F** (for the **First** line of the title), enter **Ralph Cordell Sporting Goods**, and press return. Type **T** (for **Titles**) once again, **S** (to enter the **Second** line of the title), **Quarterly Sales Data (In Dollars)**, and press return once more. Type **Q** (to **Quit**) the options menu, **V** (to **View**) the completed graph, and press **Esc** to leave the graph and return to the graph menu.

Your completed graph should now match the bar graph in Figure VP.18a which in turn corresponds to the settings in Figure VP.18b. The latter indicates a bar graph, X and A ranges of B4..E4 and B10..E10 respectively, as well as the two line title. Can you see how these settings correspond to the graph in Figure VP.18a and the spreadsheet in Figure VP.17?

Step 5: Print the Graph (VP Planner Only)

It is easier to print graphs in VP Planner than in Lotus as the print command is contained directly within the Graph menu. (The procedure to print graphs in Lotus is described in step 10). Hence, if you are using VP Planner, be sure you are still in the graph menu, then type **P** (for **Print**) and the graph will print immediately. (You may, however, encounter a problem in that the student version of VP Planner Plus does not support all types of printers; it will not, for example, print a graph on a laser printer.)

Step 6: Save the Graph

There are two distinct save operations that apply to graphs in both Lotus and VP Planner. The **Graph Save command** creates a **PIC file** (which is needed to print the graph in Lotus), but it does not allow subsequent modification of that graph. By contrast, the **Graph Name Create** command stores the graph settings for subsequent modification of the graph, but does not produce the PIC file required for printing. Hence the same graph is often saved "twice" under both **Graph Save** and **Graph Name Create** commands.

Be sure you are still in the Graph menu, then type **S** (for **Save**) whereupon you will be prompted for the name of the graph (PIC) file. Type **BARCHART** (or any other mnemonic name of eight characters or less). The Graph Save command results in the creation of a separate **BARCHART.PIC file** (in addition to the file containing the CORDELL.WK1 spreadsheet). *You must execute this command if you want to print the graph in Lotus.*

Check once more that you are still in the Graph menu, then type **NC** (for **Name Create**) to save the graph settings whereupon you will be prompted for a graph name. We suggest you use the same name as before; i.e. **BARCHART**. The significance of this command is explained in step 9.

Type **Q** to (Quit) the Graph menu and return to the READY mode. Type **/FS** (File Save) to save the graph settings within CORDELL.WK1 spreadsheet.

Step 7:   Create a Pie Chart

The best thing about computer-generated graphs is the ease with which they can be modified. You can, for example, convert the bar graph of Figure VP.18a to an equivalent pie chart, merely by changing the type of graph.

Type **/GTP** (Graph Type Pie), then **V** (to View) the graph on your monitor. The pie chart will appear immediately, without having to specify additional information, because all of the previous specifications (the A range, X range, and two line title), are retained from one graph to the next, unless you otherwise instruct the program with the Reset command).

If you are using VP Planner, you can print the graph at this time with the Graph Print command as described in step 5.

Step 8:   Save the Graph

Save the pie chart following the same procedure as in step 6. Use the **Graph Save** command to create a PIC file (required for subsequent printing in Lotus) and the **Graph Name Create** command to save the graph settings. Use the same name for both; e.g. **PIECHART**.

Type **Q** to (Quit) the Graph menu and return to the READY mode. Type **/FS** (File Save) to save the graph settings within CORDELL.WK1 spreadsheet.

Step 9:   The Reset and Name Commands

Type **/GRG** (Graph Reset Graph) to reset all settings. Type **V** (View), whereupon the computer will beep (in Lotus) or indicate that the A-F ranges are empty (VP Planner) because there are no settings in effect, and hence no graph to view. Press **Esc** to return to the graph menu.

Type **NU** (Name Use) then select either of the two graph settings (**BARCHART** and **PIECHART** from steps 6 and 8 respectively) and the indicated graph will come into view. In other words the **Graph Name Use** command retrieves the settings previously saved with the **Graph Name Create** command. Press **Esc** to return to the Graph menu.

Now you understand the significance of the **Graph Name Create** command (to save the settings), the **Graph Reset Graph** command (to cancel all graph settings) and the **Graph Name Use** command to retrieve settings previously saved.

Step 10: Print the Graphs (Lotus only)

As indicated, the procedure to print a graph in Lotus is more complex than in VP Planner and requires that you exit the spreadsheet. Type **/QY** (Quit Yes) to exit the spreadsheet and return to the Opening Lotus menu shown in Figure VP.2a on page 94. Type **P** to select the **Printgraph menu** which in turn produces the screen of Figure VP.19. (You will need a separate Print Graph Disk if you are using Lotus on two floppy drives rather than a hard drive.)

```
Copyright 1986, 1989 Lotus Development Corp.  All Rights Reserved. V2.2      MENU

Select graphs to print or preview
Image-Select  Settings  Go  Align  Page  Exit

       GRAPHS     IMAGE SETTINGS                   HARDWARE SETTINGS
       TO PRINT     Size                Range colors   Graphs directory
                    Top        .395     X Black           C:\LOTUS\SPRDSHTS
                    Left       .750     A Black        Fonts directory
                    Width     6.500     B Black           C:\LOTUS
                    Height    4.691     C Black        Interface
                    Rotation   .000     D Black           Parallel 1
                                        E Black        Printer
                    Font                F Black           HP LaserJet Med
                    1  BLOCK1                          Paper size
                    2  BLOCK1                             Width       8.500
                                                         Length     11.000

                                                       ACTION SETTINGS
                                                         Pause  No   Eject  No
```

Figure VP.19 - The Print Graph Menu

Recall that steps 6 and 8 directed you to use the **Graph Save** command to create the necessary **PIC files** (BARGRAPH.PIC and PIECHART.PIC), and further to store these files in the default directory (the same directory containing the WK1 files created throughout the Lab Manual.) Now you need to indicate to the PrintGraph program where these PIC files are stored.

Type **SHG** (Settings Hardware Graphs-directory), then type **C:\LOTUS\SPRDSHTS** as this is the default directory you established during installation. (If, however, you are using a two drive floppy system, enter the same command but type **B:** because the PIC files were saved to the disk in drive B.) Type **Q** (Quit) to return to the PrintGraph menu.

Type **I (Image-Select)** to select the specific PIC files for printing whereupon Figure VP.20 will come into view. The figure will list all of the PIC files in the default directory (e.g., C:\LOTUS\SPRDSHTS). Use the up and down arrow keys to highlight the files for printing, press the **space bar** to toggle the pound sign on and off (to select or deselect the file), and press the enter key to return to the PrintGraph menu.

```
Copyright 1986, 1989 Lotus Development Corp.  All Rights Reserved. V2.2    POINT
Select graphs to print

   GRAPH FILE  DATE      TIME     SIZE
   -------------------------------------
                                          Space bar marks or unmarks selection
 # BARCHART   08-02-90   13:28    5559    ENTER selects marked graphs
 # PIECHART   08-02-90   13:35    1886    ESC exits, ignoring changes
                                          HOME moves to beginning of list
                                          END moves to end of list
                                          ↑ and ↓ move highlight
                                            List will scroll if highlight
                                            moved beyond top or bottom
                                          GRAPH (F10) previews marked graph
```

Figure VP.20 - Selecting Graphs for Printing

Type **G (Go)** and the selected files (those preceded by a pound sign) will print. Type **E (Exit)** and **Y (Yes)** to end the PrintGraph session. Select **1-2-3** from the main Lotus menu to return to the ready mode.

Step 11: Create a Multiple Bar Graph Figure VP.21a)

Type **/FR (File Retrieve)** and retrieve the **CORDELL** spreadsheet. Type **/GRG (Graph Reset Graph)** to enter the graph menu and reset all parameters.

Type **TB (Type Bar)** to begin creating the multiple bar graph in Figure VP.21a. However, unlike the previous bar graph, we will now plot three sets of numbers for each quarter, corresponding to the quarterly sales figures for each of the three sales personnel. Thus you have to indicate three distinct data ranges (i.e. the A, B, and C ranges), for Friedel (cells B6 through E6), Davis (cells B7 through E7), and McGrath (cells B8 through E8) respectively.

Type **A** to indicate the **A** range, then enter **B6..E6** corresponding to Friedel's sales in the four quarters. Type **B** to designate the **B** range, then indicate **B7..E7** for Davis, and finally **C** for the **C** range, indicating cells **B8..E8**. Finally type **X** to indicate the **X** range and enter **B4..E4** as the range of cells containing labels for the X axis. (The Group command, available in Lotus 2.2 only, allows you to specify the X, A, B, and C ranges simultaneously.) Type **V** to **V**iew the graph which resembles Figure VP.21a, but which doesn't yet contain the title or a legend to identify the various shadings which are produced automatically by the spreadsheet program. Press the **Esc** key to return to the graph menu.

Enter the two lines of the title as you did previously in step 4. (The title has to be reentered because all parameters were erased with the reset command.)

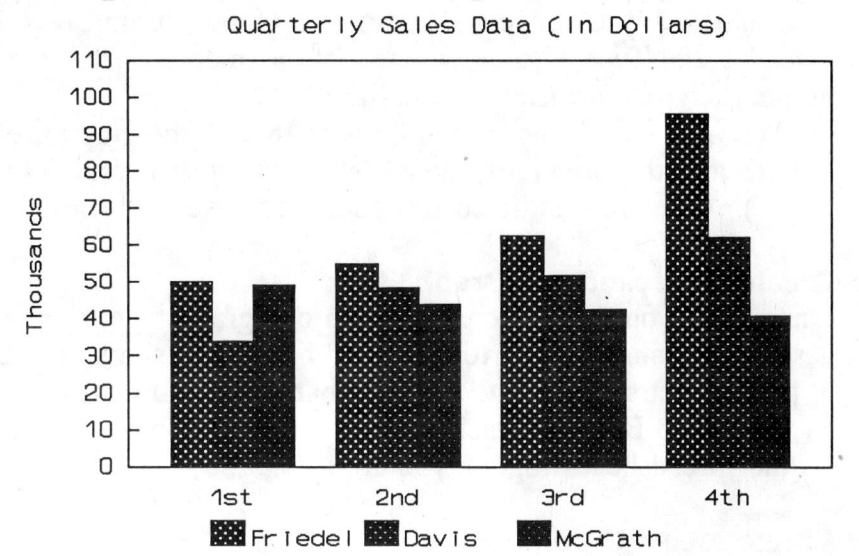

Ralph Cordell Sporting Goods
Quarterly Sales Data (In Dollars)

(a) The Graph [2]

```
Type  X  A  B  C  D  E  F  Reset  View  Save  Options  Name  Group  Quit
Use   Create    Delete    Reset   Table
─────────────────────────── Graph Settings ───────────────────────────
Type: Bar                    Titles: First   Ralph Cordell Sporting Goods
                                     Second  Quarterly Sales Data (In Do...
X: B4..E4                            X axis
A: B6..E6                            Y axis
B: B7..E7
C: B8..E8                                    Y scale:        X scale:
D:                                   Scaling Automatic       Automatic
E:                                   Lower
F:                                   Upper
                                     Format  (G)             (G)
Grid: None         Color: No         Indicator Yes           Yes

      Legend:              Format:   Data labels:            Skip: 1
A  Friedel                 Both
B  Davis                   Both
C  McGrath                 Both
D                          Both
E                          Both
F                          Both
```

(b) The Settings

Figure VP.21 - The Multiple Bar Graph

---

[2] The appearance of the scale on the Y axis will differ according to the spreadsheet you are using; i.e. Lotus indicates thousands whereas VP Planner Plus indicates millions.

166 Lotus/VP Planner Plus Hands-On Exercises

Type O (Options), **L** (Legends), **A** for the **A** legend, and **Friedel** as the legend text; type L (Legends), **B** for the **B** legend and **Davis** as the legend text; and finally L (Legends), **C** for the **C** legend, and **McGrath** as the legend text. Type **Q** to Quit the options menu. View the completed graph, then save or print as necessary.

Compare the settings in Figure VP.21b with the graph itself in Figure VP.21a and the original spreadsheet from which it was derived (Figure VP.17). Can you see the correspondence between all three figures?

Step 12: Create a Stacked Bar Graph

Once again you can move easily from one graph type to another, in this case from a multiple bar to a stacked bar graph, simply by changing the Type parameter. Create the stacked bar graph of Figures VP.22 with the Type Stacked-Bar command, then save and/or print the graph depending on the spreadsheet program you are using.

Step 13: Create a Line Graph

Type **TL** (Type Line) to change the stacked bar graph to a line graph, then View the graph to see the equivalent of Figure VP.23 on your monitor.

Print or save the graph at this time, depending on whether you are using VP Planner or Lotus respectively.

Step 14: Exit Lotus

Type **Q** (to Quit) the Graph menu and return to the READY mode. Type **/FS** (File Save) to save the graph settings within CORDELL.WK1 spreadsheet.

Type /QY (Quit Yes) to quit the spreadsheet and return to DOS.

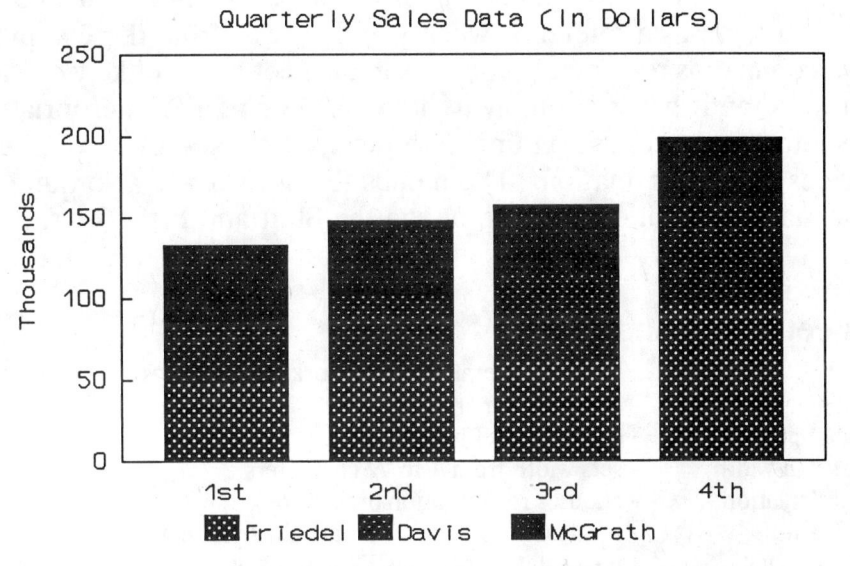

Figure VP.22 - Stacked Bar Graph

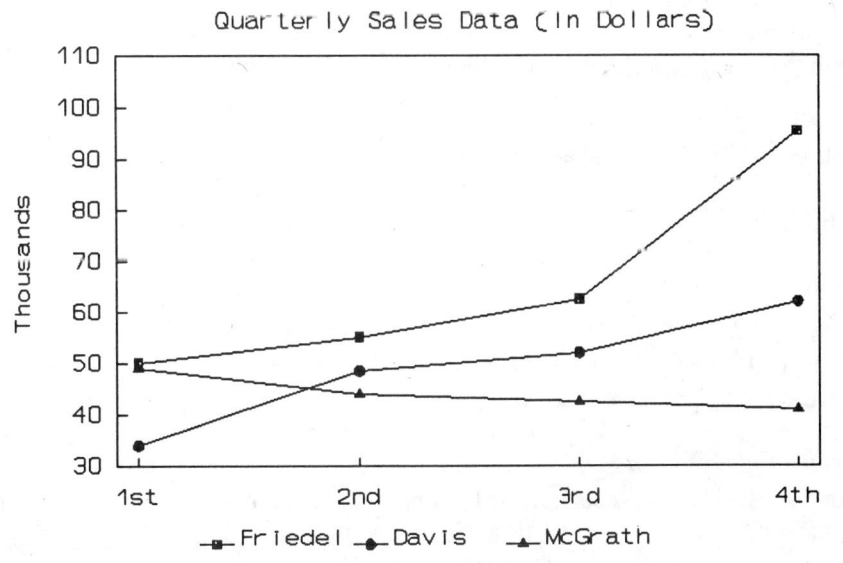

Figure VP.23 - Line Graph

Lotus/VP Planner Plus Reference

This section contains a partial listing of Lotus (VP Planner Plus) commands and is intended to serve as a reference when you are away from the computer. As you view these commands remember that the spreadsheet is most likely capable of doing what you want, and that it is simply a matter of finding the appropriate command. Remember too the excellent on-line help facility (invoked by the F1 function key) that provides more information. The menus themselves are also quite helpful and hard copy may be obtained at any time via the Shift and PrtSc keys.

/Worksheet commands

- Global - specifies overall (global) worksheet settings
  - Format - changes numeric format
  - Label-prefix - changes label alignment
  - Column-width - sets width from 1 to 72 characters
  - Recalculation - chooses recalculation procedure
    - Auto - recalculation done automatically (default)
    - Manual - recalculation requires F9 (calc) key
  - Protection - allows (prohibits) cell entries
    - Enable - does not allow entry
    - Disable - allows data entry (default)
  - Default - establishes printer settings
    - Directory - changes directory where spreadsheets are kept
    - Hardware - changes hardware configuration
    - Update - updates (changes) current default settings
- Insert - inserts rows or columns
  - Column - inserts column(s) at cursor location
  - Row - inserts row(s) at cursor location
- Delete - deletes rows or columns
  - Column - deletes column at cursor location
  - Row - deletes row at cursor location
- Column-width - sets column width where cursor is located
- Erase - erases worksheet
- Titles - freezes (clears) title settings
  - Both - freezes horizontal and vertical titles at cursor
  - Horizontal - freezes horizontal titles at cursor
  - Vertical - freezes vertical titles at cursor
  - Clear - clears titles
- Window - splits screen at cursor
  - Horizontal - sets horizontal windows at cursor
  - Vertical - sets vertical windows at cursor
  - Clear - clears windows
- Status - displays current worksheet settings
- Learn - records macro keystrokes (Lotus 2.2 only)

Examples:
- /WGC - Sets the width of all columns
- /WCS - Change width of current column
- /WGRM - Turns on manual recalculation
- /WIC - Inserts a column(s)
- /WTV - Freezes vertical titles
- /WGPE - Establishes global protection

/Range commands

- **Format** - changes numeric format
  - Fixed - fixed number of decimals shown
  - Scientific - output shown in scientific notation
  - Currency - uses dollar sign and commas with fixed number of decimals
  - Percent - displays percent; e.g. .10 shown as 10%
  - Date - changes to date format; e.g. DD-MMM-YY
- **Label-prefix** - changes alignment of labels
- **Erase** - erases cell entries
- **Name** - creates (removes) range names
  - Create - creates range name for frequently referenced cells
  - Delete - removes range name; cell contents are not affected
- **Protect** - establishes electronic fence around designated range
- **Unprotect** - dismantles electronic fence around designated range

Examples:
- /RFC - Assigns currency format to designated range
- /RU - Unprotects designated cell range
- /RP - Protects a designated cell range

/Copy command - copies entries to another location

/Move command - moves entries to another location

/File commands

- **Retrieve** - retrieves (loads) worksheet from disk
- **Save** - saves current worksheet to disk
  - Cancel - cancels save operation
  - Replace - worksheet in memory replaces worksheet on disk
  - Backup - worksheet previously on disk is stored with BAK extension
- **Combine** - combines data from disk file with current worksheet
  - Copy - file values replace current values
  - Add - file values added to current values
  - Subtract - file values subtracted from current values

Xtract	- saves portion of current worksheet (values or formulas)
Erase	- erases WK1 files on disk
List	- displays files on disk
Directory	- changes current directory

Examples:
/FSB - Saves current worksheet in WK1 file producing a BAK file with previous version
/FR - Initiates command to retrieve (load) worksheet
/FCA - Adds values in current worksheet to corresponding values in worksheet on disk

/Print commands

Printer vs File	- sends output to printer or file
Range	- indicate range to be printed
Line	- advances printer one line
Page	- advances to top of page
Options	- changes page formatting
Margins	- changes margins
Left	- changes left margin
Right	- increases right margin for compressed print
Setup	- prints control characters; e.g. specify compressed print
Other	- prints cell formulas or values
As-displayed	- prints cell values
Cell formulas	- prints cell formulas
Quit	- exits options menu
Align	- logically aligns paper to top of form
Go	- initiates printing

Examples:
/PPOOC - Prints cell formulas instead of values
/PF - Sends output to a file in lieu of the printer
/PPOMR - Changes the right margin (e.g. increase to 132 for compressed print)
/PPAG - Sets line counter to one (align), then initiates printing
/PPP - Ejects page
/PPOS - Invokes setup options; e.g. \015 for compressed print on IBM printer

/Graph commands

Type	- designates graph type
Line	- line graph
Bar	- bar chart
XY	- xy graph
Stacked bar	- stacked bar graph
Pie	- pie chart
X	- specifies x range with labels for line, bar, or stacked bar
A B C D E F	- specifies up to six ranges for the y axis
Group	- specifies ranges simultaneously (Lotus 2.2 only)

Reset	- cancels (reset) graph settings
View	- displays current graph
Save	- saves current graph in PIC file
Options	- labels graph and axes
Legend	- enters legend to explain symbols
Titles	- enters titles for axes and graph
First	- first line of graph title
Second	- second line of graph title
X-axis	- labels the x axis
Y-axis	- labels the y axis
Grid	- overlays graph with grid lines
Scale	- enters (changes) scale settings
Name	- maintains graph names
Create	- assigns a name to the current group of graph settings
Use	- reinstates the named group of graph settings
Delete	- erases a named group of graph settings
Reset	- erases all named graph settings
Print	- prints directly from graph menu (VP Planner only)
Quit	- returns to ready mode

Examples:
    /GS - Saves current graph settings in a PIC file
    /GNC - Saves current graph settings so that they can be subsequently modified
  /GOTF - Enters the first line of graph title
    /GV - Views the current graph settings

/Data commands

Fill	- initiates data fill command
Sort	- initiates sort command
Data range	- enters range of cells to sort
Primary key	- sets first column of sort
Secondary key	- sets second column (if necessary)
Reset	- erases (resets) sort parameters
Go	- sorts data
Quit	- exits sort menu

Examples:
    /DF - Initiates data fill operation (requires beginning value)
    /DSG - Performs sort after keys and range are specified

/Quit command   - returns to DOS

Lotus/VP Planner Plus Self-Evaluation

As with any other program, the best way to judge how much you have learned is to see how successful you are in using Lotus (VP/Planner) to do actual work. We expect that the use of a spreadsheet will become second nature, and that you will join the millions of others who use these programs daily. Nevertheless we have included a quiz (with answers immediately following) should you want to attempt it.

1. Starting off.
   (a) Explain how to load Lotus (VP Planner Plus).
   (b) What is the significance of the command sequence /WGDD? When should the sequence be executed?

2. Labels, numbers, formulas, and functions. Indicate whether the following entries are treated as a number, label, function, formula or error. (Your answer should be based on how the program will interpret the entries, rather than what you think was intended).
   (a) 1991
   (b) 1991 Sales
   (c) '1991 Sales
   (d) ^1991 Sales
   (e) F1 + F2
   (f) (F1+F2)
   (g) +F1+F2
   (h) MIN(A2...A4)
   (i) @MAX(A2...A4)
   (j) @AVG(A2...A4

3. Special keys. Which key:
   (a) Invokes the on-line help facility
   (b) Moves the cursor to cell A1
   (c) Moves the cursor to a particular cell
   (d) Enters the edit mode
   (e) Moves the cursor to the beginning of the line to be edited
   (f) Recalculates the spreadsheet
   (g) Returns to the previous menu
   (h) Initiates the macro recording mode (Lotus 2.2 only)

4. Functions. Given the following cell entries: A1=50, A2=40, A3=30, A4=20, A5=10, A6=0, and that A7 is empty. What value will be returned by the following functions?
   (a) @SUM(A1...A4)
   (b) @MIN(A1...A3,5,A5)
   (c) @IF(A1>0,A3,A2)
   (d) @AVG(A1...A5)
   (e) @MAX(5,@MIN(A5,A6))
   (f) @MAX(5,@MIN(@RAND,4))
   (g) @RAND*3+4
   (h) @COUNT(A1...A6)
   (i) @COUNT(A1...A7)
   (j) @AVG(A1...A6)
   (k) @AVG(A1...A7)

5. Arithmetic. Given the following cell entries: A1=5, A2=4, A3=3, and A4=2. What value will be returned by the following expressions?
   (a) (A1+A2)/A3
   (b) +A1+A2/A3
   (c) (A1+A2)^A4
   (d) (A1+A2)/A3^A4
   (e) (A1+A2)/A3*A4

6. Command sequences. What do the following command sequences do? (In most instances the command sequences are incomplete and would require additional information. Answer only to the extent of the command string).
   (a) /WGC10
   (b) /WDR
   (c) /WWV
   (d) \=
   (e) /RFF0
   (f) /WTV
   (g) /WIC
   (h) /FR
   (i) /C
   (j) /M
   (k) /FCA
   (l) /FS
   (m) /RFD

7. Manual versus automatic calculation.
   (a) What is the default mode; manual or automatic recalculation?
   (b) What does the command string /WGRM accomplish?
   (c) What prompt appears after the command string in part (b) has been issued?
   (d) Why would you want to negate the automatic recalculation?
   (e) How do you recalculate the spreadsheet when in the manual mode?
   (f) How do you turn the automatic recalculation back on?

8. File commands.
   (a) What command saves the spreadsheet currently in memory?
   (b) What is the difference between the command strings, /FSR and /FSB?
   (c) How do you retrieve a spreadsheet stored on disk?
   (d) What is the difference between the command strings, /FCAN and /FCAE?

9. Move and copy operations.
   (a) What is the difference between a move and a copy operation?
   (b) How do you invoke the copy command?
   (c) How do you invoke the move command?
   (d) What is the difference between a relative and an absolute cell address?
   (e) What is the difference between the cell address A10 and $A$10?
   (f) How many cells would be moved (copied) if the range is (A1...B4)?
   (g) Explain how pointing may be used to specify cell addresses

10. Dates.
    (a) What is the difference between @TODAY and @DATE(91,1,21) given that the current date is in fact January 21, 1991.
    (b) What value will be returned in a cell whose contents are @DATE(91,1,21)-@DATE(91,1,15)?
    (c) What is the significance of the integer value returned by all date functions?
    (d) How do you change the displayed format of a date function?
    (e) Explain how to use the various date functions to compute an individual's age given his or her birth date?

11. Macros. What is the significance of the following keystrokes used in conjunction with macros?
    (a) Alt+F2 (Lotus)
        Alt+F1 (VP Planner)
    (b) /RNLR
    (c) Alt+F5 (Lotus 2.2 only)
    (d) /WL (Lotus 2.2 only)
    (e) \0

12. More macros.
    (a) Where, within a spreadsheet, should macros be kept?
    (b) How are macros named?
    (c) How are macros executed?
    (d) Explain how to create a macro
    (e) Explain the purpose of each row in a user-defined menu.
    (f) Explain how to invoke a user-defined menu once it has been established?

13. Graphs.
    (a) Is every PC or PC-compatible computer capable of producing graphs; i.e. is any additional hardware required?
    (b) What difference, if any, is there in the procedure for printing graphs in Lotus and VP Planner Plus?
    (c) What is the difference between the /GS and /GNC commands?
    (d) What is the maximum number of quantitative variables which can be plotted on the same graph?
    (e) What does the /GR command do?

Answers to Lotus/VP Planner Plus Self-Evaluation

1. (a) To load Lotus (VP Planner) do the following:
   On systems with a hard disk:
   Type **CD \LOTUS** (VPPLUS)
   Type **LOTUS** (VPP)
   On a two drive floppy system:
   Place program disk in drive A and data disk in drive B
   Type **LOTUS** (VPP)
   (b) **Worksheet Global Default Directory** changes the default directory so that the spreadsheets are stored separately from the program files. This command is normally issued during the installation procedure.

2. (a) Number
   (b) Error (Try it)
   (c) Label (Left justified)
   (d) Label (Centered)
   (e) Label
   (f) Formula
   (g) Formula
   (h) Label (Functions begin @ sign)
   (i) Function
   (j) Error (Missing right parenthesis)

3. (a) F1
   (b) Home
   (c) F5 followed by the cell address
   (d) F2
   (e) Home (after the edit mode is entered)
   (f) F9
   (g) Esc
   (h) Alt+F5

4. (a) 140
   (b) 5
   (c) 30
   (d) 30
   (e) 5
   (f) 5
   (g) A random number between 4 and 7
   (h) 6
   (i) 6
   (j) 25
   (k) 25

5. (a) 3
   (b) 6 1/3
   (c) 81
   (d) 1 (exponentiation is done before division)
   (e) 6 (division and multiplication proceed from left to right)

6. (a) Changes the width of all columns to 10
   (b) Deletes a row
   (c) Implements vertical windows
   (d) Fills the current cell with equal signs
   (e) Formats a range to integer numbers with no decimal points
   (f) Freezes vertical titles
   (g) Inserts a column
   (h) Retrieves a spreadsheet
   (i) Initiates the copy command
   (j) Initiates the move command
   (k) Combines a spreadsheet file with current worksheet
   (l) Saves a spreadsheet
   (m) Initiates date format

7. (a) Automatic recalculation
   (b) Changes to manual recalculation
   (c) CALC appears in the lower right portion of the screen
   (d) To save time when there is significant data entry and extensive calculation
   (e) Press the F9 function key
   (f) Issue the command sequence /WGRA

8. (a) /FS (File Save)
   (b) The File Save Replace command saves the spreadsheet in memory overwriting the existing WK1 file with the same name. The File Save Backup command also saves the spreadsheet in memory, but retains the previous WK1 version with a BAK extension.
   (c) /FR (File Retrieve)
   (d) /FCAN (File Combine Add Named-Range) combines a portion (range) of the indicated spreadsheet; /FCAE combines the entire spreadsheet

9. (a) A move operation transfers cells from one place in the spreadsheet to another; a copy operation duplicates the cells in two places
   (b) /C
   (c) /M
   (d) If a cell containing a formula involving a relative cell is copied to another location the cell address changes accordingly; if however the same copy operation is done on a cell containing an absolute address, it (the address) doesn't change.
   (e) A10 is a relative address; $A$10 is an absolute address
   (f) Eight (A1 and B4 are the cell addresses in the upper left and lower right positions of the rectangle which make up the range)
   (g) Simply use the arrow keys to move to the desired cell(s)

10. (a) @TODAY returns the system date and hence changes from day to day. @DATE always returns the indicated date regardless of the system date. The two functions in the example return the same value only on January 21, 1991.
    (b) 6. The @DATE functin returns an integer number of days between the indicated date and the start of the century. Subtracting one @DATE function from another yields the number of days between the two.
    (c) It is the number of days in this century; i.e. the number of days since January 1, 1900.
    (d) Use the /RFD Range Format Date command, then select the desired format.
    (e) Subtract the @DATE function for the date of birth from @TODAY, then divide the result by 365.

11. (a) Toggles step mode on and off.
    (b) Associates the macro name with the actual keystrokes.
    (c) Toggles the recording mode on and off
    (d) Initiates the learn mode for macro recording, prompting for a range to store the subsequent keystrokes.
    (e) The name of an autoexec macro which is executed automatically when the spreadsheet in which it is contained in loaded.

12. (a) Below and to the right so that they are unaffected by subsequent insertion or deletion of rows and columns.
    (b) A backslash followed by a single letter; there is also a special macro named \0 which is an autoexec macro.
    (c) By pressing the Alt key and the name of the macro; e.g. Alt+C to execute the macro named \C.
    (d) Decide what the macro is to do; write down (record) the necessary keystrokes, then enter the keystrokes as a label in the spreadsheet; name the macro then use /RNLR to associate the name of the macro with the actual keystrokes.
    (e) Row one contains the menu choices, each of which should begin with a different letter; row two contains the associated explanation; row three contains the instructions to be executed.
    (f) A {menucall} statement invokes the user defined menu; the statement should be placed inside of its own macro, and the macro structured to reexecute itself. (See Figure VP.16.)

13. (a) All PCs do not necessarily have graphics capability; i.e. a graphics card is required which may or may not come with the machine.
    (b) VP Planner is simpler as the Print command is part of the graph menu; Lotus requires that you exit the spreadsheet and select PrintGraph.
    (c) /GS creates a PIC file required for printing in Lotus; /GNC saves the graph settings for later modification.
    (d) Six (A, B, C, D, E, and F ranges)
    (e) Resets graph parameters

dBASE III Plus[1]

Introduction

The dBASE series remains the dominant data management software for the IBM PC (see the Corporate Profile on Ashton-Tate in Chapter 11). Beginning with the introduction of dBASE II in January 1981 (before the announcement of the PC), and continuing with dBASE III in 1984, dBASE III PLUS in 1986, and dBASE IV in 1988, the dBASE series has become the standard against which others are judged.

The exercises in this section are written for the educational version of dBASE III PLUS, a fully functional version of the commercial program except that it is limited to files with 31 records. You can, of course, use the commercial version if it is available to you. You can also use dBASE IV (should you have it) to do the exercises, as all of the commands we cover will run without modification in the latter program.

Installation

You must install the educational version of dBASE prior to its initial use, in order to customize the program for your particular configuration. If, however, you are using the full blown version of dBASE III PLUS or dBASE IV, and the program has already been installed, skip this section. (If it has not yet been installed, follow the instructions in the manual.)

The installation procedure is straightforward and essentially the same for systems with or without a hard disk. To install the program boot the system, then type **A:** to change the default drive to drive A. Note too that if your computer has only 256K of RAM, you have to use DOS 2.10 and cannot use DOS 3.X or higher. Now place the first dBASE disk (disk 1) in drive A and type **INSTALL** to execute the batch file INSTALL.BAT (which is contained on the dBASE disk). You should see the following on your monitor:

---

[1] Although the exercises in this section are written for dBASE III PLUS, *they will run without modification in dBASE IV* as well. There are, however, minor differences in some of the screens which are noted as they occur throughout the hands-on exercises.

dBASE III PLUS SAMPLER INSTALLATION

MEMORY AND DRIVE SELECTION
A. 256K and 2 floppy drives
B. More than 256k and 2 floppy drives
C. 256k and 1 floppy drive and 1 hard disk
D. More than 256k and 1 floppy drive and 1 hard disk

Type the letter corresponding to your computer's configuration:

Enter the appropriate response (the system will not accept an invalid entry), then follow the indicated instructions. The installation procedure ends with instructions to reboot your computer (i.e. to press **Ctrl**, **Alt**, and **Del**) and load dBASE, a procedure which is described in the first hands-on exercise.

If you are using a hard disk, you will find it advantageous to use different subdirectories for your program files and your data files. In other words just as you use different drives to hold your program disk and your data disk in a floppy drive configuration, you should use different subdirectories on your hard disk. Accordingly, enter the command **MD C:\DATAFILE** to create the subdirectory DATAFILE on your hard disk. You should also be aware that the installation procedure has created a subdirectory named SAMPLER on your hard disk, and has copied the dBASE program files into that directory. The installation process has also placed a CONFIG.SYS file on the root directory, and has renamed the preexisting CONFIG.SYS file (if it existed) to CONFIGS.OLD. Accordingly, check the contents of the latter file to determine if any of the preexisting commands need to be added to the newer version.

Hands-On Exercise 1:
Load dBASE

Objective: Load dBASE; the procedure differs depending on your configuration (i.e., whether you are using a hard drive or two floppy drives).

Step 1a: Load dBASE (with two floppy drives)
Boot the computer with a DOS disk in drive A and a formatted disk (for your data files) in drive B. Place the first (of two) dBASE program disks in drive A. Type **dBASE** to load the program, at which point you will see the screen of Figure DB.1a.

Insert the second sampler disk as indicated and press the return key as instructed; the ASSIST menu of dBASE III PLUS will appear as shown in Figure DB.1b.

178 dBASE Hands-On Exercises

```
┌─────────────────────────────────────────────────────────────┐
│              dBASE III PLUS   version 1.0   IBM/MSDOS DEMO  │
│     Copyright (c) Ashton-Tate 1984, 1985, 1986.  All Rights Reserved. │
│            dBASE, dBASE III, dBASE III PLUS, and Ashton-Tate │
│                   are trademarks of Ashton-Tate             │
│                                                             │
│                                                             │
│     You may use the dBASE III PLUS software and  printed materials in │
│     the dBASE III PLUS software package under the terms  of the dBASE │
│     III  PLUS  Software  License Agreement.  In summary, Ashton-Tate │
│     grants you a paid-up,  non-transferable,  personal license to use │
│     dBASE III PLUS on one  microcomputer or workstation.   You do not │
│     become the owner of  the package,  nor do  you have  the right to │
│     copy or alter the software or printed materials.  You are legally │
│     accountable  for any violation of  the  License  Agreement  or of │
│     copyright, trademark, or trade secret laws.             │
└─────────────────────────────────────────────────────────────┘
```

`Command Line    |<B:>|                    |           |          |`

Press ⏎ to assent to the License Agreement and begin dBASE III PLUS.

(a) Opening Screen

```
Set Up  Create  Update  Position  Retrieve  Organize Modify Tools  10:30:31 am
┌──────────────────┐
│ Database file    │
├──────────────────┤
│ Format for Screen│
│ Query            │
├──────────────────┤
│ Catalog          │
│ View             │
├──────────────────┤
│ Quit dBASE III PLUS │
└──────────────────┘
```

`ASSIST         |<B:>|          |Opt: 1/6   |          |`
Move selection bar - ↑↓. Select - ⏎. Leave menu - ↔. Help -F1. Exit - Esc.

(b) ASSIST Mode and Opening Menu

Figure DB.1 - Loading dBASE III PLUS

Step 1b: Exit to the dBASE Prompt

Press the **Esc** key to exit from the ASSIST menu of Figure DB.1 which will bring you to the dot prompt. Your screen will be much simpler, as it contains only the dot prompt and status line as shown in Figure DB.2.

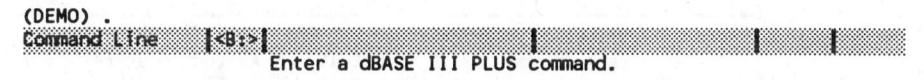

```
(DEMO) .
Command Line    |<B:>|                    |                    |          |
                    Enter a dBASE III PLUS command.
```

Figure DB.2 - Dot Prompt and Status Line

The only indication that you are running the education version of dBASE III Plus as opposed to the full blown version is the appearance of the word DEMO at the dot prompt. Note too the indication of drive B as the default drive, i.e. the drive to which dBASE will look for all of its data files. (Note, however, that when you load dBASE from a hard disk, drive C will appear as the default drive.)

Step 2a: Load dBASE (with a hard drive)

The easiest way to load dBASE on a hard drive is to log into the directory containing your data files, then load dBASE by setting a path to the directory containing the program files. Accordingly enter the commands:

CD C:\DATAFILE   to log into the DATAFILE directory created at the end of the installation procedure above

PATH C:\SAMPLER   where SAMPLER is the directory containing the dBASE educational version; you may need to indicate a different path, e.g., C:\DBASE, if you have the full blown version of either dBASE III PLUS or dBASE IV.

DBASE   to load dBASE, whereupon you will see the screens of Figures DB.1a and b (or alternatively, Figures DB.3a and b if you are using dBASE IV.)

Step 2b: Exit to the dBASE Prompt

Press the **Esc** key to exit the ASSIST menu of Figure DB.1 (or the Control Center in Figure DB.3) and end at the dot prompt shown in Figure DB.2. Note too, that if you are using dBASE IV, there will be an additional prompt asking whether you wish to terminate the operation. Answer Yes.

```
┌─────────────────────────────────────────┬───────────────────────────────┐
│                                         │              Ashton-Tate      │
│      This software is licensed to:      │              Ashton-Tate      │
│                                         │              Ashton-Tate      │
│           Robert T. Grauer              │              Ashton-Tate      │
│           Author/Consultant             │              Ashton-Tate      │
│                                         │              Ashton-Tate      │
│                                         │              Ashton-Tate      │
├─────────────────────────────────────────┴───────────────────────────────┤
│     Copyright (c) Ashton-Tate Corporation 1985,1986,1987,1988. All      │
│     Rights Reserved. dBASE, dBASE IV and Ashton-Tate are trademarks     │
│                       of Ashton-Tate Corporation.                       │
│   You may use the software and  printed  materials in  the dBASE IV     │
│   package  under  the  terms  of  the  Software License Agreement;      │
│   please  read it.  In summary, Ashton-Tate grants you a paid-up,       │
│   non-transferable, personal  license  to  use  dBASE  IV on  one       │
│   computer  work  station.  You  do  not become  the  owner  of the     │
│   package nor do  you  have  the  right  to  copy  (except permitted    │
│   backups  of  the  software)  or  alter  the  software  or printed     │
│   materials.  You are legally accountable for any violation of the      │
│   License Agreement and copyright, trademark, or trade secret law.      │
├─────────────────────────────────────────────────────────────────────────┤
│     Press ⏎ to assent to the License Agreement and begin dBASE IV       │
└─────────────────────────────────────────────────────────────────────────┘
```

(a) The Opening Screen

```
   Catalog   Tools   Exit                                      3:22:28 pm
                           dBASE IV CONTROL CENTER
                         CATALOG: C:\DBASE\SAMPLES.CAT

         Data      Queries     Forms     Reports     Labels    Applications
      ┌─────────┬──────────┬──────────┬──────────┬──────────┬──────────┐
      │<create> │ <create> │ <create> │ <create> │ <create> │ <create> │
      │         │          │          │          │          │          │
      │         │          │          │          │          │          │
      │         │          │          │          │          │          │
      │         │          │          │          │          │          │
      │         │          │          │          │          │          │
      │         │          │          │          │          │          │
      └─────────┴──────────┴──────────┴──────────┴──────────┴──────────┘

   File:         New file
   Description:  Press ENTER on <create> to create a new file

   Help:F1  Use:⏎   Data:F2  Design:Shift-F2  Quick Report:Shift-F9  Menus:F10
```

(b) Control Center

Figure DB.3 - Loading dBASE IV

A First Look at dBASE

Our approach to teaching dBASE is to get you on the computer as quickly as possible. Accordingly, rather than cover every detail of every command, we present an overview of basic commands, describe their general purpose, then turn you loose with a hands-on exercise. Programming in dBASE (or any other language) is best learned by doing, and the sooner you are on the computer the better. Table 1 contains the commands you will use in the first two exercises.

Commands affecting the file structure:
  CREATE, DISPLAY STRUCTURE, MODIFY STRUCTURE

Commands for data entry:
  APPEND, BROWSE, EDIT, DELETE, PACK, RECALL

Commands for data manipulation:
  DISPLAY, LIST, SUM, AVERAGE, COUNT

Commands associated with indexing:
  INDEX ON, SET INDEX TO

Miscellaneous commands:
  HELP, ASSIST, USE, SET DEFAULT, GOTO, QUIT

Table 1- Elementary dBASE Commands

Every dBASE application begins with the **CREATE** command to establish a file structure, which specifies the order of fields within a record, as well as the name, length, and data type for each field. Once the file structure has been created, you can **DISPLAY STRUCTURE** to see if it is correct and if not, **MODIFY STRUCTURE** to change it accordingly.

The **APPEND** command adds records to a dBASE file. You can change the data in individual records with the **EDIT** command, or view several records at once with the **BROWSE** command. You can remove records from a file, but will need two commands to do it. The **DELETE** command marks records for removal, but does not physically remove the records from the file (i.e. dBASE gives you a chance to change your mind and **RECALL** records slated for deletion). It is the **PACK** command that permanently (i.e. physically) removes the records marked for deletion.

The **DISPLAY** or **LIST** command shows some or all of the data for one or more records in the file; i.e. you can display one record, every record, or only those records which meet a specified criterion (e.g. employees in Florida). The **SUM, COUNT,** and **AVERAGE** commands are used for elementary arithmetic operations. SUM will total the value of a numeric field(s) for some or all of the records within the file; e.g. it can calculate the sum of every salary, or just the salaries of those records containing a title of "Manager". COUNT, on the other hand, will determine the number of records in the file or the number of records which meet a given criterion. In similar fashion, the AVERAGE command can be made to apply to every record within a file, or only to a subset.

The **INDEX ON** command creates an index that enables you to access records in a logical sequence different from the physical order in which records were entered initially. The **SET INDEX** command opens an existing index (as opposed to creating it) and determines the sequence in which records are accessed.

The **HELP** and **ASSIST** commands are sources of additional on-line information. HELP provides detailed information on any given command, whereas ASSIST initiates the dBASE III PLUS Assistant, which guides you via menus in the construction of dBASE commands.

The **USE** command opens an existing dBASE file for processing, the **GOTO** command moves to a specific record within a file, and the **SET DEFAULT** command establishes the default drive. (The default drive is the one dBASE searches for existing files, and/or the drive to which dBASE writes any new files it creates.) The **QUIT** command exits dBASE (closing any files which were opened) and returns to DOS.

The hands-on exercise which follows illustrates how the data entry and data retrieval functions are implemented in dBASE, and in so doing introduces you to several dBASE commands. We think you will understand what the commands do from the way in which they are used in the exercise, but we include additional explanation after the exercise.

Hands-On Exercise 2:
File Maintenance

Objective: Define a file structure, and demonstrate the ability to add, modify and delete records. (Corresponds to Hands-on Exercise 1 in Chapter 11).

Step 1: **Load dBASE**

Load dBASE as you did in the first hands-on exercise, following the steps for your particular configuration. Establish the default drive as drive B or C respectively, depending on whether you are working with two floppy drives or a hard drive. End at the dot prompt.

Step 2: **Define the File Structure**

Type **CREATE** at the dot prompt and dBASE responds by asking for the name of the file you wish to create. Enter **EMPLOYEE** (or any other suitable name).

dBASE next displays a new screen in which you are asked to enter the information for the file structure by describing each field, one field at a time. The process is interactive, easy to do, and is shown in Figure DB.4. (The upper portion of Figure DB.4 contains information on cursor control; you may remove this display, and thus have more room to view your file structure, by pressing the F1 key.)

```
                                                     Bytes remaining:    3933

    CURSOR   <-- -->      INSERT            DELETE       Up a field:     ↑
      Char:    ← →         Char:  Ins        Char:  Del  Down a field:   ↓
      Word: Home End       Field: ^N         Word:  ^Y   Exit/Save:      ^End
      Pan:    ^← ^→        Help:  F1         Field: ^U   Abort:          Esc

         Field Name   Type       Width  Dec          Field Name  Type      Width  Dec

      1  SOCSECNUM    Character     9
      2  NAME         Character    16
      3  TITLE        Character    16
      4  SALARY       Numeric       6    0
      5  HIREDATE     Date          8
      6  LOCATION     Character    12
      7               Character

    CREATE         |<B:>|EMPLOYEE              |Field: 7/7       |       | Caps
    Field names begin with a letter and may contain letters, digits and underscores
                              Enter the field name.
```

Figure DB.4 - Creating a File Structure

Enter the name of the first field, **SOCSECNUM**, and press the return key. Specify the type of field (character) by typing the letter **C** (social security number is defined as a character rather than a numeric field because it will never be used in arithmetic operations). Finally enter the width of the field as 9, then press the return key to move to the next field. (Note that for numeric fields only, e.g. SALARY, you will also have to specify the number of decimal places, if any). Repeat this procedure for the other fields in the figure.

When information for the last field (LOCATION in the example) has been entered, press the return key immediately to signify the end of the file structure. dBASE will ask you to press return a second time to confirm that you are finished. It will next ask if you wish to enter data at this time. Answer **N** (for no), and you will be returned to the dot prompt.

Step 3: Verify the File Structure

Type **DISPLAY STRUCTURE** to view the completed file structure as shown below:

```
Structure for database: B:EMPLOYEE.dbf
Number of data records:       0
Date of last update   : 05/06/88
Field  Field Name  Type       Width    Dec
    1  SOCSECNUM   Character      9
    2  NAME        Character     16
    3  TITLE       Character     16
    4  SALARY      Numeric        6
    5  HIREDATE    Date           8
    6  LOCATION    Character     12
** Total **                      68
```

The command shows the file name EMPLOYEE.DBF (note that dBASE has automatically added the extension DBF to the filename you previously supplied with the CREATE command). The command also indicates the field names you specified, the type and width of each field, the order in which the fields appear within a record, the number of records in the file (none to this point), and the date of the last file update.

Verify that the file structure is exactly as you intend it to be. (Do not be concerned that the total number of positions in the record, 68 in our example, is one more than the sum of the individual field lengths, as dBASE uses this extra position to determine if a record is marked for deletion). If you find an error, e.g. an extra or omitted field, an incorrect data type, wrong size field, etc., you can change the file structure as described in Step 4.

Step 4: Modify the File Structure

If (and only if) your file structure is incorrect, type the command **MODIFY STRUCTURE**, whereupon the original file structure will be displayed on the screen. You will then be able to add or delete fields within a record, or change the name, width, and/or type of an existing field. Do not, however, change both the name and width of a field in the same session or existing data will be lost.

The field name, type, width, and/or number of decimal places in an existing field is changed by moving the cursor to the appropriate position and entering the new value. The **Ins** key acts as a toggle switch in alternating between the insert and replacement modes. Press it once and Ins appears on the status line; press it a second time and Ins disappears. (The **Del** key removes one character at a time).

To delete a field, position the cursor on the field name and press **Ctrl U**. To add a new field, position the cursor at the location where you want the new field and press **Ctrl N**. A template line for the new field will be inserted above the field where the cursor is currently located, and the field information can be entered accordingly.

Press **Ctrl End** to save your changes.

Step 5: **Enter Data for the First Three Records**

Type **APPEND** at the dot prompt to begin entering data, bringing the input template of Figure DB.5 into view. Figure DB.5 displays the field names and input templates (as defined by the file structure) for subsequent data entry. The upper portion of this screen also contains information on cursor control.

```
CURSOR    <-- -->            UP   DOWN    DELETE            Insert Mode:  Ins
  Char:    ←   →     Field:   ↑    ↓      Char:     Del     Exit/Save:    ^End
  Word:   Home End   Page:   PgUp PgDn    Field:    ^Y      Abort:        Esc
                     Help:    F1          Record:   ^U      Memo:         ^Home
```

```
SOCSECNUM
NAME
TITLE
SALARY
HIREDATE      /  /
LOCATION
```

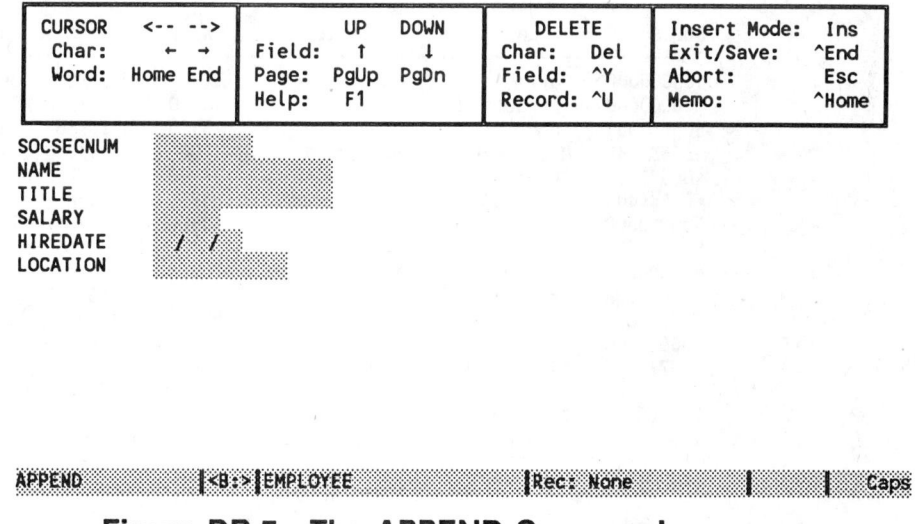

```
APPEND        |<B:>|EMPLOYEE         |Rec: None        |        | Caps
```

Figure DB.5 - The APPEND Command

Enter the data shown in Figure DB.6 (on the next page), beginning with the first record (Davis). Press the return key after completing data for one field in order to move to the next field. The only exception is if the data completely fill the template, as happens for the social security number, in which case dBASE automatically takes you to the next field without pressing the return key. In other words completion of the social security number automatically positions you in the first position of the name field, because the data entered completely fill the space allocated for social security number. You will however, have to press the return key after entering a name in order to move to the title field.

Should you make a mistake during data entry, e.g. typing a letter in a numeric field, dBASE will beep to inform you of the error and at the same time ignore the invalid character. dBASE also beeps when you come to the end of a field (e.g. social security number), to let you know you are at the end of a field, and that the next character entered will be taken as part of the next field.

When you have entered data for the last field in record 1, press the return key to move to record 2 (Friedel). After completing the entries for this individual, press the return key once more to bring up a blank input screen for the third record, and enter data for this record as well.

Press **Ctrl End** to terminate data entry at this point. (The remaining records will be appended to the file in step 9.) Be sure to press Ctrl End while still in the input template for record 3; i.e. before record 4 comes up, otherwise a blank record will be appended to the file.

```
Soc Sec Num   Last Name      Title          Salary   Hired      Location
-----------------------------------------------------------------------
100000000     Davis          Account Rep    34000    01/02/86   Boston
200000000     Friedel        Manager        48000    02/17/84   Miami
300000000     Kendrick       Account Rep    26500    02/16/86   Miami
333333333     McGrath        Account Rep    37000    04/25/86   Chicago
400000000     Cordell        Account Rep    27200    04/02/87   Boston
444444444     Facella        Account Rep    24750    01/15/87   Los Angeles
500000000     Pattishall     Account Rep    38500    11/11/84   Miami
555555555     Ferraro        Account Rep    26400    02/02/85   Miami
600000000     Tillberg       Manager        35500    10/29/82   Boston
666666666     Grauer         Account Rep    37500    03/16/85   Miami
700000000     Fitzgerald     Manager        53000    04/19/83   Chicago
800000000     Martineau      Manager        48000    02/28/83   Los Angeles
777777777     Ticich         Account Rep    27000    03/16/88   Boston
888888888     Seaman         Account Rep    29000    01/03/86   Los Angeles
900000000     Beyer          Account Rep    32900    01/19/82   Chicago
999999999     Hirschberg     Account Rep    28500    06/19/84   Miami
```

Figure DB.6 - The Employee File (for data entry)

Step 6: **Verify that Data Entry has been Successful**

It is only prudent to check that you have successfully entered records 1, 2, and 3 before expending the effort to enter the rest of the file. Type DISPLAY ALL to view the file just created. dBASE displays the contents of each record (together with its associated record number) as shown in Figure DB.7.

```
. DISPLAY ALL

Record #  SOCSECNUM   NAME       TITLE          SALARY   HIREDATE   LOCATION
      1   100000000   Davis      Account Rep    34000    01/02/86   Boston
      2   200000000   Friedel    Manager        48000    02/17/84   Miami
      3   300000000   Kendrick   Account Rep    26500    02/16/86   Miami
```

Figure DB.7 - The DISPLAY ALL Command

Step 7: Modify Data in Existing Records

Use the results of the DISPLAY ALL command to check that the data have been entered correctly. Should you notice a mistake type EDIT together with the associated record number; for example type **EDIT 1** to retrieve and edit the first record as shown in Figure DB.8.

The EDIT command displays the value of every field in the record, enabling you to change any field in much the same way as data was entered initially. (Alternatively, you can use the BROWSE command to display the contents of several records simultaneously, as opposed to the EDIT command which views only a single record.) The **PgUp** and **PgDn** keys will display the previous and following records, and allow you to continue editing.

Press **Ctrl End** when you have finished editing (or browsing) to return to the dot prompt.

```
CURSOR     <-- -->           UP    DOWN      DELETE              Insert Mode:  Ins
  Char:     ←   →    Field:   ↑     ↓         Char:    Del       Exit/Save:   ^End
  Word:   Home End   Page:  PgUp  PgDn        Field:   ^Y        Abort:        Esc
                     Help:   F1                Record:  ^U        Memo:       ^Home

SOCSECNUM   100000000
NAME        Davis
TITLE       Account Rep
SALARY      34000
HIREDATE    01/02/86
LOCATION    Boston
```

```
EDIT              |<B:>|EMPLOYEE           |Rec: 1/3            |            |
```

Figure DB.8 - The EDIT Command

Step 8: Deleting Records

Two commands, DELETE and PACK, are needed to remove a record from a file, a sequence shown in Figure DB.9. The DELETE command marks a record for deletion, but does not actually remove the record from the file (i.e. the record is logically, but not physically, deleted). In other words dBASE enables you to change your mind and RECALL (undelete) the record, should you desire. Execution of the PACK command, however, permanently (i.e. physically) removes records marked for deletion. (It is necessary however, to move the record pointer to the record in question, prior to issuing the DELETE command, a concept discussed at the end of the exercise.)

Enter the commands in Figure DB.9 to delete the third record.

```
. GOTO 3
. DELETE
   1 record deleted

. DISPLAY ALL
Record #  SOCSECNUM NAME       TITLE         SALARY HIREDATE LOCATION
       1  100000000 Davis      Account Rep    34000 01/02/86 Boston
       2  200000000 Friedel    Manager        48000 02/17/84 Miami
       3 *300000000 Kendrick   Account Rep    26500 02/16/86 Miami
. PACK
   2 records copied

. DISPLAY ALL
Record #  SOCSECNUM NAME       TITLE         SALARY HIREDATE LOCATION
       1  100000000 Davis      Account Rep    34000 01/02/86 Boston
       2  200000000 Friedel    Manager        48000 02/17/84 Miami
```

Figure DB.9 - The DELETE and PACK commands

Step 9: Enter the Remaining Records
Return to Figure DB.6 to enter the 14 remaining employee records into your file. Type **APPEND** at the dBASE prompt and you will be positioned at the third record. You will have to re-enter Kendrick prior to the remaining 13 employees.

Step 10: Exit dBASE
Type **QUIT** at the dot prompt to exit dBASE. You will see a brief message thanking you for using the program, after which you will be returned to DOS. It is extremely important that you exit properly (by typing QUIT) in order that your files are saved correctly to disk. Omitting this step can result in the loss of all records in the file.

The Basics of dBASE

The exercise just completed provides an intuitive appreciation for many commands as they are given from the dot prompt, but in no way suffices as an adequate introduction to dBASE. Indeed we expect the exercise has created at least as many questions as it has answered, especially with respect to how specific commands work.

This section begins a more detailed study of dBASE with presentation of two very basic concepts, the record pointer and dBASE notation. As you shall see, these concepts apply to all commands, and provide a firm foundation for a more formal study of the language.

The Record Pointer

The records within a DBF file are numbered consecutively, beginning with 1; i.e. the first record is record number 1, the second record is record number 2, and so on. dBASE keeps track of its position within a file by maintaining a record pointer which is continually updated as commands are executed. Even when dBASE is searching through an entire file (e.g. during execution of a DISPLAY ALL command), it still processes one record at a time, continually changing the record pointer.

The importance of the record pointer becomes apparent as you review individual commands from the hands-on exercise. The EDIT and DISPLAY commands, for example, affect only a single record, but how is that specific record chosen? The answer is that dBASE chooses whichever record is indicated by the current position of the record pointer.

You can move the record pointer with the GOTO command; e.g. GOTO 2, or simply 2, (entered at the dot prompt) moves the pointer to the second record. Enter DISPLAY at this point and the second record is shown on the monitor. GOTO TOP and GOTO BOTTOM move the pointer to the first and last records respectively.

Suffice it to say that since dBASE knows where it is within a DBF file at any given instant, it is also important for you to know this information. Accordingly you should always be thinking of the record pointer as you execute individual commands.

The dBASE Notation

dBASE uses a simple notation to implicitly explain all of the variations allowed within a given command. Consider, for example, the DISPLAY command and how it would appear in a reference manual or text:

> DISPLAY [<scope>] [<expression list>] [FOR <condition>]
>   [WHILE <condition>]   [OFF] [TO PRINT]

The notation consists of four distinct elements: upper case letters, lower case letters, angled brackets, and square brackets. Upper case letters denote a dBASE term (e.g. DISPLAY, FOR, WHILE, and so on) which must be spelled exactly as it appears within the command. Lower case letters and/or angled brackets < > indicate user supplied information; e.g. field names as they were defined within a file structure. Square brackets [ ] imply optional portions of the command; i.e. clauses which may or may not be included depending on the user's objectives.

Within the DISPLAY command every parameter is enclosed in square brackets, which according to the notation, means that every parameter is optional; in other words the only required portion of the command is the command itself.

The scope of a command refers to the records within a file that are affected by that command. Omission of this parameter (e.g. DISPLAY by itself) results in a

190 dBASE Hands-On Exercises

default value, which in the case of the DISPLAY command is one record, the record that the record pointer is on. A scope of ALL means the command is to be applied to every record in the file, whereas a scope of NEXT 5 applies to the five sequential records beginning with the current record.

The expression list indicates which fields within the file structure are to be displayed. Omission of the parameter means that every field is to be shown, whereas its inclusion states explicitly only those fields which will appear (e.g. TITLE and NAME as shown in Figure DB.10). Specification of OFF causes records to be displayed without the record numbers, whereas TO PRINT directs output to the printer.

The FOR condition further limits which records are to appear (e.g. only those records whose location field is Boston). The condition works within the scope of the command in that all records in the scope are considered, but only those meeting the condition are displayed. Note too, that the condition itself may be a simple or compound condition. The former imposes a single requirement (LOCATION = 'Boston'), whereas the latter joins two or more requirements with the logical operators AND, OR, and NOT (e.g. FOR LOCATION = 'Boston' .AND. TITLE = 'Manager'). Syntactically, dBASE requires that a logical operator (AND, OR, and NOT) be set off with periods.

Variations in the DISPLAY command (to illustrate this notation) are shown in Figure DB.10. This is followed by Table 2 containing a presentation of elementary dBASE commands, again according to this notation.

DISPLAY	DISPLAY is only required entry
DISPLAY ALL OFF	OFF omits record numbers
DISPLAY NEXT 3	Displays all fields for the next three records
DISPLAY ALL NAME,TITLE TO PRINT	Limits the displayed fields
DISPLAY ALL NAME FOR SALARY > 25000	FOR limits displayed records

Figure DB.10 - Variations in the DISPLAY Command

Table 2 contains the same commands listed previously in Table 1, but this time the formal dBASE syntax is included for each command. Were we to say nothing further about the commands in the table, you would (from your knowledge of the dBASE notation) already have a fair understanding of how these commands work.

Commands affecting the file structure:
   CREATE <new file>
   MODIFY STRUCTURE
   DISPLAY STRUCTURE [TO PRINT]

Commands for data entry:
   APPEND
   BROWSE [FIELDS <field list>]
   EDIT [<scope>] [FOR <condition>]
   DELETE [<scope>] [FOR <condition>]
   RECALL [<scope>] [FOR <condition>]
   PACK

Commands for data manipulation:
   DISPLAY [<scope>][<expn list>][FOR <condition>][OFF][TO PRINT]
   LIST [<scope>][<expn list>][FOR <condition>][OFF][TO PRINT]
   SUM [<expression list>] [<scope>] [FOR <condition>]
   AVERAGE [<scope>] [<expression list>] [FOR <condition>]
   COUNT [<scope>] [FOR <condition>]

Commands associated with indexing:
   INDEX ON <key expression> TO <file-name>
   SET INDEX TO <index file list>

Miscellaneous commands:
   HELP <command name>
   ASSIST
   QUIT
   USE [<filename>]
   SET DEFAULT TO <drive name>
   GOTO <record number>

Table 2 - Syntax of Elementary dBASE Commands

Consider, for example, the SUM, AVERAGE, and COUNT commands, and how their syntax is similar to the DISPLAY command just explained. Only the command names themselves (SUM, AVERAGE, and COUNT) are required in their respective commands; i.e. all other entries are enclosed in square brackets and consequently are optional. Hence SUM with no scope and no expression list, will total the value of each numerical field over all records within the DBF file (the default scope is ALL). Inclusion of an expression list (e.g. SUM SALARY), causes only the fields mentioned to be totaled, just as its inclusion in a DISPLAY statement causes only those fields to be displayed. The AVERAGE and COUNT commands function in similar fashion.

Return briefly to the hands-on exercise, reviewing the various commands with respect to the syntax presented in Table 2. Try to determine why individual parameters were selected (or omitted) as we sought to introduce the dBASE commands. Repeat some or all of the steps in the exercise, with additional command variations you would like to try.

The dBASE Help Facility

As you work with dBASE, questions will inevitably arise about the syntax and/or capabilities of individual commands, which can be answered in part with the dBASE HELP command. To enter the on-line help facility, simply type HELP at the dot prompt. The system returns the opening HELP main menu of Figure DB.11a, which prompts you for one of six possible responses. Entering a 6 for example, produces the Commands and Functions menu of Figure DB.11b. Enter a number from 1 to 5, to obtain additional information as indicated.

Figure DB.11c contains a list of the Starter Set Commands, many of which should look familiar. At this point you can enter any number from 1 to 44 (as shown in the command menu), to obtain detailed information on the command in question. Figure DB.11d, for example, shows the help screen associated with the DISPLAY command. (A shortcut to obtaining help on a particular command, is to type HELP followed by the name of the command; e.g. HELP DISPLAY.)

```
Help Main Menu

1 - Getting Started
2 - What Is a ...
3 - How Do I ...
4 - Creating a Database File
5 - Using an Existing Database File
6 - Commands and Functions
```

(a) Opening Help Menu
(Entered by typing HELP at the dot prompt)

```
dBASE III PLUS Commands and Functions

1 - Commands (Starter Set)
2 - Commands (Advanced Set)
3 - Functions
4 - SET TO Commands
5 - SET ON/OFF Commands
```

(b) Commands and Functions Menu
(Entered by selecting 6 in Figure DB.11a)

```
            dBASE III PLUS Commands --- Starter Set

 1 - ?          12 - DELETE FILE   23 - LABEL     34 - REPORT
 2 - APPEND     13 - DIR           24 - LIST      35 - SCREEN
 3 - AVERAGE    14 - DISPLAY       25 - LOCATE    36 - SEEK
 4 - BROWSE     15 - DO            26 - MODIFY    37 - SET
 5 - CHANGE     16 - EDIT          27 - PACK      38 - SKIP
 6 - CLEAR      17 - ERASE         28 - QUERY     39 - SORT
 7 - CONTINUE   18 - EXPORT        29 - QUIT      40 - STORE
 8 - COPY       19 - FIND          30 - RECALL    41 - SUM
 9 - COUNT      20 - GO/GOTO       31 - RELEASE   42 - TOTAL
10 - CREATE     21 - IMPORT        32 - RENAME    43 - TYPE
11 - DELETE     22 - INDEX         33 - REPLACE   44 - USE
```

(c) Starter Set Menu
(Entered by selecting 1 in Figure DB.11b)

```
                         DISPLAY
Syntax      : DISPLAY [<scope>] [<expression list>] [FOR <condition>]
              [WHILE <condition>] [OFF] [TO PRINT]

Description : Lists the current record.  Use DISPLAY with
              a scope and an expression list to see selected fields or
              a combination of fields.  Use the FOR and WHILE conditions
              to display specific contents of the records.  Use TO PRINT
              to get a hard copy of the list, and use OFF to suppress
              the record numbers.  DISPLAY lists with periodic pauses.
```

(d) DISPLAY Help Menu
(Entered by selecting 14 in Figure DB.11c)

Figure DB.11 - dBASE HELP Screens

The dBASE Assistant

The dBASE Assistant is a menu-driven feature intended to help in the construction of individual commands. Type **ASSIST** at the dot prompt and you will be presented with the opening Assistant menu of Figure DB.12. (You can press the **Esc** key to make the menu disappear). Once the Assistant is active (i.e. ASSIST has been typed at the dot prompt), the left and right arrow keys switch from one menu to the next, whereas the up and down keys go from option to option within a menu.

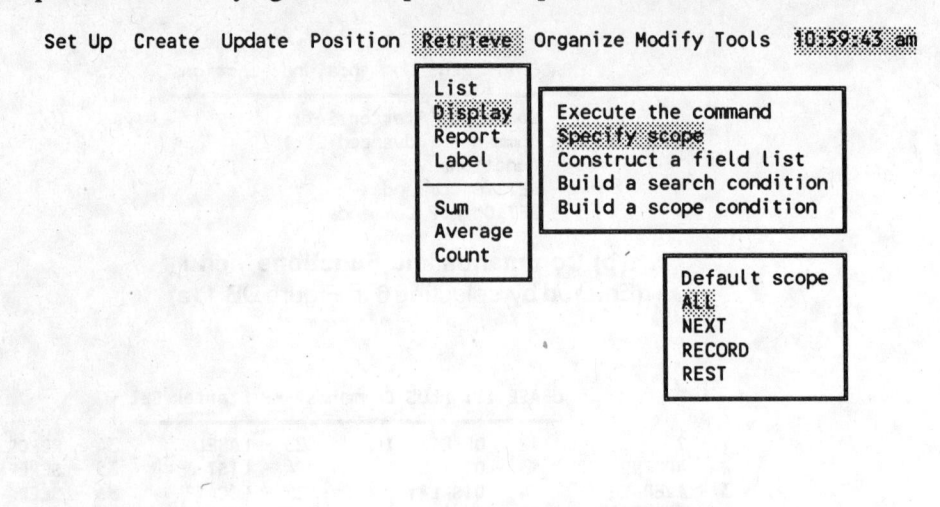

```
      Set Up  Create  Update  Position  Retrieve  Organize Modify Tools   10:59:43 am
                                 ┌─────────┐
                                 │ List    │
                                 │ Display │ ┌──────────────────────────┐
                                 │ Report  │ │ Execute the command      │
                                 │ Label   │ │ Specify scope            │
                                 ├─────────┤ │ Construct a field list   │
                                 │ Sum     │ │ Build a search condition │
                                 │ Average │ │ Build a scope condition  │
                                 │ Count   │ └──────────────────────────┘
                                 └─────────┘
                                                    ┌──────────────────┐
                                                    │ Default scope    │
                                                    │ ALL              │
                                                    │ NEXT             │
                                                    │ RECORD           │
                                                    │ REST             │
                                                    └──────────────────┘



Command: DISPLAY ALL
ASSIST         |<B:>|EMPLOYEE              |Rec: 3/3        |              |
                  Position selection bar - ↑↓.  Select - ↵.
```

Figure DB.12 - The dBASE Assistant
(Display has been selected from the Retrieve Menu)

The major advantage of the Assistant is its ability to guide you in the step by step construction of various commands as they would be entered from the dot prompt. To recreate Figure DB.12 for example, press the return key after highlighting the Display command from the Retrieve menu. A second menu (box) will appear at the right of the screen. Select "Specify scope" which in turn produces the last menu at the bottom right of the figure. You would now use the up and down arrow keys to choose the desired scope; e.g. ALL and press return.

The end result is the construction of the command, DISPLAY ALL, which appears in the lower left portion of the figure. Many people find the Assistant helpful in that it cuts down on typing, eliminates spelling errors, and "painlessly" teaches the command syntax. Our personal preference however, is not to use it as we find it just as easy to type in commands in their entirety at the dot prompt, rather than constructing them piecemeal via the Assistant. We leave you to your own conclusions. Press **Esc** to leave ASSIST and return to the dot prompt.

Hands-On Exercise 3:
Data Analysis

Objective: Use the existing employee file to demonstrate dBASE's capability to manipulate data and duplicate the reports of Figures 11.2 through 11.4 in the text. The various reports are produced through combinations of sequence, selection, and calculation. (Corresponds to Hands-on Exercise 2 in Chapter 11).

Step 1: **Load dBASE**
Load dBASE as you did previously, ending at the dot prompt.

Step 2: **Retrieve the Existing Employee File**
Be sure the status line indicates the default drive containing your data files. If necessary you can change the default drive with the SET DEFAULT command; e.g. the command **SET DEFAULT TO B** changes the default drive to drive B. Now enter the command **USE EMPLOYEE** to retrieve the EMPLOYEE.DBF file created in the first exercise. The USE command opens (i.e. uses) an existing DBF file and positions the record pointer to the first record.

Step 3: **Create an Index File**
The INDEX ON command creates an index file that allows records in a DBF file to be accessed in an order different from the physical sequence in which they were entered.

Enter the command **INDEX ON NAME TO NAME** to create the index file NAME.NDX, which is based on the key field NAME (found in the EMPLOYEE.DBF file). The syntax of the command, INDEX ON key-expression TO file-name, requires both a key expression (typically a field name) and a file-name. We like to use the same entry for both (e.g. NAME), so that the name of the index file identifies the key field on which it is based.

The results of the INDEX ON command are shown in Figure DB.13. The system indicates that 16 records have been indexed, and the subsequent DISPLAY ALL commands lists the records according to the newly created index. Remember too, that the INDEX ON command creates a separate file, NAME.NDX in the example, which exists on the default drive. Hence, once the index has been created, you can use the command SET INDEX TO NAME to list records according to the index, rather than recreating the index with another INDEX ON command.

```
. USE EMPLOYEE

. INDEX ON NAME TO NAME
  100% indexed          16 Records indexed

. DISPLAY ALL

Record #  SOCSECNUM  NAME         TITLE        SALARY  HIREDATE  LOCATION
      15  900000000  Beyer        Account Rep   32900  01/19/82  Chicago
       5  400000000  Cordell      Account Rep   27200  04/02/87  Boston
       1  100000000  Davis        Account Rep   34000  01/02/86  Boston
       6  444444444  Facella      Account Rep   24750  01/15/87  Los Angeles
       8  555555555  Ferraro      Account Rep   26400  02/02/85  Miami
      11  700000000  Fitzgerald   Manager       53000  04/19/83  Chicago
       2  200000000  Friedel      Manager       48000  02/17/84  Miami
      10  666666666  Grauer       Account Rep   37500  03/16/85  Miami
      16  999999999  Hirschberg   Account Rep   28500  06/19/84  Miami
       3  300000000  Kendrick     Account Rep   26500  02/16/86  Miami
      12  800000000  Martineau    Manager       48000  02/28/83  Los Angeles
       4  333333333  McGrath      Account Rep   37000  04/25/86  Chicago
       7  500000000  Pattishall   Account Rep   38500  11/11/84  Miami
      14  888888888  Seaman       Account Rep   29000  01/03/86  Los Angeles
      13  777777777  Ticich       Account Rep   27000  03/16/88  Boston
       9  600000000  Tillberg     Manager       35500  10/29/82  Boston
```

Figure DB.13 - The USE and INDEX ON Commands

Step 4:   Generate the Exception Reports

Enter the commands in Figure DB.14 to produce the exception reports from Chapter 11 in the text. Each report is created with a DISPLAY command and associated selection criteria (through use of the FOR parameter). Note too that a different index is used for each report, so that the selected employees are listed in different sequences.

Step 5:   Experiment

You have developed three illustrative reports, but the possibilities are endless. We showed how you can list records in a report in different sequences (ascending or descending order on any field within the file structure). We also showed how you can list only those records meeting a specified criteria or only a designated number of records in a file. Practice makes perfect, so experiment away, creating additional reports of your own design.

```
. USE EMPLOYEE

. INDEX ON NAME TO NAME
   100% indexed          16 Records indexed

. DISPLAY ALL NAME,SALARY,HIREDATE,LOCATION FOR TITLE = 'Manager' OFF

  NAME          SALARY HIREDATE LOCATION
  Fitzgerald    53000  04/19/83 Chicago
  Friedel       48000  02/17/84 Miami
  Martineau     48000  02/28/83 Los Angeles
  Tillberg      35500  10/29/82 Boston
```

(a) Employees who are Managers

```
. INDEX ON -SALARY TO SALARY
   100% indexed          16 Records indexed
```
to sort salaries in descending order

```
. DISPLAY ALL NAME,SALARY,HIREDATE,TITLE,LOCATION FOR SALARY > 35000 OFF

  NAME          SALARY HIREDATE TITLE         LOCATION
  Fitzgerald    53000  04/19/83 Manager       Chicago
  Friedel       48000  02/17/84 Manager       Miami
  Martineau     48000  02/28/83 Manager       Los Angeles
  Pattishall    38500  11/11/84 Account Rep   Miami
  Grauer        37500  03/16/85 Account Rep   Miami
  McGrath       37000  04/25/86 Account Rep   Chicago
  Tillberg      35500  10/29/82 Manager       Boston
```

(b) Employees earning more than $35,000

```
. INDEX ON HIREDATE TO HIREDATE
   100% indexed          16 Records indexed

. DISPLAY ALL NAME,SALARY,HIREDATE,TITLE FOR LOCATION = 'Miami' OFF

  NAME          SALARY HIREDATE TITLE
  Friedel       48000  02/17/84 Manager
  Hirschberg    28500  06/19/84 Account Rep
  Pattishall    38500  11/11/84 Account Rep
  Ferraro       26400  02/02/85 Account Rep
  Grauer        37500  03/16/85 Account Rep
  Kendrick      26500  02/16/86 Account Rep
```

(c) Miami Employees by Seniority

Figure DB.14 - Exception Reports

Hands-On Exercise 4:
Menu Driven Programs

Objective: To demonstrate the dBASE command mode through the development of a menu-driven program. (Corresponds to Hands-on Exercise 1 in Chapter 12, although the data are different. This program is based on 30 arbitrarily chosen countries, rather than the 50 United States as the latter exceeds the 31 records permitted with the student version of dBASE, and hence is not suitable.)

Step 1: **Create the Menu-Driven Program**
Use a word processor to create the menu driven program of Figure DB.15, saving it as the file MENU.PRG. (The vertical lines in Figure DB.15 are only to facilitate your understanding of the program and are not to be typed in.) *Be sure to save the file as an ASCII file.*

The procedure you use to load the word processor will depend on whether or not you are using a hard disk. Accordingly:

With two floppy drives:
Place the word processing program in drive A and a formatted data disk in drive B. Eventually you will replace the word processing disk in drive A with the (first) dBASE program disk; you will, however, continue to use the same data disk in drive B with both the word processor and dBASE.

With a hard disk:
Enter the command **CD C:\DATAFILE** to change to the directory containing your data files. (This is the same command you have been using prior to loading dBASE.) Now set the appropriate path to your word processor; e.g. PATH C:\WP51, then load the word processor.

Try to gain a conceptual understanding of the program. It is not necessary to understand the precise syntax of dBASE, but you should be able to follow the program's logic. Observe how the program is restricted to the basic building blocks of structured programming (sequence, selection, iteration, and case), and how the logic flows from the top, down.

Step 2: **Load dBASE**
Exit from the word processor, then load dBASE as you did in the previous hands-on exercises.

```
CLEAR
SET BELL OFF
SET TALK OFF
@ 3,23 SAY 'WORLD DATABASE REPORT MENU'
@ 6,23 SAY '   A) AREA REPORT'
@ 7,23 SAY '   B) 1989 POPULATION REPORT'
@ 8,23 SAY '   C) DATE OF ADMISSION REPORT'
@ 9,23 SAY '   D) POPULATION DENSITY REPORT'
@ 13,23 SAY 'WHICH REPORT DO YOU WISH TO SEE: '
STORE 'no ' to mrepmenu
DO WHILE mrepmenu = 'no '
   STORE ' ' TO mselect
   @13,56 GET mselect PICTURE 'A'
   READ
   @18,20 SAY SPACE (50)
   STORE UPPER (mselect) to mselect
   IF mselect < 'A' .OR. mselect > 'D'
      @18,20 SAY 'Please choose one of the options listed!'
   ELSE
      STORE 'yes' TO mrepmenu
   ENDIF
ENDDO
CLEAR
@ 9,23 SAY 'ASCENDING OR DESCENDING SEQUENCE?'
@ 11,23 SAY '         ENTER A OR D:'
STORE 'no ' to morder
DO WHILE morder = 'no '
   STORE ' ' TO mchoice
   @11,47 GET mchoice PICTURE 'A'
   READ
   @18,20 SAY SPACE (50)
   STORE UPPER (mchoice) to mchoice
   IF mchoice = 'A' .OR. mchoice = 'D'
      STORE 'yes' TO morder
   ELSE
      @18,27 SAY 'Please enter A or D only!'
   ENDIF
ENDDO
CLEAR
@ 9,23 SAY 'HOW MANY COUNTRIES DO YOU WANT LISTED?'
@ 11,23 SAY '         ENTER NUMBER: '
STORE 'no ' to mnumber
DO WHILE mnumber = 'no '
   STORE 0 TO mnum
   @11,47 GET mnum PICTURE '99'
   READ
   @18,23 SAY SPACE (50)
   IF mnum < 1 .OR. mnum > 30
      @18,23 SAY 'Please enter a number from 1 to 30 only!'
   ELSE
      STORE 'yes' TO mnumber
   ENDIF
ENDDO
```

Figure DB.15 - Menu-driven Program (1 of 2)

```
        CLEAR
     ┌─ DO CASE
     │     CASE mselect = 'A'
     │        STORE '        AREA REPORT' to mheading
     │        USE world INDEX area
     │     CASE mselect = 'B'
     │        STORE '  1989 POPULATION REPORT' to mheading
     │        USE world INDEX popltn
     │     CASE mselect = 'C'
     │        STORE 'DATE OF ADMISSION REPORT' to mheading
     │        USE world INDEX yradmtd
     │     CASE mselect = 'D'
     │        STORE 'POPULATION DENSITY REPORT' to mheading
     │        USE world INDEX density
     └─ ENDCASE
        ? '              ',mheading
        ? ' '
     ┌─ IF mchoice ='A'
     │     GO TOP
     │  ELSE
     │     GO BOTTOM
     └─ ENDIF
        STORE 0 TO mcounter
     ┌─ DO WHILE mcounter < mnum
     │  ┌─ DO CASE
     │  │     CASE mselect = 'A'
     │  │        ? '          ',country,'            ',area
     │  │     CASE mselect = 'B'
     │  │        ? '          ',country,'         ',popltn
     │  │     CASE mselect = 'C'
     │  │        ? '          ',country,'         ',yradmtd
     │  │     CASE mselect = 'D'
     │  │        ? '          ',country,'         ',popltn/area
     │  └─ ENDCASE
     │     STORE mcounter + 1 TO mcounter
     │  ┌─ IF mchoice = 'A'
     │  │     SKIP
     │  │  ELSE
     │  │     SKIP-1
     │  └─ ENDIF
     └─ ENDDO
        CLOSE DATABASES
        RETURN
```

Figure DB.15 - Menu-driven Program (2 of 2)

Step 3: Create the File Structure

Create the WORLD.DBF file structure of Figure DB.16a, then enter data for the 30 countries as shown in Figure DB.16b. Check that your data have been entered correctly.

```
Structure for database: C:WORLD.dbf
Number of data records:      30
Date of last update   : 06/02/90
Field  Field Name  Type         Width    Dec
    1  COUNTRY     Character       14
    2  YRADMTD     Numeric          4
    3  POPLTN      Numeric         10
    4  AREA        Numeric          8
** Total **                        37
```

(a) File Structure for WORLD.DBF

Country	Year Admtd to UN	Population (1989)	Area (sq miles)
Algeria	1962	25063000	918497
Argentina	1945	32617000	1065189
Bangladesh	1974	112757000	55598
Brazil	1945	153992000	3286470
Canada	1945	25334000	3851790
China	1945	1069628000	3705390
Congo	1960	2031000	132046
Egypt	1945	54779000	385201
Finland	1955	4990000	130119
France	1945	55813000	220688
Germany, East	1973	16736000	41768
Germany, West	1973	60162000	95975
Ghana	1957	13754000	92098
Greece	1945	10048000	51146
Hungary	1955	10571000	35919
India	1945	833422000	1266595
Israel	1949	4477000	7847
Japan	1945	123231000	145846
Kenya	1963	23727000	224960
Mexico	1945	88087000	761604
Portugal	1955	10240000	36390
Spain	1955	39784000	194896
Sweden	1946	8371000	173731
Switzerland	1945	6485000	15941
Togo	1960	3423000	21622
USSR	1945	287015000	8649496
United Kingdom	1945	56648000	94226
United States	1945	247498000	3615123
Vietnam	1977	66708000	128401
Zaire	1960	33991000	905563

(b) Data for WORLD.DBF

Figure DB.16 - WORLD.DBF File

Step 4: Create the Supporting Index Files

The menu driven program uses four different indexes, corresponding to the type of report chosen. Create the indexes as follows:

```
. INDEX ON AREA TO AREA
  100% indexed          30 Records indexed
. INDEX ON YRADMTD TO YRADMTD
  100% indexed          30 Records indexed
. INDEX ON POPLTN TO POPLTN
  100% indexed          30 Records indexed
. INDEX ON POPLTN/AREA TO DENSITY
  100% indexed          30 Records indexed
```

Your directory should contain now contain six files; MENU.PRG (the program file), WORLD.DBF (the data file), and four supporting index files: YRADMTD.NDX, POPLTN.NDX, AREA.NDX, and DENSITY.NDX. Verify that these files are in fact present with the command, **DIR *.***

Step 5: Execute the Menu-Driven Program

Type the command **DO MENU** at the dBASE prompt, whereupon your program will take over and you will be prompted for three responses:

1) The Report Type (Enter A, B, C, or D)
2) The sequence in which countries are to be listed (Enter A or D)
3) The number of countries to include (Enter a number from 1 to 30)

Supply appropriate answers, relax, and enjoy the results. Figure DB.17 contains four examples of various reports which can be produced.

Step 6: Debugging

The program in Figure DB.15 is long and essentially unfamiliar, with the potential for error too great to ignore. In all likelihood you will omit apostrophes, spell words incorrectly, or otherwise fail to enter statements in the precise format expected by dBASE. When mistakes occur (and they will) dBASE will try its best to help you in the form of diagnostic messages.

Assume, for example, that you incorrectly omitted the closing apostrophe in the very first print message, to which dBASE responds as follows:

```
Unterminated string.

a 3,20 SAY '   WORLD DATABASE REPORT MENU
Called from - C:menu.prg

Cancel, Ignore, or Suspend? (C, I, or S)
```

dBASE Hands-On Exercises 203

In essence dBASE is telling you that there is a problem with this statement, and that the nature of the problem is an Unterminated string. It is then up to you to realize what the error is, and to proceed accordingly (note the appearance of a question mark where dBASE expected the closing apostrophe). After listing the error, dBASE gives you the option to Cancel the program (terminate processing), Ignore the error (and continue processing), or Suspend processing (and return to the dot prompt, and later back to this point in the program.)

Our suggestion is to temporarily ignore the error messages and continue executing the program as long as it is productive, realizing that you must note all problems as they occur. Eventually you will have to cancel execution, exit dBASE, return to your word processor to fix the errors, re-enter dBASE, and finally reexecute the corrected program.

```
          AREA REPORT                        1989 POPULATION REPORT

Israel              7847            China               1069628000
Switzerland        15941            India                833422000
Togo               21622            USSR                 287015000
Hungary            35919            United States        247498000
Portugal           36390            Brazil               153992000
Germany, East      41768            Japan                123231000
                                    Bangladesh           112757000
                                    Mexico                88087000
                                    Vietnam               66708000
```

(a) Area Report
(6 Countries, Ascending)

(b) Population Report
(9 Countries, Descending)

```
    DATE OF ADMISSION REPORT              POPULATION DENSITY REPORT

Argentina           1945            Bangladesh              2028.08
Brazil              1945            Japan                    844.94
Canada              1945            India                    658.00
China               1945            Germany, West            626.85
Egypt               1945            United Kingdom           601.19
France              1945            Israel                   570.54
Greece              1945            Vietnam                  519.53
India               1945            Switzerland              406.81
Japan               1945            Germany, East            400.69
Mexico              1945            Hungary                  294.30
Switzerland         1945            China                    288.67
USSR                1945            Portugal                 281.40
United Kingdom      1945
United States       1945
```

(c) Admission Report
(14 Countries, Ascending)

(d) Density Report
(12 Countries, Descending)

Figure DB.17 - Reports Produced by the Menu-driven Program

dBASE Reference

Although dBASE provides an excellent on-line help facility, you will find it useful to have a printed copy of some of that material, and hence we include our own highly condensed dBASE reference. We do not intend however that this section be a substitute for the Ashton-Tate manual. Accordingly we do not list the more esoteric options of the commands we discuss, nor do we even list all of the available commands. You are of course referred to the Ashton-Tate manual and/or the on-line help facility for complete information.

APPEND Command

Description: Adds records to the end of a database file; may also add records from other database files to the current file

Syntax: APPEND

Examples: APPEND

AVERAGE Command

Description: Computes the arithmetic mean of a numeric expression.

Syntax: AVERAGE [<expression list>] [<scope>] [FOR <condition>]
 [WHILE <condition>]

Examples:
AVERAGE	Averages all numeric fields
AVERAGE FOR CITY="Miami"	Averages all numeric fields for Miami
AVERAGE SALE	Averages only the SALE field
AVERAGE SALE FOR CITY="Miami"	Averages the SALE field for Miami

BROWSE Command

Description: A menu-driven command allowing full-screen editing of up to 17 records per screen. The FIELDS option views and edits selected fields. BROWSE uses standard full-screen cursor controls. To exit:
   ^W to save the changes
   ^Q to save all changes except to the current record.
dBASE makes use of internal buffers to temporarily record changes made during editing; hence the drive light may not come on when you exit this command.

Syntax: BROWSE [FIELDS <field list>]

Examples:	BROWSE	Enters browse mode at current position of the record pointer
	BROWSE FIELDS NAME,SALARY	Enters browse mode, displaying only the indicated fields for each record

CLEAR Command

Description: Erases the screen and repositions the cursor.

Syntax: CLEAR

Examples: CLEAR

CLOSE Command

Description: Closes specified types of files.

Syntax: CLOSE <file type>

Examples: CLOSE DATABASES   Closes all DBF and NDX files

COUNT Command

Description: Counts the number of records in the currently selected DBF file

Syntax: COUNT [<scope>] [FOR <condition>] [WHILE <condition>]

Examples:	COUNT	Returns a single number, equal to the number of records in the file
	COUNT FOR TITLE="Mgr"	Counts the number "Mgr" records

CREATE Command

Description: Defines the structure for a new database (.dbf) file and adds the file to the directory. All commands are menu driven.

Syntax: CREATE [<filename>]

Examples:	CREATE	dBASE will prompt for the file name of the resultant DBF file
	CREATE EMPLOYEE	dBASE will assign the name EMPLOYEE.DBF to the resultant file

DELETE Command

Description: Marks records for subsequent removal in the DBF file in use. Records slated for deletion are identified by an asterisk and may be displayed with the command: DISPLAY FOR DELETED( ). Deleted records may be subsequently recalled prior to being physically deleted.

Syntax: DELETE [<scope>] [FOR <condition>] [WHILE <condition>]

Examples:

DELETE	Deletes the record at the current position of the record pointer
DELETE NEXT 3	Deletes the next 3 records starting at the position of the record pointer
DELETE ALL FOR CITY="Boston"	Deletes all records for Boston

DIR Command

Description: Functions differently from the DOS command as DIR (issued from the dBASE prompt) displays only the DBF files in the default directory. DIR, in conjunction with other parameters, can display or other types of files.

Syntax: DIR [<drive:>] [<path>] [<skeleton>]

Examples:

DIR	Lists the names of all DBF files in the current directory
DIR *.NDX	Lists the names of all NDX files in the current directory
DIR *.*	Lists the names of all files in the current directory

DISPLAY Command

Description: DISPLAY with no parameters lists only the current record. The FIELDS option lists selected fields. The OFF option causes record numbers not to be shown. The structure parameter can be used to display the structure of a dbf file.

Syntax: DISPLAY [<scope>] [<expn list>] [FOR <condition>] [WHILE <condition>] [OFF] [TO PRINT]

Examples:

DISPLAY	Displays all fields for the record at the current position of the record pointer
DISPLAY NEXT 3	Displays all fields for the next three records beginning at the current position of the record pointer
DISPLAY ALL	Displays all fields for all records, pausing at each screen

DISPLAY ALL OFF	Displays all fields for all records, *without* record numbers
DISPLAY NAME,CITY	Displays the NAME and CITY fields for the current record
DISPLAY ALL NAME,CITY	Displays the NAME and CITY fields for all records
DISPLAY ALL FOR CITY="NY"	Lists all fields for those records whose city is NY

DO Command

Description: Causes a program file to be executed

Syntax: DO <program file>

Examples: DO MENU   Executes the program MENU.PRG on the default drive

DO CASE Command

Description: Permits the execution of one of several possible paths (cases) with one alternative (otherwise). A DO CASE statement must end with an ENDCASE.

Syntax:
```
DO CASE
   CASE <condition₁>
      commands


   OTHERWISE
      commands
ENDCASE
```

Examples: See the MENU.PRG program in exercise 4

DO WHILE Command

Description: Repeats a list of commands while the stated condition is true. DO WHILE must end with ENDDO.

Syntax:
```
DO WHILE <condition>
   commands
ENDDO
```

Examples: See the MENU.PRG program in exercise 4

EDIT Command

Description: A full-screen command for making changes to a specified record in the database. EDIT uses the standard full-screen cursor controls. To exit:
^W to save the changes

Syntax: EDIT

Examples: EDIT   Enters the edit mode at the current position of the record pointer

EJECT Command

Description: Issues a form feed to the printer.

Syntax: EJECT

Examples: EJECT

FIND Command

Description: Positions the record pointer at the first record whose index value matches the specified character string. The FIND command is case sensitive, requires an active index, and is typically followed by a DISPLAY command to show the indicated record. FIND utilizes a binary search algorithm and is significantly faster than a corresponding LOCATE command.

Syntax: FIND <character(s)>

Examples:

FIND Miller	Positions the record pointer at the first occurrence of *Miller* (according to the active index)
FIND MILLER	Positions the record pointer at the first occurrence of *MILLER* (according to the active index)

GO/GOTO Command

Description: Positions the record pointer to a specific record number. GO TOP (BOTTOM) moves the record pointer to the first (last) record.

Syntax: GO <expression>

Examples: GO 1   Moves the record pointer to record number 1

dBASE Reference 209

GO TOP	Moves to the first record in the file (according to the master index)
GO BOTTOM	Moves to the last record in the file (according to the master index)

IF Command

Description: Allows conditional execution of commands in a program, with an optional alternative path (ELSE). An IF statement must terminate with ENDIF.

Syntax:
IF <condition>
   commands
[ELSE
   commands]
ENDIF

Examples: See the MENU.PRG program in exercise 4

INDEX ON Command

Description: Creates an index (NDX) file from the database (DBF) file in use in which the key fields are alphabetically, chronologically, or numerically ordered.

Syntax: INDEX ON <key expression> TO <index file>

Examples:

INDEX ON NAME TO NAME	Creates an index on the NAME field, in the file NAME.NDX
INDEX ON -SALARY TO SALARY	Creates an index on the SALARY field which will list records in *descending* order according to salary
INDEX ON CITY+NAME TO CITY	Creates a concatenated index with city as the primary key and name as the secondary key (both keys must be character fields)

LIST Command

Description: Lists the contents of a database (DBF) file. The FIELDS option displays selected fields. The OFF option causes record numbers not to be shown.

Syntax: LIST [<scope>][<expression list>][FOR <condition>][WHILE <condition>] [OFF][TO PRINT]

Examples:

LIST	Lists all fields for all records (since the default scope of the command is ALL)

	LIST OFF TO PRINT	Lists all fields for all records without displaying record numbers, displaying the output on both the monitor and printer
	LIST NEXT 10 NAME,CITY	Lists the NAME and CITY fields for the next 10 records
	LIST FOR SALARY>40000	Lists all fields for all records whose salary is greater than 40000

LOCATE Command

Description: Initiates a sequential search through the database (DBF) file in use and positions the record pointer at the first record satisfying the specified condition. Additional records meeting the search condition are found with the CONTINUE command; i.e. CONTINUE causes dBASE to search for the next record meeting the same condition. LOCATE is typically followed by a DISPLAY command to display the record.

Syntax: LOCATE FOR <condition>

Examples:

LOCATE FOR NAME="SMITH"	Positions the record pointer at the first record whose name is SMITH
LOCATE FOR NAME="Smith"	Positions the record pointer at the first record whose name is Smith (the command is case sensitive)
LOCATE FOR NAME="S"	Positions the record pointer at the first record whose name begins with S

MODIFY Command

Description: Invokes the dBASE editor. We suggest, however, that since the dBASE editor is somewhat limited, you use the word processor you already know (e.g. WordPerfect) to create the program file, and the dBASE editor only for modifications.

Syntax: MODIFY COMMAND <filename>

Examples:

MODIFY COMMAND MENU	Invokes the dBASE editor for the file MENU.PRG (the PRG extension is assumed)
MODI COMM MENU	Identical to previous example; only the first four letters of this (and all commands) are required

PACK Command

Description: Permanently removes all records marked for deletion.

Syntax: PACK

Examples: PACK

QUIT Command

Description: Closes all open files, exits dBASE, and returns control to the operating system. The QUIT command is the only safe way to exit dBASE and guarantee that all modifications made during the session will be written to disk.

Syntax: QUIT

Examples: QUIT

READ Command

Description: Permits data entry in a field in conjunction with the @... GET and @ SAY commands. The READ command initiates the actual data entry, whereas the @SAY and @GET commands merely map the screen with prompts and input templates.

Syntax: READ

Examples: See the MENU.PRG program in exercise 4

RECALL Command

Description: Reinstates records that have been marked for deletion which appear with an asterisk (*) next to the record number.

Syntax: RECALL [<scope>] [FOR/WHILE <condition>]

Examples:
RECALL	Recalls the record at the current position of the record pointer
RECALL NEXT 3	Recalls the next 3 records starting at the position of the record pointer
RECALL ALL FOR CITY="Boston"	Recalls all records for Boston

REINDEX Command

Description: Rebuilds open index (NDX) files in use

Syntax: REINDEX

Examples: REINDEX

SET Command

Description: Establishes (sets/resets) various parameters, several of which are illustrated below.

Syntax: SET <parameters>

Examples:

SET BELL OFF	Suppresses the beep during data entry
SET DEFAULT TO <drive>	Establishes default drive
SET INDEX TO <.ndx file list> first of which is the master index	Opens one or more index files, the
SET PRINT ON	Directs all output displayed on the screen to the printer as well
SET TALK OFF	Used within a program file to suppress dBASE messages

SKIP Command

Description: Moves the record pointer forward or backward relative to its current position.

Syntax: SKIP [[+/-] <expression>]

Examples:

SKIP +1	Moves pointer one record forward
SKIP -1	Moves record pointer one record back

STORE Command

Description: Initializes one or more memory variables, simultaneously creating the variables if they do not exist; used within a program file.

Syntax: STORE <expression> TO <memory variable>

Examples:

STORE 0 TO mcounter	Stores zero in the numeric memory variable, *mcounter*
STORE 'yes' to morder	Sets the alphanumeric (character) memory variable *morder* to 'yes'

SUM Command

Description: Computes and displays the sum of an expression for specified database records

Syntax: SUM [<scope>] [<expression list>] [FOR <condition>] [WHILE <condition>]

Examples:
SUM	Sums (totals) all numeric fields for all records in the file
SUM SALARY	Sums only the SALARY field for all records in the file
SUM SALARY FOR TITLE="Mgr"	Sums only the SALARY field for all records whose title is "Mgr"

USE Command

Description: Opens a database (DBF) file and optionally any named index file(s) associated with that DBF file, while closing the file currently in use.

Syntax: USE [<database file>] [INDEX <index file list>]

Examples:
USE EMPLOYEE	Opens the EMPLOYEE.DBF file
USE EMPLOYEE INDEX NAME	Opens the EMPLOYEE.DBF file according to the NAME index

WAIT Command

Description: Suspends program processing until a key is pressed. The default prompt is: Press any key to continue...

Syntax: WAIT [<prompt>]

Examples: WAIT

? Command

Description: ? evaluates and displays value of the expression list on the next/current line.

Syntax: ? <expression list>

Examples:
? NAME,SALARY	Prints the NAME and SALARY fields for the current record
? NAME,SALARY/12	Prints the NAME field and indicated computation for the current record

dBASE Self-Evaluation

The best way to judge how much you have learned is to see how successful you are in using dBASE to do actual work. As with the other programs however, we have included a quiz (with answers immediately following) should you wish another means of evaluating your progress.

1. Answer True or False for the following:
   __ (a) The student version of dBASE III plus is limited to a maximum of 31 records.
   __ (b) A file structure cannot be changed after it has been created and saved.
   __ (c) The DELETE command permanently deletes a record.
   __ (d) The EDIT command displays multiple records simultaneously on the screen.
   __ (e) A file contains one or more records.
   __ (f) A record contains one or more fields
   __ (g) Ctrl Exit exits a dBASE session and saves all changes.
   __ (h) The prompt characters for DOS and dBASE are the same.
   __ (i) The APPEND command always adds records to the beginning of a file.
   __ (j) Every record within a file has the same number of fields.
   __ (k) Output of the DISPLAY command can be directed to the printer.
   __ (l) Records listed by the DISPLAY command must be shown with their record numbers.
   __ (m) The USE command establishes the default drive.
   __ (n) Information on the DISPLAY command can be obtained with the command, HELP DISPLAY.
   __ (o) The PACK command physically deletes all records marked for deletion.
   __ (p) The ASSIST facility must be used to create a DBF file.
   __ (q) The SUM and COUNT commands are equivalent.
   __ (r) The SUM command must include values from every record.
   __ (s) The USE command positions the record pointer to the first record within a file.
   __ (t) All dBASE commands operate independently of the record pointer.

2. Which dBASE command will:
   (a) Correct individual records
   (b) Display multiple records on the screen, allowing you to correct any of the displayed records?
   (c) Modify a file structure
   (d) Add records to the end of an existing data file
   (e) Mark a record for subsequent deletion
   (f) Physically delete records marked for deletion
   (g) Save changes and exit from the edit or browse modes
   (h) Position the record pointer at the first record in a file
   (i) Deactivate the dBASE Assistant
   (j) Obtain additional information on the EDIT command
   (k) Establish drive B as the default drive for all files?
   (l) Change the index associated with the current data base file?
   (m) Direct output to the printer?
   (n) Suppress the beep in data entry?
   (o) Obtain a directory of all DBF files on the default drive?
   (p) Obtain a directory of all NDX files on the default drive?

3) Distinguish between:
   (a) Data entry and data retrieval
   (b) Operating with and without the dBASE Assistant
   (c) Editing and browsing
   (d) DISPLAY and DISPLAY ALL
   (e) A field and a file
   (f) Upper and lower case letters within the dBASE syntax
   (g) The DOS and the dBASE prompt
   (h) The SUM and COUNT commands
   (i) The PgUp and PgDn keys

4. Given the file in Figure DB.18, what will happen as a result of the following commands executed at the dot prompt. (Assume the commands are executed in succession, so that the answer to part b may depend on part a, and so on).
   (a) 3
   (b) DISPLAY
   (c) GOTO TOP
   (d) DELETE
   (e) LIST ALL
   (f) RECALL
   (g) PACK

5. Given the dBASE file in Figure DB.18. Indicate which records (and fields within each record) will be displayed as a result of the following commands. Assume in each instance that the record pointer is positioned at the first record in the file prior to the list command being issued.
   (a) LIST ALL
   (b) LIST ALL FOR CITY = 'Miami'
   (c) LIST NEXT 5
   (d) LIST NAME,TITLE NEXT 5
   (e) LIST NAME FOR CITY = 'MIAMI'
   (f) LIST NEXT 5 FOR CITY = 'Miami'

6. Given the dBASE file in Figure DB.18, what will happen as a result of the dBASE commands? (In each instance the number prior to the particular command is intended to position the record pointer to the indicated record)
   (a) GOTO 1
       LOCATE FOR CITY = 'Boston'
   (b) GOTO 5
       LOCATE FOR CITY = 'Boston'
   (c) FIND Boston (Assume that an index file on city is open)
   (d) FIND BOSTON (Assume that an index file on city is open)

7. The file structure below is associated with a list or companies (e.g. the Fortune 500), and contains for each company its revenue, net income, and number of employees.

```
Structure for database : B:company.dbf
Number of data records :     20
Date of last update    : 03/07/88
Field  Field name  Type        Width   Dec
  1    COMPANY     Character     32
  2    SALES       Numeric       12     0
  3    INCOME      Numeric       12     0
  4    EMPLOYEE    Numeric        6
```

Provide the necessary command(s) to create the following reports:
   (a) All 20 companies in increasing order of income (include the commands to create any required index files)
   (b) All 20 companies in increasing order of sales (include the commands to create any required index files)
   (c) The 10 largest companies (in terms of employees) in decreasing order
   (d) All companies with net income of more than $30 million (list companies in descending order of net income)
   (e) All 20 companies in order of decreasing sales/per employee, listing the company name and the sales/per employee.
   (f) Explain why you cannot create a report listing the companies with the highest percentage increase in net income from last year to this year.

Record #	NAME	CITY	TITLE	SALARY
1	Adams	Boston	Programmer	30000
2	Baker	Miami	Programmer	29000
3	Brown	Miami	Sr. Programmer	38000
4	Charles	Boston	Analyst	39000
5	Edwards	Miami	Proj Leader	43000
6	Frank	Miami	Programmer	24000
7	George	Miami	Analyst	38000
8	Hathaway	Miami	Analyst	41000
9	Michaels	Boston	Sr. Programmer	37000
10	Newton	Miami	Analyst	39000

Figure DB.18 - File for Problems 4, 5, and 6

8. Answer the following questions with respect to the file structure of problem 7.
   (a) Consider the command INDEX ON INCOME TO INCOME in which "INCOME" appears twice. Explain the difference between the two usages.
   (b) What is the difference (if any) between the statements:
   ```
   USE COMPANY INDEX INCOME,SALES
   ```
   and
   ```
   USE COMPANY
   SET INDEX TO INCOME,SALES
   ```
   (c) In which order would the records in COMPANY be listed if the statements in part b were immediately followed by the command LIST ALL?
   (d) What is the difference (if any) between the statements:
   ```
   USE COMPANY INDEX INCOME,SALES
   ```
   and
   ```
   USE COMPANY INDEX INCOME,SALES
   SET INDEX TO INCOME
   ```

9. Consider the following program fragment:
   ```
   SET TALK OFF
   USE DPCOMP
   INDEX ON NET TO NETNDX
   GO TOP
   DO WHILE .NOT. EOF()
       ? NAME
       SKIP +1
   ENDDO
   ```
   (a) In which order (ascending or descending) will the records be listed?
   (b) What would happen if SKIP+1 were replaced by SKIP -1?
   (c) What would happen if the SKIP +1 statement were eliminated entirely?
   (d) What changes would you have to make to the program to have the records listed in the opposite order of part a? (Do not create additional indexes)
   (e) The following program fragment is intended to print every record in a particular file. There are two distinct logic errors. What are they?
   ```
   USE B:DPCOMP
   DO WHILE EOF()
       DISPLAY NAME
   ENDDO
   ```

10. Describe what will be printed as a result of the following statements with respect to the WORLD.DBF of exercise 3. In each instance indicate precisely what will print, rather than what was probably intended. Note too that some of the statements are syntactically invalid and will produce dBASE error messages.
    (a) ? country
    (b) ? county
    (c) ? 'country'
    (d) ? 'county'
    (e) ? 'country
    (f) ? country,area,population
    (g) ? 'country, area, population'
    (h) ? country,' ',area
    (i) ? 'country   area'

11. The program fragment below contains a portion of *modified* code from the original MENU.PRG program. This erroneous code causes the program to accept the user's response as valid (i.e. it does not display an error message), but instead of requesting the next response, the program remains in a loop requesting the number of countries. Identify the cause of the problem.
    ```
    @ 9,23 SAY 'HOW MANY COUNTRIES?'
    @ 11,23 SAY '        ENTER NUMBER: '
    STORE 'no ' TO mnumber
    DO WHILE mnumber = 'no '
        STORE 0 TO mnum
        @ 11,47 GET mnum PICTURE '99'
        READ
        @ 18,23 SAY SPACE(50)
        IF mnum < 1 .OR. mnum > 30
            @ 18,23 SAY 'Enter from 1 to 30!'
        ELSE
            STORE 'yes' TO number
        ENDIF
    ENDDO
    ```

    Hint: The error is subtle and requires you to carefully go through the existing code. The best way is to "play computer" and enter the value for each variable as it is established in the program fragment.

Answers to dBASE Self-Evaluation

1. (a) True.
    (b) False. The MODIFY STRUCTURE command enables you to change an existing file structure.
    (c) False. The PACK command permanently deletes a record.
    (d) False. The BROWSE command displays multiple records for editing.
    (e) True.
    (f) True.
    (g) False. The Quit command exits dBASE and returns to DOS.
    (h) False. The period and greater than sign are the dBASE and DOS prompts respectively.
    (i) False. It adds records at the end of the file.
    (j) True.
    (k) True.
    (l) False. The OFF parameter will suppress the record numbers.
    (m) False. The SET DEFAULT command establishes the drive.
    (n) True.
    (o) True.
    (p) False. The ASSIST facility can be suppressed with the Esc key
    (q) False. SUM totals the values in a numeric field; count totals the number of records.
    (r) False. The FOR condition can restrict the records which are included.
    (s) True (assuming that the command is specified without an index.
    (t) False. The record pointer is essential.

2. (a) EDIT
    (b) BROWSE
    (c) MODIFY STRUCTURE
    (d) APPEND
    (e) DELETE
    (f) PACK
    (g) Ctrl End
    (h) GOTO 1 or GOTO TOP
    (i) The Esc key
    (j) HELP EDIT
    (k) SET DEFAULT TO B
    (l) SET INDEX TO new index
    (m) SET PRINT ON
    (n) SET BELL OFF
    (o) DIR
    (p) DIR *.NDX

3. (a) Data entry implies the initial entry of data into a record; data retrieval suggests the display of existing data.
    (b) Operating without the Assistant places the user at the dot prompt where complete commands are entered.
    (c) The edit mode displays only a single record whereas browsing displays multiple records at one time, generally with fewer fields on the screen.
    (d) DISPLAY displays only a single record (at the current position of the record pointer); DISPLAY ALL displays all records in the file.
    (e) A file consists of multiple records; a record contains multiple fields.
    (f) Upper case letters imply dBASE reserved words; lower case letters indicate a user supplied element.
    (g) The DOS prompt consists of the drive followed by the greater than sign; e.g. A>. The dBASE prompt is a period or a period preceded by (Demo) in the student version.
    (h) SUM totals the value of a numerical field, whereas COUNT computes the number of records.
    (i) PgUp moves to the previous record; PgDn moves to the next record.

4. (a) Positions the record pointer at the third record
    (b) Displays the current record (Brown)
    (c) Positions the record pointer at the first record
    (d) Logically deletes Adams
    (e) Lists all ten records, positioning the record pointer at the end of the file
    (f) Does not recall Adams as the record pointer is not at record 1
    (g) Physically deletes Adams and renumbers the remaining nine records

5. (a) Lists all fields for all records
    (b) Lists all fields for records 2, 3, 5, 6, 7, 8, and 10; i.e. records in Miami
    (c) Lists every field in records 1 through 5
    (d) Lists only the name and title fields for records 1 through 5
    (e) Does not list any records; records in the file contain Miami whereas the specified condition was MIAMI
    (f) Lists records 2, 3, and 5 as dBASE considers only the next five records

6. (a) Positions the record pointer to the first record.
    (b) Positions the record pointer at the first record. (The LOCATE command begins its search at the beginning of the file).
    (c) Positions the record pointer at the first record.
    (d) Returns a "no find" condition as the FIND command is case sensitive.

7. (a) USE COMPANY
        INDEX ON INCOME TO INCOME
        LIST COMPANY,INCOME OFF
    (b) USE COMPANY
        INDEX ON SALES TO SALES
        LIST COMPANY,SALES OFF
    (c) USE COMPANY
        INDEX ON -EMPLOYEE TO EMPLOYEE
        LIST NEXT 10 COMPANY,EMPLOYEE OFF
    (d) USE COMPANY
        INDEX ON -INCOME TO INCOME
        LIST COMPANY,INCOME FOR INCOME>30000000
    (e) USE COMPANY
        INDEX ON -SALES/EMPLOYEE TO SALESPER
        LIST COMPANY,SALES/EMPLOYEE
    (f) The report cannot be produced because it requires additional data (last year's net income) which is not present in the DBF file.

8. (a) The first occurrence is the name of a field as it exists within the structure of a DBF file; the second occurrence is the name of an index (NDX) file.
    (b) No difference
    (c) According to the order in the primary index which is the first file listed (INCOME in the example)
    (d) The first statement leaves both indexes open with INCOME as the primary index; the second leaves only the INCOME index open. A SET statement implicitly closes all other indexes which were previously open.

9. (a) Ascending order according to the variable NET
    (b) Only the first record. (Since the record pointer is on the first record skipping backward would immediately reach the beginning of the file.)
    (c) The program would be in an infinite loop and would continue listing the first record in the file indefinitely.
    (d) Substitute GO BOTTOM for GO TOP and SKIP -1 for SKIP +1; also BOF (beginning of file) for EOF
    (e) EOF should be replaced by .NOT. EOF and a SKIP +1 statement inserted in the loop. These changes would list the file in ascending order.

10. (a) The value of COUNTRY for the current record.
    (b) An error would result since the existing file structure does not contain a COUNTY field.
    (c) The word (literal) "country"
    (d) The word (literal) "county"
    (e) An error since there is no closing apostrophe
    (f) The value of the three fields COUNTRY, AREA, POPLTN for the current record
    (g) The literal, "country, area, population"
    (h) The value of the COUNTRY field, followed by the spaces, followed by the value of the AREA field
    (i) The literal, "country   area"

11. The loop is controlled by the variable *mnumber* which is initially set to 'no ' and which is supposed to be set to 'yes' when a valid response is entered. The problem is in the STORE statment which sets *number*, rather than mnumber, to 'yes', and hence the loop never ends.

Retrieve
List
Build a Search Condition — select field
— criteria
— execute command

Retrieve
List
Construct a field list — specify fields
— execute command

✗ didn't press enter, use arrows to move out of field etc.

Organize - Index — salary
to salary
Retrieve List Search condition salary >35000

esc. to dot prompt
up arrow
end key

takes 1, 2, off 3

LIST FOR SALARY >35000 off

enter to print